The LUCKY ONE

The LUCKY ONE

A story of courage, hope & bright pink lipstick

KRYSTAL BARTER

with Felicity McLean

First published in 2014

Copyright © Krystal Barter 2014

All rights reserved. No part of this book may be reproduced or transmitted in any form or by any means, electronic or mechanical, including photocopying, recording or by any information storage and retrieval system, without prior permission in writing from the publisher. The Australian *Copyright Act 1968* (the Act) allows a maximum of one chapter or 10 per cent of this book, whichever is the greater, to be photocopied by any educational institution for its educational purposes provided that the educational institution (or body that administers it) has given a remuneration notice to Copyright Agency Limited (CAL) under the Act.

Allen & Unwin
83 Alexander Street
Crows Nest NSW 2065
Australia
Phone: (61 2) 8425 0100
Email: info@allenandunwin.com
Web: www.allenandunwin.com

Cataloguing-in-Publication details are available
from the National Library of Australia
www.trove.nla.gov.au

ISBN 978 1 74331 730 3

Set in 13.5/17 pt Granjon by Midland Typesetters, Australia
Printed and bound in Australia by Griffin Press

10 9 8 7 6 5 4 3

The paper in this book is FSC® certified. FSC® promotes environmentally responsible, socially beneficial and economically viable management of the world's forests.

This book is dedicated to my beautiful husband and babies—you are my heart, my soul, my everything. I love you to the moon, the stars and back again.

Courage doesn't always roar, courage is sometimes the little voice at the end of the day that says 'I will try again tomorrow'.
Mary Anne Radmacher, author

PROLOGUE

'How do you feel about your breasts?' The question hung in the air. In front of me, a cameraman shuffled his feet awkwardly on the timber floor of my lounge room and skilfully readjusted the bulky camera on his shoulder without interrupting his shot. He was a blokey guy, all blue chinos and *'maaate'* when the camera was switched off, and I could tell he was embarrassed and wanted to turn away now but it was his job to remain looking down the barrel at me.

'I hate them,' I said.

A few weeks later when the interview went to air around Australia, 1.4 million viewers glanced up from their Sunday night television dinners, they paused from feeding their fidgety baby in their high chair and they put down the kettle from where they stood making a cup of tea in the kitchen; they stopped and they turned and they stared at the TV. At me.

'What do you mean?' probed the journalist, Ellen Fanning, a seasoned reporter and a familiar face on the Nine Network's *60 Minutes* program. I'd watched Ellen countless times before on the program, hounding shady politicians or revealing medical breakthroughs or reporting live from natural disaster zones, but I'd never seen her cry on screen. Not until my story.

'I feel like a ticking time bomb,' I explained. 'Like my breasts are going to betray me. Ever since I found out that I've got up to an 80 per cent chance of developing breast cancer, well, I've lost all closeness to my breasts. They're a part of me that I don't want.'

Ellen looked sombre and we finished filming. 'Thanks, Krystal, that's great,' she said and she reached forward and placed a hand on my knee. 'The program will jump to a voice-over now to give the viewers a little more of your back-story. So why don't you take a breather for a few minutes before we head over to the next location?'

I nodded, distractedly. I could already imagine what the voiceover would say: 'Krystal Barter, ticking time bomb, inherited a genetic mutation that is almost certain to cause her to develop breast cancer.' Or, 'Lose your breasts or lose your life? This young mother of two faces a devastating choice.'

Turns out I wasn't far wrong. When the program was shown on TV, Ellen's honeyed tones reported: 'At 25, Krystal Barter has grown up living with what can only be described as a sense of doom. Her family carries a flawed breast cancer gene so ferocious it has struck down at least twenty women in three generations.

The Lucky One

'Krystal's great-grandmother died of the disease aged 69, her grandma Val was 44 when diagnosed, her mum Julie was just 36 years old. Each of them carries the burden of having passed on the gene to their daughters.'

The camera panned out then, before cutting to another shot and my mum's distraught face filled the screen. 'We're so strong as a family but this is breaking us at the moment,' she wept.

Poor Mum. Just half an hour earlier the two of us had been silly and giggly with excitement as we sat on twin bar stools in the kitchen while the *60 Minutes* makeup artist got the pair of us 'camera ready'.

'Sit still, Krystal!' Mum had admonished as she sat unnaturally straight-backed, surrounded by brushes and eyeshadow pots and cotton balls.

'Which lip gloss?' the makeup artist had asked. 'Love that Pink? Or Pink Velvet?' And she'd held out two near-identical tubes for my mum to choose.

'Er, Krystal?' Mum deflected the question to me.

'Pink Velvet,' I'd said decisively. I was fast becoming an expert in all things pink as it was the colour adopted by breast cancer charity organisations.

'Great choice,' the artist replied and, holding Mum gently but firmly by the chin as she steadied her face, she got to work. 'And we'll be using blue-black mascara on your eyes.'

Now, though, that mascara was perilously close to running down Mum's face. She had been so determined not to cry on national television and yet here she was, her voice trembling with emotion, as she sat between my nan and me. She clutched our hands.

Krystal Barter

'We've talked about this,' Mum said, indicating towards Nan. 'In the past I've said, "I feel like I've given this to my daughter."' Here, her voice trailed off and Nan smiled grimly. Mum went on: 'And she replied, "Well, what about me? I've given this cancer to you."'

Then Mum let out a desperate, gasping laugh, as though torn between putting on a brave face for the camera and simply taking in air. But sitting to her left, just off-screen at this point, I certainly wasn't laughing.

As Ellen explained to her viewers, after I'd finally made the agonising decision to have my breasts removed, a pre-surgery check-up with my surgeon delivered shocking news: pre-cancerous cells had already appeared in my breasts. In a final mammogram before my surgery, linear lines of calcification were detected. 'Early breast cancer' was how it was described to me.

'It may be too late,' reported Ellen gravely. 'Doctors have found changes in Krystal's breast tissue. They say that probably means the start of cancer. For Krystal it was devastating; she might have waited just one month too long to have surgery.'

Here, the program cut to me as I struggled to keep my emotions under control. 'I just didn't think something like this would happen so soon and it upsets me because I just …' I trailed off as tears spilled over.

'It's okay, do you want to stop?' asked Ellen.

'No, it's alright.' I was determined to continue. 'I just thought I was finally beating cancer …' I paused and blinked and looked at the ceiling, willing the tears away. 'And that traumatises me even more so than losing my breasts.'

'That you thought you were in control?' asked Ellen.

The Lucky One

'I did! I did!' I was angry now. 'And it … aggravates me!' I couldn't find the words to express the depth of my fury. 'I just don't know when it's going to end! When is this cancer in our family going to end?'

Ellen turned to face the camera head-on and I could almost hear the deathly crescendo that would surely provide the soundtrack to this moment: 'The surgery is now urgent. Krystal's operation is pushed forward as her doctors are keen to get the tissue out before any suspected cancerous cells can spread.'

◆ ◆ ◆

Two days later, Ellen Fanning and her crew were back again, only this time we were filming at North Shore Private Hospital in Sydney while I was being admitted for a risk-reducing double mastectomy. At just 25 years old, I had elected to have both of my healthy breasts removed and replaced with silicone implants in order to mitigate the risk of developing breast cancer. No breasts, no breast cancer, right? If only the decision was that simple. In reality, I had never been so petrified in my life.

As I sat propped up in a hospital bed, I did my best to look good for the camera in a flaming red hairnet (they didn't come in breast-cancer pink—I asked) and a regulation-blue hospital gown. No easy task. It was a strange sensation to feel the rough cotton fabric—to feel any fabric—resting against my breasts for the last time. I'd still have (most of) the same skin there when I woke up after the operation, but the breast tissue underneath would be gone. Beside me stood an obviously emotional Ellen, decked out in similar hospital garb, her pearl necklace stark against the sanitary blue of her scrubs.

'You seem very calm,' she said encouragingly while she clutched my hand in support. On the far side of the bed a cameraman captured everything.

'I have to be,' I said shakily.

'Well, you're doing very well,' she soothed.

I took a deep breath and powered on. 'I said goodbye to my boobs last night and my husband, Chris, took photos of them.' Though my voice began to crack as I recalled our farewell ritual of the night before. Chris and I had tucked our two boys into bed at my parents' house then gone home and put Beyonce's *I Am ... Sasha Fierce* on the stereo. Loud. While Chris snapped away on our camera, I pranced around the lounge room wearing just my knickers, preening and posing and doing my best impersonation of a Victoria's Secret catwalk model. 'If you liked it then you shoulda put a ring on it ...' I crooned along with Beyonce, squeezing my breasts together to accentuate my cleavage and pouting for the camera.

'That's it, baby!' yelled Chris, laughing. 'Work it! You look beautiful!'

My glass of champagne sat untouched on the kitchen bench. I wasn't nil-by-mouth for another hour or so yet, but there was only so much of a party atmosphere a girl could muster. Still, Chris and I had done our best to make the night a celebration and not a wake for my boobs.

'So I'm not sad; just nervous,' I said to Ellen.

'Wait till I get my calmative,' I added, thinking of the sedative that was coming my way. 'Then I'll be right; I'll be talking gibberish.'

Ellen laughed then leaned over and kissed my cheek; it was a move that surprised us both. This wasn't what I'd expected when I'd invited a film crew along to follow my surgery and clearly Ellen hadn't planned on being so affected by my story, either. She smiled sheepishly and I was grateful to see her let her guard down at a time when I was feeling so incredibly vulnerable. It lasted only briefly, however, as she was suddenly all concentration and well-articulated vowels again the instant my surgeon entered the room.

'Ellen Fanning, *60 Minutes*. Nice to meet you,' she offered her hand.

'Dr Mark Sywak, breast and endocrine surgeon.' They shook hands and Ellen began to run through her list of questions for her story.

'Am I right in thinking Krystal's surgery today will be minimally invasive?'

'That's right; what we'll do is make a small incision, dissecting under the skin and removing all the breast tissue that puts her at risk of developing breast cancer.'

'And with modern plastic surgery techniques, removing that risk no longer means terrible disfigurement?'

'Correct. The nice thing about this approach is that Krystal comes to hospital with breasts and she leaves hospital with breasts. And with a very reduced risk of breast cancer in the future.'

At this, Ellen smiled at me. 'Fantastic,' she said, trying to sound upbeat.

Dr Sywak moved over to my bedside. 'How are you feeling, Krystal? Ready to do this?'

I could only nod in reply. I wanted Chris; I wanted my mum. But I had already said goodbye to both of them out in the corridor. I felt scared and nervous and anxious about the pain I would face when I woke up.

'Well, your stats are all fine,' said Dr Sywak. 'So if you don't have any questions then I'll see you in theatre shortly.'

'Good luck,' I managed to say to him, smiling weakly, and he patted my hand and strode out of the room.

I turned to Ellen for the final time before I was wheeled into theatre and found, to my surprise, that she was crying.

'Are you okay?' I asked her.

'I'm okay,' she choked back, laughing through her tears. It wasn't lost on her that here was a possible cancer sufferer and the subject of her report checking that *she* was alright. 'I'm okay,' she said again and patted my hand tenderly.

Minutes later I was face-to-face with my anaesthetist and the reality of what I was about to do hit home. *I am having my breasts cut off! Forever!* Panic rose until I could taste it in my mouth. I tried to think about Chris and about my beautiful boys, Riley and Jye. They were the reason I was doing this. I thought back to yesterday when Mum and Nan had ambushed me as I packed my bag for hospital and, giggling, they'd both lifted their tops and revealed their own war-torn breasts: 'Your boobs will look so much better than ours!' they'd chorused. 'We're so proud of you, Krystal. You're going to beat this!' I almost smiled thinking about it.

'I've got some great drugs here for you today, Krystal,' interrupted my anaesthetist. We'd met several times before and had developed quite a rapport by now. 'Top quality stuff. Some of my best work. So why don't you start counting backwards from ten for me.'

I felt the stab of the needle pierce my arm and my head began to swim.

'These drugs are awesome,' I slurred to the camera crew

poised faithfully beside my trolley. 'I could do with a nightclub right about now because I feel like going out dancing ...'

Their laughter was the last thing I remember hearing.

◆ ◆ ◆

Four excruciating days later I was desperate to hear it again. As I lay in my hospital bed in agonising, post-surgery pain, I was surrounded by my family and by the *60 Minutes* team. We were waiting for Dr Sywak to arrive with the results of the pathology tests performed on the breast tissue that was removed during my surgery. This would tell us, definitively, if my breasts contained cancer.

Riley and Jye, who were aged three and one at the time, had a book at home called *There's a Hippopotamus on Our Roof Eating Cake*. Right then, I felt like that hippo was sitting on my chest. And not just because of my surgery. My breasts were bound up tighter than a mummy. Flimsy blue tape poked out from the white crepe bandages and my mind conjured up all sorts of horrific images of what lay hidden beneath. Stitches? Bloodied gauze? Heavy scarring? Macerated breast tissue? Who knew what I looked like under there. But the dread I felt about what my breasts might look like was nothing compared to the fear I felt for my future.

Dr Sywak knocked and then entered.

I later watched myself on TV as Ellen intoned here: 'For Krystal, the surgery has gone well. But in her case, there's so much more at stake. She still doesn't know whether her cancer has begun.'

The hippo shifted uncomfortably on my chest as Dr Sywak smiled curtly and immediately began inspecting my breasts.

'Good morning, Krystal. How's the pain today?' He ignored the rest of the room as he expertly pressed and prodded my wounds.

'Fine,' I croaked. I was desperate for him to get on with it.

Dr Sywak cleared his throat: 'Your pathology results arrived this morning …'

The hippo began doing aerobics then; my breathing became shallow and blood pounded in my ears. This was the moment I had feared my whole life. I was staring cancer straight in the eyes and I was terrified about who would blink first. Regardless of what Dr Sywak said next, my life would already never be the same.

CHAPTER 1

I feel lucky I was born with cancer in my DNA. Crazy as it sounds, I consider myself fortunate that, when I was just 22 years old, I discovered I had up to an 80 per cent chance of developing breast cancer; the same insidious disease that attacked my mum, and my nan before her, and my great-grandma before her.

I feel lucky that a gene test revealed I carry the rogue BRCA1 genetic fault which poisons our family tree, because knowing this gave me the chance to *do* something about it, rather than sitting around and waiting for this relentless cancer to come and get me. So, yes, I feel lucky that our particular brand of gene mutation—the one parcelled out to me the very instant my DNA began twisting into its double-helix ropes—causes a type of cancer that can be tested and treated and even possibly avoided. Eventually, I even learned to feel lucky that when I went into hospital to have both of my breasts permanently removed my surgery was elective, not emergency. (Or worse: too late.) And I guess I'm lucky, too, as my girlfriends often point out, that with my silicone implants I'll have the best breasts in the nursing home one day.

But don't get me wrong, I'm no Pollyanna. And I sure as hell didn't always feel this way.

In fact, I've spent a lot of my life not feeling this way—*really* not feeling this way—like, for instance, around the time I was fourteen years old and my mum was diagnosed with cancer. Rage, disbelief, pure hatred; these were the emotions I felt back then. Although, pre-diagnosis, they had nothing to do with Mum's cancer and everything to do with teenage hormones.

'I hate you, Mum!' I screamed through the keyhole of the bathroom door.

There was no response from inside, just the steady sound of running water. *I hate you, I hate you, I hate you*, it hammered onto the tiles. She was washing my fury down the plughole.

'I said *I hate you!*' I upped the volume, and then kicked the door for good measure. Still nothing. She had probably pulled her shower cap over her ears and shoved her head directly under the shower spray so the sound of the water drumming against the plastic was amplified enough to drown out my voice. It wasn't like she hadn't done it before.

'You're not the boss of me!' I tried again. 'If I want to go to Lisa's house, you can't stop me!'

And yet there I was (fully clothed and able to walk outside at will) standing at the bathroom door arguing about it, while Mum (naked and unable to go anywhere fast) showered inside.

The Lucky One

Somehow it made sense in my teenage mind. I aimed another kick at the door, right in the bifold where it was weakest, when the phone in the kitchen started to ring.

'Leave it! It's for me!' Mum yelled loudly and the water in the shower stopped abruptly.

She could hear the phone? *She was ignoring me!* I was incensed.

'Muuuum!' I squealed in frustration, punctuating it by stamping my foot. Then I debated with myself, briefly, whether or not to race her for the ringing phone.

'I said leave it!' she called out again and I paused. If I waited just a few more seconds, Mum would emerge from the bathroom, dripping wet, and I could step towards the kitchen, neatly blocking her path, and then scoop the phone out of the cradle right in front of her face. Maximum. Aggravation. Achieved. The phone kept ringing.

Of course, then I'd get stuck speaking to one of her friends (who loved a chat) and I wasn't sure it was worth the pain.

'Leave it!' she yelled once more. The bathroom door snapped open and Mum dashed across the floorboards to where the phone was still crying out from the wall beside the kitchen doorway. 'Hi, it's me,' she said into the receiver, curling the cord absently around her finger as she spoke. She was expecting one of her friends to be on the line.

'Oh!' She untangled her finger. 'Yes, this is Julie speaking.' A change of tone now: more professional, less Mum.

I hung around in the hallway, not especially curious to see who was on the phone but not done with our argument, either. Suddenly Mum buckled, slumping to the floor like she'd been taken out by a sniper.

'No!' she screamed in horror. 'No! No! Oh, my god! No!'

I froze in the hallway, stricken. Behind me, somewhere, I heard a door fly open and my nan must have emerged from the bedroom that she always stayed in while she holidayed with us from her home in New Zealand.

'No!' Mum screamed again and she was crying now, too, as she sat in a crumpled heap in the kitchen doorway, her head against the doorframe, one leg straight out in front of her, the other bent up underneath. Her hair was still dripping from the shower.

What the hell was going on?

Nan pushed past me and stumbled towards the kitchen, where she dropped to her knees and held Mum's wet head against her chest, rocking her back and forth while Mum continued to sob and sob. It would have looked comical in any other situation: my mum, who's so tall, being cradled by my nan; the two of them sprawled on the floorboards in a tangle of phone cord and bath towel, a flash of white flesh from Mum's exposed thigh. But in my memory the image is simply macabre. As I was about to find out, it was one cancer victim nursing another down the same path.

◆ ◆ ◆

I can still remember the smell of Mum's shampoo that day. It was apple, which is galling when I think about it. Why should apple—fresh, sweet apple—be the smell that I associate with cancer? It should be something rotten or putrid or decaying. Still, the smell of synthetic apple will always take me back to that day when we learned Mum had cancer, just like

The Lucky One

so many others in our family. We pumped them out, alright: cancer victim after cancer victim, our family produced them with factory-like precision. For as far back as we have information, breast cancer has cursed our family (with the occasional case of ovarian or other cancers, too). At last count, 25 women in my immediate family have suffered breast cancer to some extent, and what's more, the age of diagnosis is getting younger in each new generation. Ours is a story of hereditary cancer so frighteningly ferocious that no single generation of my family is safe. It's a curse that won't stop.

So it's hardly surprising that Nan claims she knew straight away that Mum's phone call that day was one of a breast cancer diagnosis. After all, what other bad news would there be in our family? The rest of us, though, had no idea what was happening at the time. I don't know how long I stood sentry in the hallway that day; a hallway I'd skipped through a thousand times as a child and where I'd dragged my feet on the way out the door to school and where I'd chased my younger brother, Andrew, even though we weren't supposed to run in the house. Now, all those memories had been replaced and the hallway of our family home became the place where I saw Mum's life—all our lives—change forever. And right after I told Mum I hated her.

On the floor, however, Mum was still screaming and tears streamed down her face. Strangely enough for a family like ours, this was all so horribly unexpected. You see, at the time when Mum received her diagnosis we didn't know anything about BRCA1 (or breast cancer susceptibility gene 1), which is the genetic fault plaguing our family. BRCA1 is part of a class of genes known as tumour suppressors and mutations in this gene (and the BRCA2 gene) have been linked to hereditary breast and ovarian cancer. But back then genetic testing wasn't readily available and the test for our particular gene didn't even exist. All we knew was that a week earlier Mum had gone in for a routine lumpectomy, a common procedure used to remove a small lump on one of her breasts. It was no big deal, especially not to a teenage girl living in her alternate universe of parties and boys and sneaking out for cigarettes. Mum had been through nine or ten lumpectomies for various lumps and bumps in her breasts over the past decade, so we were hardly keeping a family vigil by the phone to hear the results of this latest test. We simply expected someone from the surgery to notify us with another standard, 'No; nothing to worry about,' and then we could all forget about it until the next time Mum found something in one of her apparently lumpy breasts.

And Mum certainly never believed she was going to get cancer. She just never did. She thought, 'We can't be *that* unlucky, can we?' It would be like winning some deranged lottery twice (or 25 times in our case). How many families have to endure that amount of suffering? It simply wasn't going to happen to Mum and to the women of her generation in our family. At least, that's what she thought back then.

Mum's breast cancer was detected in its very early stages so it was a best-case scenario as far as breast cancer diagnoses go. But the fact it was 'early cancer' didn't matter much to us. Here was *another* incidence of cancer, another woman in our family who would have to face the pain and emotional turmoil of losing her breasts and all the complications that come with that, another woman whose life could be cut terribly short by this same damn disease. Even now, after she has successfully beat breast cancer once and for all, Mum's had an ovarian cancer scare, plus she has spots on her kidneys and her skull that have to be constantly monitored and we do so, always, with some trepidation. Sadly, since her initial breast cancer diagnosis, Mum's developed a habit of saying: 'I just have a feeling I'm not going to live a full life.' Quite a turnaround for the woman who never seriously thought she'd get cancer.

◆ ◆ ◆

Immediately following the fateful phone call that day, my nan retreated to her bedroom for an entire three days. She wouldn't come out, she couldn't eat and she was constantly in tears. We'd leave trays of food outside her door for her and they'd sit there untouched until we came and collected them again. It was a devastating time for all of us but particularly for Nan, because she blamed herself that Mum—her only daughter—was going to suffer like she had, and like her mother before her.

Nan lived her whole life on dairy farms in Matamata, on the north island of New Zealand. The area is now mostly known as Hobbiton, thanks to filmmaker Peter Jackson, and this is a source of immeasurable pride to my nan. To say Nan's life has been one of rural domesticity is nothing short of understatement. It was all cows and cooking casseroles for her family's dinner and Nan wanted nothing more. Cows and casseroles, cows and casseroles, and then, wham!, suddenly one day it was cows and casseroles *and cancer.*

When Nan's mother, my great-grandmother Annie Bergman, was 68 years old, she was diagnosed with terminal breast cancer. Both breasts; no hope. In fact, by the end the cancer had spread throughout much of her body. And so Annie was admitted to hospital and simply never left, and it was up to my nan to help nurse her through the final months of her illness and try to make her days as comfortable as possible. Only then the unthinkable happened. As her mother lay dying from this terribly aggressive form of the disease, Nan became sick and received her *own* shocking diagnosis: Nan had breast cancer, too. (In fact, this was the second time: Nan was first diagnosed with breast cancer when she was just 44 years old.)

So now my nan had to get out of bed each morning, no longer simply racked with grief but also paralysed with fear, as she watched her mother die from the same disease that was growing in her own chest. Plus, my poor nan was suffering awfully due to chemotherapy and at one stage it looked like it could be the chemo, and not cancer, that might just kill her. Then, as if this wasn't enough, it was around this time my nan found out that her husband had been having an affair for the past eleven years. Grandad had been secretly seeing a woman who was the same age as my mum, and so half the age of my devastated nan. It was to be years before Nan and Grandad reached a point where they decided to try and retrieve their marriage, and just as they did my grandad suffered a massive stroke and died. He was only 53 and he died before Nan had the chance to forgive him.

And yet throughout the whole time Annie was dying, when Nan herself was suffering from cancer and enduring chemo and heartbroken and deceived, Nan lied to her mother, telling her she was only sick with the flu. She didn't want Annie to be on her deathbed knowing that she had passed this terrible cancer curse on to her daughter. Just like Nan had now passed it on to Mum.

The Lucky One

But before Mum's cancer, before Nan's cancer and even before Annie's, the disease was already rife in the Codlin family. Annie's mother, my great-great-grandmother Ada (Tottie) Codlin (later Bergman), was the youngest of ten children born with Jewish heritage and raised in rural New Zealand. A staggering ten out of ten of those children passed on the cancer gene to their children. The 'Codlin curse', as it was known locally, was the stuff of legends but for all the wrong reasons. Even now Nan says not a week goes by when she doesn't get a call from someone in the family. 'Did you hear Pam's been diagnosed? Left breast; like her sister …' One of Nan's uncle's had three daughters, two out of three got cancer (one breast, one ovarian) and they died a year apart. We lost count long ago of the number of cancer cases in our extended family, but soon gene-mapping will be able to provide us with the sobering tally to date and it's well into double digits by now.

Which is unbelievable, really. Especially given that medical experts liken finding our particular gene fault to spotting a single spelling mistake within the Yellow Pages phone directory. It's *that* incredibly small. And yet a gene fault in BRCA1 pops up again and again with deadly regularity. As with many hereditary gene faults (of which BRCA1 and the closely related BRCA2 are the most common), it doesn't matter if you're male or female. Regardless of gender, if you come from a family that's 'cursed' like ours, then you face a 50 per cent chance that you will inherit the mutation at the time you're conceived. While rare, the men in our family can pass on the fault and are at personal risk of developing breast and prostate cancer, but it's the women who mostly develop breast cancer (and occasionally ovarian cancer) as a result.

Krystal Barter

When Mum was diagnosed with cancer back in 1995 we didn't know about our genetic mutation—yet it didn't take a genius to work out that, generation after generation, we were dropping like flies. My nan was certainly finding the whole thing hauntingly familiar. For her, it was like some ghastly ground-hog day when my mum received her diagnosis. Having nursed her own mother to death from the disease, and then suffering breast cancer in both breasts herself, it was no wonder Nan broke down and retreated to her bedroom when the lump in Mum's right breast was found to be malignant.

♦ ♦ ♦

Me? My reaction was more complicated than that. I was shocked. And when the shock wore off, I was devastated. I was terribly, horribly frightened for Mum. Would she have to have chemotherapy? Would she lose her hair? Lose her breasts? Was she scared? Was she in pain? I worried about her until I nearly made myself sick. Most often, I was afraid of the physical suffering she might have to go through: the surgeries, the drugs, the radiation, the dreaded mastectomies. But my darkest fear and the one I never dared put into words, not to myself as I lay in bed at night and cried for Mum, and certainly not to anyone else, was: 'Would she make it?' Because she *had* to make it; she was my mum. *My mum.* And I couldn't live without her.

On the outside, though, it was a vastly different story. My tough-girl exterior went into overdrive. Here I was, a 14-year-old kid, who had only just started to grow breasts at the same time as Mum was discovering cancer in hers, and I was woefully ill-equipped to cope. I was in just my second year of high school (and a new school, at that) and yet I was witnessing the strong women in my family—my mum and my nan—fall apart in front of my eyes. What was I meant to do?

Deny it, that's what.

I'm ashamed to admit it but my first response, as far as anyone else could tell, was to pretend as though Mum's cancer simply didn't exist. It was as if I woke up and decided: 'You know what? I refuse to think about this; I'm going to socialise and have fun and be a normal teenage girl. This isn't my problem.'

In reality, the fear factor had well and truly set in. Fear for Mum, fear for our family, plain old fear of death. Because whenever I was alone, and trying desperately not to think that Mum could die, my mind would then distract itself by doing the most dreadful calculations: 'If Annie was 68 when she died of cancer, and Nan was 44 when she was diagnosed, and now Mum is 36 ... Then how old am *I* going to be when *I* get cancer? Twenty-five? Twenty?' There was no 'if' in my thinking; it was only ever a case of 'when'—and that's the sort of maths problem no kid should ever have to solve. It's a terrifying thing to have to stare at your image in the mirror each morning as you get into your school uniform and wonder: *How soon is this cancer coming for me?*

CHAPTER 2

As Mum tells it, on the eve of my thirteenth birthday I morphed, overnight, into Linda Blair from the horror film *The Exorcist*. Green projectile vomit and all. It was like I went to bed a normal human being and woke up as the devil's spawn. (Mum was about to come up against her own terrifying medical demons, although she didn't know that then.) It's hard to say what flicked my switch—the 'bitch switch', as my family called it. Puberty? Or hormones? Or I just felt like it so why don't you shut up/get out of my room/get out of my face/I hate you?

Mum says that at this point in my life I didn't resemble anyone or anything she'd ever seen before, and certainly not the sweet daughter she thought she'd raised. And this came as an especially rude shock to my parents because I'd been so perfect in primary school. Just twelve months earlier I'd been elected sports captain of Kendall House at Harbord Public School (which was just five minutes from our home in North Manly). I was one of the leading debaters in my age group in New South Wales, and I was selected for gifted and talented programs in the performing arts. I could sing, I could dance and I was near the top of my class academically but, most of all, in what was now a distant and very rosy memory for my parents, I was always impeccably behaved. I know; sickening, right? I even matched my socks to my hair-scrunchie each day. And I was a sweet kid, too. One you couldn't help but indulge.

Take my obsession with pop princess Kylie Minogue. From about eight years old, I began saving all my pocket money to go down to the local music store and purchase Kylie's latest single. I had boxes of the yellow cassettes. And I would sit in my room for hours and hours, hairbrush-microphone in hand, blissfully singing along to every memorised word. Such was my obsession that my parents suffered through a severe bout of gastro just to take me to a Kylie concert for my ninth birthday; with plastic buckets tucked under their arms—now that's what I call parental love. Of course, I was shocked to hear of Kylie's breast cancer diagnosis in 2005. Here was this beautiful, healthy pop star fighting the same cancer as my mum, and at the same age that my mum was diagnosed: 36 years old. If Kylie was an inspiration to me before, she was truly a star in my eyes now. (I still buy all her music and am a massive fan.)

But it might be said that a rebellion was always on the cards and that diligence like mine was unsustainable. Even in my former, more golden years, I'd had the good grace to temper my glowing behaviour by being a bit of a drama queen (you didn't, for instance, want to be around if I stubbed my toe or sustained a paper cut). It seems that, even at being endearingly flawed, I was an overachiever of the highest order. Until I started high school, that is. Then I was just a plain old pain in the arse.

To begin with my crimes were fairly vanilla. Exhibit A: I liked to wag school and go shopping at Chatswood Westfield instead. Or, exhibit B: I used my pocket money to buy alcohol for the Year 7 school dance. Then there were exhibits C, D and E: I began to smoke; I locked my teacher out of the classroom (more than once); and I regularly bought cigarettes at the corner store using a (forged) note from my mother asking me to purchase them on her behalf. Individually, none of these things was worth calling Department of Community Services over. But, by the time I was racking up offences Y and Z (drinking and smoking marijuana), this new routine of mine was starting to wear thin with my parents and my school, and quite possibly the other kids in the playground.

Then, of course, there was the time I was busted for drug possession by the cops but this sounds a lot worse than it was. And, to this day, I'm still not sure who it reflects worse on: Me? Or my parents (who, I later discovered, were the ones who dobbed me in)?

When I was away overnight at Year 7 school camp my parents decided to investigate the contents of my makeup case. This was no ordinary makeup case, mind you. Supersized, bulletproof and Barbie pink, this thing came complete with security-code facilities and was just crying out to be filled with pot. Or maybe that was just me. Anyway, Mum and Dad must have had their suspicions because they called in a friend of theirs who was an employee of the police force to see what he could make of the contents. Quite a lot, as it turned out.

On arriving at our house, this cop cracked the foolproof '000' security code on my makeup case in no time—hell, he wasn't a cop for nothing—and inside discovered a few precious buds of marijuana. (This would have been about one week's supply for me at that time and, I should point out here, that I never, ever, at any point in my life, pushed drugs. Anything I possessed was purely for my own enjoyment.)

Now, this guy had seen a lot of pot (see above: he wasn't a cop for nothing) but even so, at my parents' urging, he checked my stash to make sure what it was. Trouble, wrapped in Barbie-pink, that's what it was.

When I returned home from camp the next day it was to very angry, very disappointed parents. They immediately shipped me off to stay with my nan in New Zealand for three weeks ('Do not pass go, do not collect $200') where, it was thought, all that fresh country air and grass of the dairy-farm variety would do me some good.

When they weren't calling in the cops, however, my parents' response to my behaviour was far more predictable. Those first few months of misdemeanours, after years of near-faultlessness, led Mum and Dad to what they believed was the only possible conclusion: It wasn't my fault.

'Krystal's fallen in with the wrong crowd at school!' they'd say, when other kids' parents rang up to express their concern.

'It's peer pressure!' they'd chorus, as they were dragged into yet another parent/teacher conference at school.

'It's her friends making her do these things; it's not her!' they'd assure anyone who'd listen.

Heart-warming testaments to their faith in me, sure. But in truth? Hell, the problem was me.

◆ ◆ ◆

Things really started to get interesting around the time I got expelled from school. At least, that's what it sounded like to me when the principal suggested: 'Krystal, we think the best option is for you to leave our school.'

Best option? For who? The school? Because that felt a lot like expulsion and that surely wasn't the best option for me. And yet there I was. Less than a year after I started high school, and a fleeting four months since my thirteenth birthday, fate conspired against me and I was asked to leave Mackellar Girls High. And by fate, I mean my own stupidity.

It went like this: It was a stinking hot December day, the kind of day that's only good for eating Icy Poles and working on your tan, so a group of about five of us decided to wag school and wander down to Forty Baskets, a picturesque private beach near Balgowlah, flanked on one side by bushland and the other by the pristine waters of Manly Cove. The location was just perfect for smoking Winnie Golds and drinking the bottle of Midori I'd nicked from my mum. Perfect also, it turns out, for attempting to steal a dinghy that was moored on the beach and just begging to be taken out on a joy-ride round the bay. But try as we might, the thing wouldn't budge and so we flopped into it instead to sun ourselves as it sat on the sand.

The Lucky One

Lying back against the side of the boat, the PVC surface pleasantly hot through the cotton of my tunic, I let my hand fall against the cool wet sand below us. This beat sitting in a stifling-hot history classroom any day. But you know what was not so hot? Not so hot was doing all this in your school uniform, during school hours, like some sort of beacon for the authorities. We'd just failed Wagging 101.

As we lounged around in the dinghy, getting drunk and getting loud, someone nearby inevitably spotted us and helpfully phoned our school to report us. Who knows, maybe that someone had come down to the beach to take out their dinghy and found it full of pissed, pre-pubescent girls? Whoever it was, it didn't take them long to recognise our school colours and raise the alarm. Just as it didn't take our principal and vice-principal long to jump in a car and drive down to Forty Baskets to try and catch us at the scene of the crime.

Now, I can't recall if I was the ringleader this particular day—and, in defence of my memory, I was pretty drunk—but for a moment it looked like I'd be the scapegoat regardless. When the principal and vice-principal arrived at the beach, my friends and I were lazy with sunshine and languid with alcohol and were unhurriedly stuffing our salty feet back into our school shoes and beginning to amble up the beach.

'Stop!' the principal shouted, spying us from the footpath above the beach, as if that directive has ever halted any criminal anywhere and we might just freeze in our tracks.

We grabbed our school bags and bolted. Fast. Slipping through a row of upturned tinnies and running from the beach in the direction of Balgowlah, we scrambled up an embankment with our teachers in pursuit. But coming down the other side of the hill I tripped on a rock, hit the dirt and went tumbling down the slope, grazing the skin on my arm and my leg as I went. *Damn it!* As I lay sprawled among the rocks and sticks at the bottom of the hill, I felt like the stupidest person in the world. Blood streamed down my shin and my forearm as I hauled myself up and took off again, now trailing my friends but still safely ahead of the principal and vice-principal. Pausing a safe distance on, I turned and checked behind me and saw them awkwardly coming down the hill, puffing and red-faced as they negotiated the loose surface. That was the last we'd see of them that afternoon. Or so I mistakenly thought.

When I got home there was no hiding my injuries from Mum. 'What happened to you?' she asked suspiciously as I hobbled through the back door. The numbness from the afternoon's Midori had worn off and my arm and leg were stinging badly now.

'Rough game of soccer,' I lied and retreated to my bedroom.

I might have got away with it, too, you know, if the principal hadn't already phoned Mum and given her a blow-by-blow of what I'd been up to when she thought I was at school. I was sitting on my bed, rummaging through the first-aid kit, when Mum came barging into my bedroom, shouting: 'I know what bloody went on today, Krystal! And I'm taking you into the principal's office *this instant*! You're for it now!'

To his credit, the principal asked me to leave his school, rather than outright expel me (as expulsion would go on my school record). But this was of little solace to Mum. After we pulled into the driveway at home, following our short but tense car ride, following our short but tense meeting, Mum turned to me in fury and she slapped me on the arm.

The Lucky One

'Expelled!' she exploded. 'Who *are* you? And what have you done with my daughter? I can't believe you were expelled!'

Asked to leave, I wanted to correct her but I was too busy raging against that slap. This wasn't the first time that Mum had slapped me and I think we both knew it wouldn't be the last. Don't get me wrong, it wasn't like Mum's blows were hard enough to actually *hurt* me, not by a long shot; they were more a desperate expression of her total frustration with me. But, naturally, I slapped her right back.

And so there the two of us were, sitting side-by-side in our car seats, still restrained by our seat belts, slapping ineffectually at each other. The blows barely made contact with skin and we were both squealing and slapping and sobbing: 'I'm sorry! I'm sorry!' We must have looked like something from an episode of *Comedy Capers*. Very rarely would Mum and I ever get to the point where we would have a full-on screaming match, a real proper argument. It was more common for us to have these slap-a-thons. Mostly, though, our showdowns either took the form of the 'silent treatment' (which was infinitely worse than arguing *or* slapping), or else Mum simply declared, 'That's it: you're grounded until you're 21, young lady!' And she'd mean it, and I would be. Then a week or so later I'd be straight back at it again, doing the very first dumb-arse thing I could think of. It's no wonder the poor woman tried to slap some sense into me from time to time.

Now, though, I was less than a year into high school and without a high school to go to. Hardly ideal. In desperation, Mum and Dad readied themselves to fork out a mountain of their hard-earned cash and applied for me to attend Manly's premier all-girls Catholic school, Stella Maris, in what I can only assume was an attempt to exorcise some of my demons. That, and they were running out of options. First, however, I had to be accepted by Stella Maris which, as a private school, isn't required to take in any old riff-raff that turns up on its doorstep. And so Mum and I set off for another meeting with another school principal.

♦ ♦ ♦

It's funny, I regularly go back to Stella Maris these days as part of my role as Director of Pink Hope, the charity I founded. As an ambassador for cancer awareness, I speak at assemblies on the issue of hereditary cancer and of the importance of prevention and vigilance in fighting cancer, and I talk to the girls about what they can do to help raise funds to support charities like ours. My principal is no longer there but that doesn't mean there's not plenty that's still unnervingly familiar about the place today. (Some of my old teachers, for instance, are still there.) Looking out at that sea of maroon and green uniforms, from my viewpoint high up on stage, it's easy to see that some of the girls are bright-eyed and empathetic and just itching to get involved with our important work. The others? They're the ones with their heads resting on their friend's shoulder or examining their nails or picking at their tunic hem while they plan what they're going to wear to whatever party tomorrow night. Not long ago, that was totally me.

When I visited Stella Maris for the first time, to meet the principal and to see if I would make an acceptable 'Stella Girl', I can remember exactly what Mum said to me in the car on the way there because it struck fear into the very core of my being.

The Lucky One

'Krystal,' Mum announced, 'today you're going to have to take responsibility for your bad behaviour.' I gawped. '*You,*' she said, 'are going to have to sit down in front of this new principal and tell him exactly why you're looking for a new school. *You* will have to list each and every one of the things you've done to get yourself into so much trouble. And *you* are going to have to ask him whether he is prepared to accept you into his school.'

Ask? Me? I didn't like the sound of this.

'Because he doesn't have to take you, you know,' Mum added for good measure. 'And if he doesn't, who knows where you'll end up?'

The rest of the trip took place in stony silence as Mum sat contemplating my future and I sat scrolling through my recent past. Drinking? Check. Drugs? Check. Wagging school? Check. The thought of sitting in some stale principal's office and running through my list of misdemeanours for the benefit of some intimidating, middle-aged man I'd never met filled me with dread. As did the outcome. No school? Versus a *Catholic girls school*? I wasn't sure which was worse.

After what seemed like eternity (is there any other way to get to such forgiveness as Stella Maris was offering?), we pulled up at the school gates and made our way towards the front office. 'Remember,' Mum said, 'you're the one that has to do all the fast talking today.' And with that, I promptly puked into the principal's office garden. 'Krystal!' Mum was mortified. She yanked me up and wiped me down and frog-marched me into reception.

As it turned out, Stella Maris accepted me with open arms. I think I was too irresistible a prospect for the nuns. They were probably rubbing their hands together with glee as they saw me walk through their gleaming school gates that day. 'Hallelujah!' they would have praised. 'Rehabilitation time!' Because if there was one soul in that Year 7 cohort that needed shepherding onto the straight and narrow, then it was surely mine. What they didn't know, of course, was that it would be many, many years to come before that miracle ever took place.

In the meantime, however, I took to Stella Maris College with gusto. In those first few months at my new school I was elected to the Student Representative Council, I quickly settled in with a big group of friends and I even started achieving again on the academic front. On one occasion, my dad bribed me to do something outlandish and try studying for a class maths test. Given it was rare for me to open a textbook of any description, let alone actually read it, Dad offered me $200 to really work my arse off for an upcoming algebra test, if only to see for myself what I might be able to do. Turns out I could do quite a bit if I put my mind to it. I aced the test, scoring 98 per cent and topping my class. Poor Dad was torn between being disgusted and impressed: 'See what you can do if you try! You've got no excuse, Krystal, you've got to work harder. Even after rotting your brain with trashy magazines and pot, you can still come top of your class.'

When I decided to be, I was surprisingly adept at academic achievement; the problem was I so rarely decided to be. But in those early months at Stella Maris I really knuckled down, I studied hard and got good results, and my parents must have thought they'd solved the problem of what to do with their wayward teenage daughter.

But then I got bored. Ugh, it was all so tedious! Roll-call and chapel and homework and Saturday morning sport and

The Lucky One

blah, blah, blah. Fed up with doing what I was supposed to be doing, I fell back into my cycle of old. Drinking and smoking and skipping school and dabbling in pot again. Only now my parents were paying school fees—really expensive school fees—for the privilege of my misbehaviour. I smuggled alcohol into class and I snuck out on the balcony at home to smoke cigarettes. I bought pot from my friends' older siblings then smoked it at the park and came home reeking of bubblegum and Impulse deodorant in a pathetic attempt to try and mask the gunja scent. Just as soon as I'd showed some signs that I might be getting my act together, I turned around and stuffed things up again.

And then my mum got cancer.

CHAPTER 3

I was in Year 8 when Mum received her diagnosis: malignant tumour, right breast, requiring immediate breast removal due to our family history and the high risk of bilateral cancer (cancer in both breasts). The cancer was detected early enough that Mum had a really good prognosis. And yet, I don't know whether it was the weight of *another* instance of cancer in the family, or just the fact this thing had finally, inevitably, come for her, but Mum didn't cope at all with her diagnosis and subsequent surgery. Emotionally or physically.

Having suffered from anxiety in the past, Mum was now deeply distressed and would frequently break down into uncontrollable crying. She locked herself in her bedroom for hours and just sobbed. She was having panic attacks that were so severe her doctor was talking about admitting her to hospital to help her recover. The surgery itself, while traumatic, was a success. The cancer hadn't spread to Mum's lymph nodes and doctors were confident they had removed all existing breast tissue, on both sides, and with it all traces of cancer. Yet after the surgery, things were worse than before.

Mum woke up in terrible emotional shock at having had her breast removed, plus she reacted very negatively to her painkillers. We have a history—my nan, my mum and me—of responding badly to painkillers and anaesthetics. Several years after Mum's mastectomy I had a regular knee reconstruction and wound up in intensive care because my body couldn't handle the morphine. I'd only had 2.5 milligrams and still my blood pressure plummeted and my breathing slowed to the point that I was placed on oxygen and nurses had to monitor my condition every few minutes. (You'd think this drug-intolerant family history might factor in my decision to dabble in recreational drugs, but apparently not.) But this was small fry compared to Mum's reaction to her post-surgery drugs.

To start with she developed a rash on her neck, then she began vomiting violently and this continued for the entire week or so that she was in hospital. She suffered severe hallucinations; most often she believed that rats were being flung at her face and she would scream in fear at all hours of the day and night. Then one afternoon, eight days after her mastectomy had been deemed a success and less than four hours after she'd arrived home, Mum suffered a severe and adverse drug reaction.

◆ ◆ ◆

Krystal Barter

I was sprawled on the couch just outside my parents' bedroom at the time, and Mum was holed up inside, resting in bed, with Dad hovering nearby. Nan was pottering around in the kitchen somewhere and my little brother was off at Cub Scouts. Suddenly, I heard Dad swear, quietly, from Mum's bedside. Dad never swore. Dad was calm and placid and logical and even-tempered; he didn't get flustered, he just got on with it. Dad was not a swearer. Next, I heard him pick up the phone from the bedside table and punch in three short numbers: beep, beep, beep. I held my breath. 'Ambulance, please.'

They say that in instances like this time slows until it's practically standing still. Seconds take an age, as if they've been spilt from a great height and as they fall they elongate, liquid and languorous, before they pool on the floor. That's sure as hell not how it felt to me. As we waited for the ambulance to arrive that day, Mum catatonic on her bed, Dad prowling between her bedside and the window overlooking the street, and Nan holed up in the kitchen in immobilised panic, I stopped and started and stopped and started about a million different useless tasks. *I know! I'll get some water. No, no, I'll stand out the front waiting for the ambos. Or, should I stay here and see if there's any change in Mum's breathing?* I scuttled in ever-decreasing circles, doing nothing much of anything at all, and the minutes simply evaporated in front of me until two burly ambulance officers bustled into the house. The second ambo, in particular, was impossibly tall and he had to duck to avoid hitting his head as he came in the front door.

'Through here?' They started towards where Dad was hovering in the bedroom doorway. I nodded.

The Lucky One

'She'll be right,' the tall officer said, winking kindly to me, and I desperately wanted to believe him. But I had my doubts. From where I was standing it seemed that, when it came to our family, anything that *could* go wrong, *would* go wrong; and anything that would go wrong was going really pear-shaped right now.

'Breathing?' It was the tall ambo and he threw the question at his shorter colleague, who was a few steps ahead of him, already bent over Mum's impassive face.

'Breathing. Airway clear. Pulse present. Unresponsive. Dissociative state,' came the staccato reply. Tall officer nodded as he crouched down in one surprisingly smooth movement and began unpacking supplies from his backpack with expert efficiency.

If this was anyone else's mum, in anyone else's family, she would go through cancer surgery and then come home and get better, I raged to myself, my fear giving way to fury now. *There'd be no panic attacks or hallucinations or collapsing dramatically; for anyone else this would all just go smoothly. End of story. But, no; not for us. It could never be that simple for us.*

'Oxygen?'

'Active.'

'Blood pressure?'

'50/30.'

The ambos volleyed information back and forth as Dad and I watched on, bewildered. Mum didn't stir.

Of course, years later I've come to realise that there are many, many families out there who suffer just as much as we seemed to. Some suffer even more. I know people whose mother was taken away by an ambulance and never brought back again.

Ever. But at the time it was beginning to feel like maybe we really *were* cursed and that the possibility of Mum never coming back to us might be exactly where we were headed.

'IV line?'

'Stabilising now.'

The medics began to administer clear fluid through a drip they'd set up in the middle of the bedroom. At the same time they continued to check Mum's pulse and to monitor her breathing. For two large guys, working under pressure and in an overcrowded bedroom, they were impressive. Seeing them move around in their matching white uniforms was like watching some strange but highly choreographed ballet.

And then slowly, so slowly, Mum appeared to regain consciousness. Her eyes, which had been spookily open the entire time, like some unblinking doll who was made without eyelids, now flickered slightly. For a moment she seemed to be aware of what was going on around her, although her body was still rigid and unmoving and she made no attempts to speak.

'Julie-Anne!' Dad said and rushed over to her bedside.

It was strange to see Dad cut up like this. Normally he was Mum's rock; he was everybody's rock. I wasn't sure how to react to Dad being exposed. I felt like I should look away. Dad was such a man's man—all motorbikes and beer and Sky News—it was like I was intruding somehow by seeing this vulnerable man who was hovering at Mum's bedside. Mum and Dad were like two halves of the one coin. Dad cooked and Mum cleaned; Dad drove and Mum navigated. They seemed to do everything together and I just didn't know what Dad would ever do without Mum.

The Lucky One

'Mum?' I asked warily, but she just stared blankly in Dad's general direction, her eyes as frozen and unmoving as the rest of her body.

'See? Told you she'd be apples,' the tall ambo said brightly as they continued to busily inject and insert and administer and monitor and all with no less urgency than before. 'Reckon we might whack her into Manly Hospital for a bit, though, just to keep an eye on her.'

I watched in silence as they wheeled Mum outside to the waiting ambulance. Her face was deathly pale. She didn't look very apples to me. Dad clambered into the back of the vehicle next to her and the last I saw of them he was gripping her hand tightly and looking grim-faced. Then the doors slammed shut and I was left alone on the kerb.

I sat in the gutter for a while after the ambulance had gone. I wasn't sure what else to do so I just sat, stabbing uselessly at the warm concrete with a broken stick I picked up off the lawn. Mum was gone again. And Dad this time, too. Nan was still inside somewhere. My brother would be home later and after mooching around the house for a while might come and shout through my bedroom door: *Where's Mum and Dad?* I tried not to think of what my friends' families would be doing today.

Not dying, that's for sure.

◆ ◆ ◆

As it turns out, our mum wasn't, either. When Dad rang from the hospital later, it was to tell us that Mum was doing okay. She'd woken up and had stabilised nicely. Talking to me afterwards, Mum said that the closest thing she could equate the whole episode to was an out-of-body experience. Despite being seemingly unconscious, she could, as I suspected at one point, hear a little of what was going on around her. She said she felt as though she had drifted in and out of consciousness and did, for instance, remember the ambulance officers arriving. Mostly, however, everything was a blur and she certainly couldn't have responded, even if she'd wanted to; her mouth was rigidly shut. The strangest and most frightening part for her, though, was the way in which the whole thing came on. Mum said she knew something was wrong when she suddenly felt no pain for the first time since her operation. Having been in the most terrible pain for more than a week, Mum recalls how a beautiful, serene feeling came over her and how she felt like she was hovering several centimetres above her body.

'Mark, I think I'm dying,' she'd said calmly to Dad. 'I feel like I'm drifting away.'

Dad, practical as ever, had rushed over to her bedside and grabbed her wrist to feel for a pulse.

'You're not dying, Julie-Anne,' he told her firmly. But he'd immediately snatched up the phone and called the ambulance.

◆ ◆ ◆

After being rushed back to the hospital only four hours after she left, it took another four hours for Mum to regain full consciousness. Her doctors determined that it *was* one of the post-operation drugs she'd been prescribed which had caused her reaction, as well as all of her other preceding symptoms, and so they immediately removed it from the cocktail of medications she was taking. They were confident, now, that they had her medication right and so they assured us that today's emergency was unlikely to happen again.

I was relieved, of course; we all were. But I didn't go to the hospital to visit Mum. I figured she'd be home soon enough. And after that? Well, she'd probably be back in hospital again before too long, I thought bitterly. So if I really wanted to hang out in Manly's intensive care unit I was sure I'd still have plenty of opportunity.

Back in the gutter, I stood up and kicked the concrete. Twice. Stupid family, stupid Mum, stupid, stupid cancer. I hated them all and I walked around the front yard now, slashing at things with my stick. Stupid tree, slash. Stupid letter box, slash. Stupid, stupid white pillar. Slash, slash, slash. I left a satisfyingly long scratch in the paintwork on the veranda pillar. It felt good to be the one breaking things for once, rather than sitting around waiting for the next blow to land on us. I was so scared and so distraught and so utterly miserable these days that I didn't know what to do with myself. I was scared of Mum's cancer and I was scared of Mum dying. I was scared that she'd had to have her breasts removed and I was scared *witless* at having just seen her collapse. There had been some strange delineation in my mind that hospitals were the place for sickness and death but at home we were somehow protected from all that. Now, though, having just seen Mum unconscious in her own bedroom—having seen her look, for all intents and purposes, like a corpse lying there on her bed—it broke down some final barrier in my mind. Nowhere was safe anymore.

Most all of, though, I was scared of sitting alone in the gutter outside our house, with its neatly tended lawn and its wide, welcoming veranda, but with no living people inside.

No Mum, no family, no cancer survivors to speak of. And one day, I figured, I wouldn't be there, either. This stupid cancer would come for me, too, and then our house would finally be empty.

◆ ◆ ◆

The way I articulated these fears, however, was to behave worse than ever before. Sure, I realise that *before* Mum got sick I was never a contender for Daughter of the Year. But after her diagnosis I really took things up (or, more correctly, down) a notch.

Mum's cancer was just the excuse I needed to truly start rebelling. I had no shame exploiting her illness to my advantage and I regularly used it to get out of trouble. Failed to hand in an assignment? My mum has cancer. Busted smoking? My mum has cancer. Absent from school? Drunk again? Rude, argumentative, annoying as all hell? My mum has cancer, my mum has cancer, my mum has cancer!

Whatever my latest offence, I would simply pull my teacher aside and have a quiet word with them. 'Look,' I'd say sagely, acting as though I was letting them in on this for their own benefit, 'I don't know if the school has explained my situation to you but … my mum has breast cancer. In fact, she's at home right now recuperating after having had her breast surgically removed. So hopefully that sheds some light on my current behaviour.' Then the two of us would perform this ludicrous dance: me, the overwrought daughter, only driven to misbehave by fear for my mother; and the teacher, guilt-stricken and paralysed from punishing me out of concern for my welfare.

When in reality we both knew I was just being a shit.

The Lucky One

The best example of this, and the one I'm nearly too ashamed to write down, is the day Mum was admitted to hospital to have her mastectomy. On that day, my brother and I were instructed to stay at home with my nan but, unimpressed at being 'babysat', I decided I'd rather go and hang out with my friend Lisa at her house. Watching *Rage* and reading *TV Week* sounded like a better option than being stuck at home with my nan. Nan, on the other hand, was (understandably) distressed at the time and so any complications—even complications that involved getting her delinquent teenage granddaughter out of her hair for a few hours—were a no-go.

'I'd rather you just stayed here with me and Andrew,' she said. 'At least that way, I know where you are.' (And 'what you're up to' was the subtext, although she didn't need to say it.)

Not one to take 'no' for an answer, I immediately phoned my parents at the hospital. 'Nan won't let me go to Lisa's house!' I screamed at my startled parents. The outrage needed no preamble in my mind; the facts, well, they spoke for themselves. 'It's like a jail here!' I shrilled. 'Nan's not the boss of me!' On this, I was indignant.

Now, there's a right and a wrong time to call your parents with this type of gripe. And the few precious moments your mum and dad have together before your mum is wheeled away to have cancer surgery is surely not the right time. Mum and Dad patiently explained to me that, while they weren't there, Nan was in charge, but that things would be back to normal soon and I could hang out with Lisa as much as I liked then. I'm sure they were trying to convince themselves as much as me that better days were just around the corner, but all I heard was 'hang out with Lisa' and 'soon' and 'as much as I liked' and so I gave in and grudgingly agreed to wait it out with Nan. We hung up then and I returned to the minutia of my teenage-girl day, while my parents prepared for my mum to have her breast cut off.

It's amazing to think I could be so insensitive to their trauma, but at the time I never gave it a second thought. And I'm afraid, even now, I couldn't tell you why, other than to offer my age as some sort of lame and shameful explanation.

◆ ◆ ◆

And yet it *was* hard to be a 14-year-old kid with a mum who had cancer. To an outsider seeing me at that age, I was cocky and confident and not intimidated by anything. But I could get embarrassed just like any other teenager and, despite my shows of bravado, in truth I found it mortifying to have to go to school and tell people that my mum had been diagnosed with cancer. I hated their sympathy and their well-meaning arm around my shoulders and their saccharine quotes about strength and perseverance and footsteps in the sand. I was fourteen years old, for godssake, and all I wanted was to be like everyone else in my class. I didn't want the boy I had a crush on finding out my mum was having her *breasts* removed (breast cancer was such an *embarrassing* cancer). I didn't want to be separated from my friends to 'take time out in the library' if I needed it. I didn't want to go home from school to a mum who was sick and pale and clinically depressed; who couldn't come to my netball matches; who couldn't yell at me to stop watching *Neighbours* and go and do my homework; who couldn't nag me about my uniform being too short.

The Lucky One

I wanted my mum, my normal old mum, and not a mum who had cancer *all the time*.

Looking back, it seems ridiculous that I was ever worried about stuff like having to say '*breast* cancer' in front of boys, especially when Mum was suffering the way she was. But the universe according to a teenage girl is a strange place and, much as I'd like to, I can't change how I felt back then, and how I felt was embarrassed.

To make things worse than they already were, the blame for Mum's cancer lay squarely with me. And for once this wasn't something dreamed up or exaggerated by my adolescent mind; it was the actual accusation flung at me by distraught family and friends.

'The reason your mum is in hospital is because of all the stress you put her through!' was the charge.

'Your poor mother wouldn't be going through this now if you hadn't worried her half to death!' they'd say.

I guess I can hardly be surprised that this is the conclusion people came to. After all, these same friends and family had watched me torture my parents with my misbehaviour. They'd seen my parents arrive at work with bags under their eyes after staying up all night waiting for me to come home, or they'd listened to my mum pour her heart out over the phone about her out-of-control daughter. So I guess it was only fair that when things got really dark for Mum, and when those closest to her flailed around looking for someone or something to blame, that finger of blame inevitably landed on me.

Some people, I'm sure, only said it in an attempt to shock me into improving my ways. For others, it was a completely unintentional outburst, usually uttered through tears in some dreaded, sterile hospital room as we waited to hear Mum's latest prognosis, or stood around anxiously for her to be wheeled back to us after surgery, pale and frail and unconscious. Whatever the reason, each time it was uttered I felt like it was my own strange, black tumour eating me up inside. To be the reason for my mother's cancer was a devastating thing to have to carry around with me and I didn't realise till much later how deeply it affected me. At the time I mostly brushed it off, denying it to myself and even, on occasion, openly challenging the person who said it. Even as a kid I knew enough about medical science to know that my wagging school didn't cause a malignant lump in Mum's breast. But that doesn't mean I didn't take at least part of what they said to heart, and it would be years before I could begin to let that go.

I'm not, for one second, saying 'poor me'. Not at all. And I realise that emotional damage, if you want to call it that, is vastly different to the devastating physical wreckage that I was seeing all around me. It's just that to understand the person I am today, you need to see how much cancer has shaped me, in so many ways, and from such a young age.

For as long as I can remember, cancer has been part of my life. Some of my earliest memories are infected with cancer, though I couldn't see it at the time. I remember having baths with my nan when she came to stay with us from New Zealand. Sitting opposite me in the tub, surrounded by a flotilla of cheerful plastic bath toys, Nan had nothing where her breasts should have been, only ribs and skin. She'd undergone a double mastectomy in the late 1970s and early 1980s after being diagnosed with a malignant tumour in her right breast and back then the surgery was pretty primitive: no cosmetic consideration, no prosthetic inserts. As a result her chest was in pretty bad shape, with one side completely flat and the other devastatingly concave. Yet, to me, her barren chest was totally normal; I never realised that a nan might look any other way.

After our bath I used to think it was fun to slip Nan's rubbery prosthesis down my cotton pyjama top and parade around the house pretending to be Dolly Parton. 'Look at me; I'm wearing Nan's boobs!' I'd say as I posed in front of the full-length mirror in my parents' room.

It was only when I was much older that I realised how bizarre this was and understood just what it means for a family to be surrounded by so much cancer. You mean other kids don't play dress-ups with prosthetic body parts? Or don't know how to spell 'malignant'?

And if my childhood was infected with cancer, then my teenage years were riddled with it. Once, when I was fifteen and after Mum had endured her mastectomy, I convinced myself that I'd found a lump in my own breast. Images of my devastated future flashed through my brain. Spending 'Work Experience Week' in oncology but as a patient and not a budding surgeon ... wearing a wig to my Year 12 formal after losing my hair to chemo ... missing Schoolies Week on the Gold Coast while I was hospitalised for a double mastectomy ... It's laughable, now, to think I might have been harbouring a tumour in what little breast I had inside my training bra, but at the time I was near-hysterical with fear.

Clutching my breast I ran screaming to Mum, who was chopping vegetables in the kitchen (and probably near-sliced a finger off). 'I've found a lump! I've found a lump!' I screamed in panic and slumped dramatically onto the kitchen floorboards.

Krystal Barter

Crying and pounding the timber, I wailed: 'I've got cancer like you! I just know it!' My adolescence, just like anyone else's, was a highly emotionally charged time. The only difference was that mine had a nucleus and that nucleus was cancer. It defined me; and in an exclusively negative way.

Years later, when I held my firstborn, Riley, I finally understood just how much a parent loves their child, but as a teenager I had no real concept of this. Or, if I did, I chose to ignore it. When she was first diagnosed with cancer and she was fearful she would die, Mum sat down and wrote me a heartfelt (heartbreaking) letter. As it turned out, she didn't give it to me until many years later because there simply wasn't any need to and in hindsight I'm glad that she didn't. Because until I was older I would never have appreciated just how very special it was. It read:

To my darling precious daughter Krystal,
My heart is breaking writing this letter, my tears are falling wondering if I will survive this dreadful disease. I want so much to see you marry and have children of your own. I should have written this letter years ago, bad health or not. I have had an amazing life, I am very grateful for that. I married, had babies and I'm very grateful for that reason. This letter is to give you courage and strength. I want you to never give up on the power of hope.
When your wedding day comes, erase your memory, do not mourn me on this special day, and embrace this beautiful day. This is your journey now, I dreamt of this day watching you walk down the aisle on your father's arm. I will hold that thought in my heart forever.

The Lucky One

Remember, health and happiness is far more important than wealth. Listen to your husband, take guidance, give love, be understanding, forgive, be positive and supportive. Work things through, it's too easy to walk away from problems, work through them. And, most of all, respect one another.

Your babies: how I dream of their smell holding them in my arms. The happiness of their births. The gift of a child is an amazing precious journey. Now you will know how I felt when I gave birth to you, I felt peace when I looked into your eyes, I felt brave beyond words. I was exhausted after a long difficult labour but when I saw you for the first time I felt calm, free of pain and instantly in love. I wanted you so much it hurt in my heart, I asked for a little girl and I got you. You were my childhood dream.

I was given two beautiful gifts from your dad and that's you and Andrew.

A mother is so protective; have patience, give your children opportunities in life, be observant, listen. You will feel sometimes you are on a rollercoaster but you will get off that rollercoaster, never forget that. Be creative with them, give them wisdom, you will be an inspirational mother, you will dazzle, my darling.

I will hold you in my heart forever when you are thinking of me, I will be thinking of you, my baby girl. Be brave, my darling, and have courage; you are not alone. Remember the journey of a thousand miles must begin with a single step.

I will love you forever.
Mummy x

When I was a teenager I placed no value on my own life, which allowed me to act as badly as I did. And it wasn't until after those first few precious hours of holding my son Riley in my arms that I turned to Mum and Dad and said, 'Oh my god, I'm so sorry.' I put my mum, in particular, through such a terribly tough time and, awful as the truth is, it wouldn't have made any difference whether she had been diagnosed with cancer or not. I was out of control and Mum's cancer wasn't the reason. My teenage years were spent not coping; not coping with cancer, but also not coping with just being me. It would be a long and very rocky road before I accepted this, and to get where I am now. But first there was much worse to come.

CHAPTER 4

During my childhood I spent almost every weekend visiting my Nanny Beryl. Now, this was no cup-of-tea-and-if-you're-lucky-a-biscuit affair. No keep-your-voice-down-Nanny's-sleeping (or speak-up-Nanny-doesn't-have-her-aids-in) effort. Not even close. No, my Nanny Beryl was, and still very much is, fabulous.

Beryl is my dad's mum and she lives in Frenchs Forest, a leafy suburban idyll about twenty minutes drive from our house. For the longest time she was the sole carer for my grandpa, Dudley, who had suffered from Parkinson's Disease since he was 36 years old. So when I was a kid and went to visit my grandparents I loved seeing my grandpa, but it was really Nanny Beryl who was the star of the show. And with good cause.

Krystal Barter

Nanny Beryl was a grandma without limits. If I told her I wanted to be a hairdresser then she'd rummage through her kitchen drawer for a pair of scissors and brandish them in the air, saying, 'Well, let's get started! Come on, show me how good you are!' Then she'd plonk herself down at the dining room table and let me, five-year-old me, hack at her hair. 'You can only cut this much,' Nanny would instruct me, holding her thumb and index finger a centimetre apart, but 'this much' can quickly become 'that much' when you're five and often I'd be left with a hefty chunk of hair in my chubby apprenticed hands. But Nanny never seemed to mind and so I'd be employed as her hairdresser, weekend after weekend, until I was on to my next phase.

Like, being an actress. My favourite thing to do at Nanny Beryl's was to watch 'olden-day' movies with her. *Gone with the Wind*, *Calamity Jane*, *The Wizard of Oz*: I adored them all and knew every word. Still do. When *Oklahoma!* came on TV recently and I broke into (word-perfect) song, my husband looked at me like I was mad. 'How can the same person love Britney Spears *and* Rodgers & Hammerstein?' he asked, shaking his head. What can I say? I'm a sucker for the classics. And with Nanny Beryl on the couch beside me, these old technicolour relics became magical. We'd be watching *Meet Me in St Louis* and Nanny would turn to me and say, 'See Judy Garland there, Krystal? She looks just like you do.' And I believed her, as I imagined my life with Tom Drake, dancing at the Christmas Eve ball in St Louis.

We'd play banks and I'd be the teller whose name was always 'Rose' and, years later, I discovered Nanny had kept all the 'cheque books' I'd scribbled in when doling out my millions.

The Lucky One

I was really into drama as a kid and Nanny Beryl always encouraged me here, too. When I was in primary school I was selected for the Metropolitan North Drama Ensemble and chosen for the role of Dorothy in *The Wizard of Oz* (there was Judy Garland again). As Dorothy, I performed solo at Sydney's State Theatre and then at the Sydney Opera House and I firmly believe it was my Nanny Beryl who gave me the skills and the confidence to do that.

Together Nanny Beryl and I performed the canon of great theatrical works: *Sleeping Beauty*, *Little Red Riding Hood* and, let's not forget, *Cinderella*. Naturally, I would be Cinderella, in all her glass-slipper-shod glory, while Nanny took on the supporting roles of the Ugly Stepsisters and Prince Charming and the pumpkin coach and every single other cast member I could dream up. Or, in *Sleeping Beauty*, I would lie (*dramatically*) on the couch, concentrating on looking beautiful while Nanny put the rest of the characters through their paces, until I deigned to be woken from my slumber.

Nanny Beryl was my best friend.

I remember being nine years old and going into hospital to have my tonsils removed. Nanny Beryl never left my side the entire three days I stayed at Mona Vale hospital. She sat with me all day, tickling my arm and reading me stories, and then at night she slept in a chair by my bedside. I always hoped if I ever had children that my mum would love them like Nanny Beryl loved me (and, of course, she does).

But perhaps the best thing about Nanny was her stories. At night Nanny used to lie down on my bed with me and tell me all about my dad's side of the family, the Barters. We were of French stock, Nanny told me, from the medieval fortress city,

Krystal Barter

Carcassonne, in the south of France; although the first Barters arrived in Australia as free settlers as early as 1838. Nanny's father, my great-grandad Colin Whitfield, fought at Gallipoli during World War I. 'He was a war hero, my dad,' Nanny would tell me proudly, before regaling me with stories of his adventures at Lone Pine after he lied about his age and enlisted with the Anzacs before he'd even turned eighteen. He survived, too, which was no mean feat at Gallipoli. (I guess they make them pretty tough on *both* sides of my family.)

'Tell me about our bushranger again,' I'd boss Nanny. *Our* bushranger was Flash Dan Charters, who was my third great-uncle (my grandfather's great-uncle).

'Oh, you don't want to hear that silly story again,' Nanny would tease. 'Ole Flash? You mean Flash Dan, right-hand-man to the great bushranger Ben Hall, the biggest, baddest bushranger this side of Forbes? *That* Flash Dan? The one who was right there by Ben Hall's side when he bailed up the Cobb & Co and stole all that gold? The one who was there when Ben Hall was hunted down by the troopers, one, two, three? You mean, that Flash Dan? The one who was a local hero, who robbed the rich to feed the poor, is that the one you're talking about?'

'Yes! *That* one!' I'd shout, exasperated, my Annie Hall finger-pistols hooked into the elastic waistband of my PJs. 'I said, tell me about *our* bushranger!'

Now, I don't know exactly how much of Nanny Beryl's bushranger stories were fact and how much were fiction. I've never since asked and she's never divulged. There's no denying Flash Dan Charters is my third great-uncle and that he was friend enough to Ben Hall that he was godfather to Hall's firstborn child. But from there the details become a little hazy. Did he bail up stagecoaches? Was he the Robin Hood of Central Western New South Wales? Who's to say? But none of that really mattered to me, what mattered was the hope that Flash Dan brought me; hope that I might grow up to one day be just like him, or like my great-grandad Colin Whitfield, our hero of Gallipoli, or, hell, like Nanny Beryl herself. Like anyone, in fact, from any branch or from any limb of the Barter family tree, anyone that grew up and did something fantastic *other* than beating cancer.

Because that was the difference.

While my dad's family all seemed to be out having heroic adventures or achieving amazing thing—things worthy of a Nanny Beryl bedtime story—Mum's family fought cancer. That's unfair of me, I know. Mum's mum (my nan), for instance, ran a farm and raised two children, both of which are important things and things to be very, very proud of. She has had the toughest life (only recently, for example, she recovered from major heart surgery to repair her aorta which was damaged as a direct result of radiotherapy) and she has experienced so much. And yet she's the kindest person you could ever hope to meet. But what defines Nan's life, her salient achievement, has been battling and beating that bloody cancer. All the women in the Codlin family, all those victims of the 'Codlin cancer curse', they fought cancer. That was their life's work simply because they didn't have the chance to do anything else; they were too busy just surviving. And our family stories reflect that. On Mum's side we focus on cancer, not on achievements or milestones or those hilarious personal anecdotes that all families tell and re-tell even though they aren't really amusing to anyone who's not blood related to you. No, the Codlin family history has been completely overshadowed by cancer. That's it; that's all we talk about.

So it was good to hear Nanny Beryl's stories and to learn that I had a history beyond disease and maybe a future, too. That I might grow up to be an actress or a bankteller or a bushranger or, hell, anything other than sick. Until one day, when I must have been about twelve years old, I announced to Nanny Beryl that I wouldn't be going to visit her anymore.

'I'm grown up now,' I explained. 'So I don't want to come over here, I'd rather stay at my friends' houses now, thanks.'

And so that was the end of my weekends at Nanny Beryl's. She told me, much later, that she'd sobbed for weeks after my grand announcement, but I had no inkling of it at the time. I simply turned on my newly independent heel and trotted off into the next stage of my life. Although, at various times over the next few years, I would have done just about anything to be back, safe, on Nanny Beryl's mustard-coloured velour couch, waiting for Scarlett O'Hara to realise her love for poor Rhett, or holding my breath while Nanny Prince Charles fitted my glass slipper.

◆ ◆ ◆

'Krystal, where are your shoes!'

It wasn't a question, just a statement of exasperation. And as the words left her mouth, Mum's outstretched arms flailed out from her sides, as if she was trying to demonstrate the enormity of her frustration. Those arms swam before my eyes like jellyfish tentacles. I giggled, then gasped in pain.

The Lucky One

'Krystal! Get up!' Mum was sliding from frustration to anger and fast. So fast, in fact, she hadn't realised the ridiculousness of what she'd said. Because if there was one thing I *wasn't* going to be doing that night, it was getting myself up from where I was splattered across the slimy floor of the Newport Arms women's toilets, my face streaked with mascara, my skirt hoiked up around my underwear, and my shoes? I had no idea where my shoes were.

'Mark? You'd better come in here,' Mum shouted to my poor dad, who was hovering awkwardly in the doorway of the ladies bathroom, trying not to look like a middle-aged man who was hovering awkwardly in the doorway of the ladies bathroom. He shuffled inside.

'Shit,' Dad said, assessing the situation and hitting the nail on the head in more ways than one. For a man who didn't swear he was becoming quite adept at it. 'What the hell have you done to yourself?'

'Meneeeeee,' I groaned.

It was true; I'd finally done my knee. For the past few months I had been regularly injuring my left knee while I was out partying. It was nothing major, or so I thought at the time, just a case of tripping over some (ill-placed) furniture or stumbling up some (ill-placed) steps when I was drunk. Easy enough to do. The problem was that I was drunk *a lot,* like, every night on the weekend (and by weekend I mean Thursday through to Sunday nights, inclusive, with the odd Wednesday night thrown in for good measure). And if I wasn't drunk, I was on ecstasy or speed (except for the times I was drunk *and* on ecstasy or speed). In short, that knee of mine copped a battering.

Krystal Barter

But was that going to stop me? Hell no! By the time I was eighteen and I had finally left school (as in: graduated, I didn't leave via expulsion this time), I was partying like it was 1999 even though it was well into the new millennium. I was a party animal, the party starter, the party queen, never a party pooper. My phone rang almost 24/7 with friends checking up to see what was going down. I was fun with a capital 'F'.

'Be at the party tonight, Krystal?'

'Gunna see you at Charlie Bar?'

'Not having a quiet one, are you, Krystal?'

'Hey, know where I can get it on tonight?'

Yes, yes, hell no, and, of course.

I never wasted a second that could have been better spent getting wasted and if that pesky knee popped out of alignment, as it did on seven or eight occasions, well then, I simply whacked it back in again on the spot and got back to enjoying myself. Until that night at Newport Arms. It took several attempts for me to crack my knee back into place and when I finally did it was with a stomach-churning 'crunch'. *The pain!* It sliced through my drunken haze and I cried out in agony. My friends, unable to get me to stand or move, were forced to phone my parents to come and get me.

'Can you stand?' my dad asked optimistically.

'Do you think she can stand?' Mum snapped, glaring at me. I pressed the heels of my hands into the putrid green tiles and made a show of trying to put weight through them.

'Uuuuugh,' I slurred dramatically, as if I'd somehow managed to move myself even a centimetre.

'Come on then,' Dad said and he shoved his hands under my armpits and hoisted me up off the ground. 'We can't leave you here.' (Both he and Mum looked tempted.) Then the three of us headed out through the throbbing bar like some strange five-legged animal: me, slumped drunkenly all over Dad, my injured leg dangling uselessly at a right angle ahead of us. We led the way, while Mum hustled behind us, shouldering my ludicrously tiny handbag. I never did find my shoes from that night.

My parents drove me straight from the pub to Manly Hospital, where the prognosis wasn't pretty. Neither was its delivery. 'You've obviously been drinking,' the doctor said curtly. It was a statement of fact (with a side-order of judgement). He was as unimpressed as my parents were.

'Wannagooome,' I replied.

'You're not going anywhere fast,' he said. 'So I hope you had a good night; it'll be your last for a while. You've stuffed that knee good and proper.'

He wasn't wrong. I'd dislocated my knee so severely this time that a full knee reconstruction was required. And while a knee recon isn't life-threatening surgery, it did mean I needed a general anaesthetic and several days stay in hospital (especially after I had that allergic reaction to the morphine, as I mentioned before). As I sat up in my hospital bed, surrounded by septuagenarians who were having various decrepit joints replaced after a lifetime of vigorous lawn bowls, I pondered what it means to need a knee reconstruction when you're just nineteen years old. But, then, I was hammering my body with so much drink and drugs and drunken dancing and a drunken diet that, I suppose, something had to give and that something was my knee. For anyone that hasn't had a knee reconstruction, let me tell you now: it bloody hurts. On a scale of one to child birth, knee surgery and its associated rehabilitation is up there at the kill-me-now end of things. So you'd expect that excruciating pain of this degree, and for what was ostensibly a self-inflicted injury, might be enough to make me stop and think about my life. Or not.

In my case: not. Hell, I wasn't pausing long enough to think or to reflect or to see the error of my ways and take up Bikram yoga and bircher muesli. There was still fun to be had (with that capital 'F'!) and it wasn't long before I was out of my hospital gown and back on the dance floor. Because if there's one thing that's hot, fellas, it's a drunk girl in a miniskirt wearing a knee brace!

◆ ◆ ◆

At this stage of my life getting wasted *was* my life. If you'd sat next to me on a plane and watched me fill out one of those 'Incoming Passenger' cards, then you would have seen me write 'Partying' in the little empty boxes next to 'Occupation'. After completing the Higher School Certificate, I was accepted into the Australian Catholic University at Strathfield to study a Bachelor of Teaching in Primary School Education. (Fancy leaving your kids in my care for the day?) For six studious weeks there, I was a model university scholar. I attended lectures and contributed to class discussions in my tutorials; I read my course handouts and queued dutifully to buy textbooks from the Co-Op Bookshop. And then someone invited me to a Subski party at Sydney University. Real. Bad. Idea.

Subski, for the uninitiated, is like every tasteless American college movie you've ever seen, but all rolled together, oh, and on crack. Short for 'Sydney University Boarders and Ski Society', Subski specialised in social skiing, with the emphasis on social (I knew club members who had never seen snow). Subski was known for hosting the wildest parties at Sydney Uni's vast campus. Parties such as their infamous traffic light parties, where you had to wear red, yellow or green depending on your romantic status in order to shout to the world, without the need for annoying conversation, just how available you were right then and there. Theirs were parties where the decorations were inflated goon bags and the beer was measured in kegs. I had found my spiritual home.

It's fair to say that I had a massive night at my first Subski party. So massive, in fact, that when I woke up the next morning I had something of an epiphany on the careers front.

'That's it!' I decided. 'I've found my true calling. I'm not going back to study teaching, in fact, I'm not going back to uni at all. I'm going to spend my life partying! And when I'm not partying, I'll be working to *pay* for my partying.' Because even through a hangover I had the clarity of vision to see that getting wasted on the scale that Subski had revealed to me was going to require some funds.

So I dropped out of my course. I had lasted six measly weeks at university before I threw it all away to work in various, entry-level jobs so I could earn enough money to buy the outfits, alcohol and drugs that my all-important lifestyle demanded. Looking back, I really regret not persevering with my teaching degree because I wouldn't have made a bad teacher, eventually. But at the time I couldn't have been happier with my newfound 'career choice' because it got me out of the classroom and back on the dance floor and that's where I thought I belonged.

Krystal Barter

◆ ◆ ◆

It wasn't long before this that I broke up with my first boyfriend, Tyrone. Tyrone and I met through our mutual mate Peter, and we'd been together since I was fifteen. A Holden-driving, party-going Northern Beaches surfer, Tyrone was a couple of years older than me (important) and easily the best-looking guy me and my friends knew (even more important). He had finished school by the time we started dating but he was the boy most girls at my high school dreamed about.

'Gotta go, Tyrone's here,' I'd say casually to my friends as he cruised by the school gate to pick me up after I finished school for the day. With the skirt of my school uniform rolled up at the waistband to shorten it as far as it would go, I'd saunter over to this rust-bucket of a car (complete with surfboard strapped to the roof) and slip into the passenger seat like I was slipping into a Rolls. Classy.

Mostly, Tyrone and I spent our time hanging out with his friends, who had that shimmering and perpetually unattainable appeal of being two years older than me, and therefore two years cooler in my teen mind. I went to parties with this crowd, got drunk with this crowd and yet, throughout it all, I couldn't for the life of me work out why Tyrone chose me as his girlfriend.

Why does he want to go out with me? I wondered. *I'm not attractive. I'd even go as far to say I was funny-looking. (Although, I never seemed to have any trouble getting boyfriends; and cute ones, too.) Yet the hottest guy I know has chosen to be my boyfriend.* It made no sense. Still, I wasn't stupid enough to ever point this out to Tyrone. If he was so blind to his own attractiveness (and

The Lucky One

to my relative *un*attractiveness), then who was I to come along and clear things up with my twenty-twenty vision?

It did come with its fair share of problems, though.

Tyrone was a really nice guy but throughout our relationship we fought, *a lot*, and even at the time I could see it was mostly my fault. *Oh, god, he just looked sideways at that other girl!* I would screech inside my 16-year-old head. *That's it; that's it! I can't cope with this any longer! He doesn't really love me!* And down and around my thoughts would spiral until Tyrone and I would wind up embroiled in yet another argument about yet another girl who may or may not have caught my boyfriend's eye as we walked past her at the beach/shops/movies/insert your own option here. Everywhere, basically.

It was my insecurities that caused us to break up in the end. One of the sorer points in our (at times, very sore) relationship was the fact that Tyrone turned eighteen two years before I did and so was legally able to go to pubs and clubs while I was still too young. For a couple of years there Tyrone would abandon me, infuriatingly underage, in order to go out drinking with our friends. And then a day or a week or a month later it would inevitably be reported back to me just how much fun Tyrone had while he was out clubbing and exactly how he'd been spotted tearing up the dance floor with some other girl while I wasn't around. The rage I experienced was insane! I could barely see straight for the lurid green lights beaming out of my eyes. And somehow this all feels especially brutal when you're a crazy teenage girl. At the time I was so unsure of who I was, and so afraid of disliking who I'd become, that life was a constant battle to fit in. I was always trying to be someone I wasn't. And when I wasn't trying to *be* someone else, then I was busy worrying that someone else was lurking around the corner waiting to steal my boyfriend away. So, when I was only a few weeks shy of my eighteenth birthday, and on a night when I was fed up with Tyrone going out without me *again* (and when I was tempted by the notion of going to Schoolies Week happily single), I issued an ultimatum: 'You go out tonight and we're done.'

And he did, and we were.

It was that simple. No tears or tantrums or impassioned speeches. At the end of the day it was the best thing for both of us (and, fast forward a few years, and I was on the dance floor at Tyrone's wedding, having introduced him to one of my friends who he ended up marrying). Back then, though, I don't think Tyrone really believed I would break up with him. I'm not sure I believed it myself. But, by the time our relationship ended, I was finally—incrementally—starting to gain some self-confidence. Which could have gone one of two ways. Path A: I might finally grow up, ditch the drugs and booze completely (I had cut back on the pot while with Tyrone), and then emerge from the mire of my teenage years as a confident and articulate young woman, wiser for the mistakes of my youth. Or Path B: I could be worse than ever; worse *with added confidence*. I chose B.

◆ ◆ ◆

So I drank, I smoked, and I took drugs with true abandon. I started my day with Baileys Irish Cream Whiskey on my cornflakes and things went steadily downhill from there. I drank vodka from a recycled 250-millilitre water bottle and, at the rate I was going through it, it may as well have been Mount

The Lucky One

Franklin I was sculling. In addition to this, and as well as my longstanding pot practice, I now dabbled in ecstasy and speed in more worrying amounts. While my friends were happy to pop pills at parties on weekends, I was increasingly using these drugs throughout the working week. In fact, at the height of my habit (or the nadir, depending how you look at it), I was taking eccy most weekend nights (that's Thursday through to Sunday inclusive), as well as speed every second day. Every day, at my worst. Occasionally, I showed some class (and some cash) and got myself some cocaine. But I drew the line at heroin because, in my drug-addled brain, I still considered my behaviour to be normal enough, whereas heroin was strictly for junkies. Everything else, though, was fair game. And the effects were undeniable.

For instance, I'm not a naturally energetic person; I suffer from low blood pressure, I often feel lethargic, hell, I can drink coffee and still want to go to sleep. But when I was on speed I was a woman possessed! After popping just one of those magical tabs, I could dance all night, I could talk for Australia, I would move and think and feel like someone had plugged my index finger into an electrical socket and there were 100 000 volts of pure, exhilarating energy flowing through my veins. (Note: kids, don't try this at home; the drugs or the electrical socket.) I would, for instance, come home at four or five in the morning, after hours and hours of uninterrupted dancing and partying, and decide to clean the house. Scrubbing and mopping and dusting my way around my parents' place, I must have looked like some demented fairy godmother, or I would have done if there was anyone else stupid enough to be awake at that hour. It's laughable now—especially when you see the messy state of my house (maybe that's because my drug of choice these days is a double espresso, though don't think I haven't toyed with the idea of dropping a couple of tabs just to get some housework done occasionally ...).

But the real appeal of speed wasn't the 'pick-me-up'. No, it was the 'let-me-out': the escape hatch it offered. Drugs allowed me to run away from my life. They let me create my own version of reality, where happiness and pleasure-seeking were sharply in focus and cancer was some blurred abstraction in the background.

And when I came down? Well, I just went straight back up again. I yo-yo'ed between manic hyperactivity and melancholy comedowns, but I never allowed myself to actually bottom out and wake up back in reality. Throughout this whole time I was so rarely 'straight' that I forgot what being 'Krystal' was supposed to feel like. Speed turned me into a space cadet, like some strange carbon-copy of myself, as if someone had Photoshopped my image, but ever so slightly, so that I couldn't quite put my finger on the bits that weren't right or real. I was never truly happy but I was never truly sad; I lived in some strange muted limbo in-between the two, as if I had no real feelings at all.

Of course, this was exactly what I craved: a release from the worry and the anguish and the pain that cancer brought into my family. I know, cancer was no excuse, but perhaps it goes some way to explaining why I was so keen to pump myself full of methamphetamines. It makes me shudder now when I consider how regularly I was taking stuff that was cooked up in some random backyard who-knows-where and cut with who-knows-what. It was pure luck that I never got a bad batch.

The Lucky One

But the truth is, my drug abuse has had a very tangible and very negative impact on my health.

Where I was once really coordinated (sports captain, remember?), I now struggle with catching a ball. And before drugs I never had to wear glasses, whereas now I can barely drive at night as the streetlights and traffic lights swim before my eyes and I find it impossible to focus. Plus, there was the vast amounts of alcohol I was drinking. (After all that I've put it through, I'd hate to bump into my liver in a dark alley nowadays.)

I used to carry a water bottle full of neat vodka with me at parties and neither the taste nor the vodka sweats the next day ever stopped me from draining the bottle. I'd scull anything, from tart cider to sickly sweet Passion Pop, and my favourite party trick was downing my friends' unattended drinks before they had the chance to do it themselves. Being 'straight' at parties was never an option for me but, more than that, I always had to be the person to take things one step further. You can scull that beer? I'll do two. You're popping pills? Not as many as me. You're messy and crazy and fucked up and wild? You ain't got anything on me, baby. I'm all that and more.

I should mention here, too, that, like so many teenagers, I battled a bad relationship with my body. For me this started in the latter part of my childhood and continued well into my twenties (and really didn't end until I became a mum, and had other precious little bodies to look after, and then realised the importance of being healthy). My eating problems began when I had glandular fever while I was in primary school and I was so sick I could barely eat; my stomach shrunk as a result and I never really ate properly again for years after that. And, while the glandular fever wasn't the underlying *cause* of my eating disorder, it was the initial trigger. Yet again, it was illness that shaped my life.

In my teens I controlled my body weight by going for days without eating then bingeing for days afterwards. I used to skip meals and hide food then gorge in secret and make myself vomit. I would throw out my school lunches and count calories fastidiously. Then later, when I was older, I would use drugs to suppress my appetite and go for days and days existing on nothing more than an apple and some crackers, or Cheezels and creaming soda (a breakfast of champions, if ever there was one). I morphed from being an overachieving perfectionist of a child into an obsessively skinny young woman (at my worst I weighed less than 50 kilograms). Such a cliché would be laughable if it wasn't so sad. Because as all the textbooks will tell you: my attempts to control my diet were a reaction to the fact I couldn't control anything else in my life. Not my genes, not my health, not my longevity, not my future; as I was to discover when I entered the brave new world of genetic testing when I turned eighteen.

CHAPTER 5

Taking a genetic test to see if you're carrying a cancer gene is an experience like no other. Even through my teenage drama-queen fog—where a pimple is a trauma, and boyfriend troubles a catastrophe—I knew I wasn't overreacting by being spooked at the thought of a BRCA genetic test. And by spooked, read: scared stupid. With one single blood test, one quick sample sent off to a lab somewhere, I would know, with near-certainty, exactly how likely I was to develop breast cancer in the future. And the odds didn't look good. Around 12 per cent of all women will get breast cancer at some point in their lives, versus up to 80 per cent of women who have inherited the BRCA1 or BRCA2 gene mutation (although, only 10 per cent of families fall into this 'high risk' category).

Krystal Barter

To test positive to the BRCA1 gene which my family carried was about the least positive thing that I could think of. Which is why, when I was eighteen years old and only recently out of high school, it was Mum's idea, and not mine, to book me in for genetic testing.

'We're here for a blood test at three o'clock. It's booked under the name Krystal Barter,' Mum instructed the receptionist. I could hear the nervousness in her voice.

'I can do this myself, you know.' Irritation was my default setting with Mum.

'I know, darling,' soothed Mum. 'Let's go in there together and get this test out of the way then we can go home.'

Sure, I thought, only you're omitting one small detail there. You know, the one where I test positive to the BRCA1 genetic mutation and then spend the rest of my life waiting for my breasts to suddenly sprout cancerous tumours that will eat away at me from the inside out until I'm dead and buried and rotting in the ground? Remember that old chestnut, Mum?

I folded my arms sullenly across my chest as I sat in the plastic waiting-room chair. Mum sat next to me, forcibly acting blithe, as she flicked through the surgery's tattered copy of *The Women's Weekly*. It was like we were on some cosy mother–daughter excursion to get our nails done and there'd be champagne and cupcakes coming up next.

'Krystal Barter?' The doctor called my name out into the waiting room.

Mum and I scuttled into his surgery.

'Now, you understand the implications of today's blood test, don't you, Krystal? We may well find out that you have a significantly heightened risk of breast cancer.' These were the first words out of the guy's mouth and each one landed on me like a physical blow.

Even though I didn't really understand the ramifications of what he was saying at the time, the severity of his tone couldn't be missed. Clearly, whatever these choices involved, it was scary. Nevertheless, I tried to appear nonchalant.

'Sure, whatevs.'

'And it may take several months before we receive the results from the lab,' he went on, before explaining the inner workings of the laboratory's testing process.

I shrugged.

'Okay, well, if you're ready to do this, then it's just a case of a simple blood test.' He stood up and began going through the motions. 'Just a quick prick,' he muttered, pulling the cap off the needle with his teeth.

Mum gripped my left hand. It wasn't like I hadn't had a blood test or injections before, but this time I watched the tip of the needle with detached fascination. Who'd have thought that a small vial of my blood could predict my whole future? A few dark red stains on a glass slide under a microscope (specifically, a gene DNA analyser) and some doctor could tell me with confidence whether I was free to get married and have kids and enjoy a long life uninterrupted by disease, or if I was destined to live a lifetime condemned to sickness and chemo and losing my hair and dying young. It's like I'd stepped into some strange parallel universe where suddenly my whole existence was mapped out for me and I had no choice but to follow the yellow brick road that lay in front of me. Only, unlike my beloved Judy Garland, I wasn't off to see the wizard, I was more than likely off to be diagnosed with cancer, if not now then someday soon. It was too much.

'Stop!' I yelled. 'I can't do it!'

The doctor froze, needle mid-air, his face one of astonishment.

'Krystal!' Mum admonished.

'Don't make me do it! Don't make me do it!' I shouted and burst into tears as I stood up. 'I'm not ready for this!'

In a hysterical state I raced to the surgery door and yanked it open. Mum and the doctor just looked at one another in stunned silence.

'I don't want to do this!' I yelled, and ran through the waiting room full of now-surprised patients and out of the building. My drama queen had taken over.

❖ ❖ ❖

I never did go back to that doctor to have my BRCA test. In fact, it was years before I went to any doctor to try the test again. As I pointed out to Mum that day (albeit, at about 100 decibels and in an embarrassingly public place), I just wasn't ready to handle that sort of information. I wouldn't have coped. If I *was* going to follow in my mother's footsteps and develop early-onset breast cancer—as all the signs, terrifyingly, indicated I would—then I simply didn't want to know about it yet. People would often comment how I looked so much like Mum, or how we had the same voice, so it made sense to me that I'd inherited her cancer gene as well. And if I did? Well, I preferred to live in blissful ignorance. Even though *my* version of blissful ignorance about cancer-induced early death was, ironically, to party like there was no tomorrow.

The Lucky One

And so I continued as I had before: going out (to excess), drinking (to excess) and taking drugs (to, well, you guessed it). 'Wild abandon' is probably not too strong an expression for it all. A psychologist would probably draw a neat connecting line between me failing to take the BRCA test (and so avoiding the chance that I might learn of any future cancer) and my reckless behaviour. You dodge the test, you dodge the cancer, right? And it's not such a big leap from here to think: Hell, if I can dodge death from cancer, then why not elsewhere in my life?

In truth, though, I don't think I ever gave it that much thought. I was eighteen years old and having too much fun to stop. It was that simple. And, anyway, doesn't every teenager think they're invincible?

A few years earlier, when I was about fifteen, a couple of my friends were involved in a horrific, life-altering car accident. Chris, the driver, was a particularly close friend and he'd called my house on the day of the crash to ask if he could take me out for a spin that night.

'Mrs B!' he'd said affectionately when my mum answered the phone. 'It's my birthday today! So I'm going for my P's this arvo and then we're having a bit of a shindig tonight to celebrate. Howsabout I drive Krystal home for you after the party?'

'Howsabout no,' was Mum's response. Driver's licence or not, she wasn't about to let me get into a car with someone who'd so recently qualified (and who'd been partying to celebrate). Turns out Mum probably saved my life.

That night, despite failing to get his provisional licence, Chris and another mate, Pete, took a friend's Commodore for a spin, lost control of the car coming around a sweeping left-hand bend and ploughed into a power pole, shearing it off at the base. The force of the crash was such that Chris was thrown from the car and found by the emergency rescue team lying, face down, on the bitumen ahead of the vehicle. He suffered a depressed fracture to the skull; they didn't know if he'd live. His passenger, Pete, was wedged between the dashboard and his seat and had to be cut free from the car with the 'jaws of life'. He had a fractured arm and leg, facial injuries and a ruptured spleen and was in a critical condition. Debris from the crash landed as far as 40 metres away and the power pole was so decimated that 3300 homes were blacked out in Warriewood that night.

Miraculously, both Chris and Pete survived and were taken to Royal North Shore Hospital's intensive care unit. Here, family and friends took turns keeping vigil at their bedsides, willing them to wake up. Both boys had staples across their foreheads which were the size of footballs and both boys were never expected to make a full recovery.

It was while we were standing by their beds one night that Mum turned to me and said: '*Now* do you understand how precious your life is, Krystal? There are consequences for all our decisions in life and you need to have a think about some of the decisions you're making.'

Mum wasn't callously using my friends' dire situation for point-scoring; she was just so desperate to get her message across to me. That is, I had to stop before it was too late.

I remember staring down at my unconscious friends and truly fearing they'd never wake up. I felt squeamish and faint at the sight of Chris's injuries but I forced myself to visit him, day after day, when I would just sit by his bed, willing him to suddenly open his eyes and recognise me. It was devastating to see him like this.

And then one day, nearly two weeks after the accident, Chris woke up and said my name.

I wasn't at the hospital at the time but Chris's mum rang to tell me his fragile body had suddenly come alive and he'd opened his eyes and said: 'Krystal?' The word was barely discernible but that didn't matter. Chris was conscious! What's more, he was able to remember me, which was a positive sign in terms of brain function. I was elated. I laughed and cried tears of relief at the same time. I wish I'd seen the look on his mum's face when she first saw Chris was awake. I'd lost count of the times his mum and his sister and I had stood in that hospital room desperately hoping and praying for Chris and Pete to wake up. And now Chris had finally opened his eyes. Pete also regained consciousness a few days later. It was nothing short of incredible.

Over the next few weeks both Chris and Pete began the long, hard slog of rehabilitation. They were both hugely messed up by the accident—physically and emotionally—and it took years for them to painstakingly piece their lives back together. I still can't quite believe my own luck at escaping injury that night. If it hadn't been for Mum putting her foot down, I would definitely have been in that car when they crashed, and who knows what state I would have been in when I was pulled out. My uncle was a local firefighter with the Mona Vale brigade and he was called out to the accident that night. He later said that any girl of my (petite) size would never have survived an accident of that magnitude. He's probably right.

But even though the accident occurred when I was fifteen years old, and truly shocked me, here I was at eighteen, still partying like I had a death wish. (I'd like to point out that, to my credit, I never got in a car with a drunk driver or drove recklessly myself; I preferred to take my risks *outside* the vehicle.) I'd been exposed to my nan's cancer scars from before the time I could walk; I'd experienced my own mother diagnosed with cancer when I was just fourteen years old; and then I'd seen my friends' lives shattered (in an accident I could have been involved in) only one year after that. And none of these things had any bearing on my behaviour. In fact, if anything, they made me party harder than ever. Life's short, right? So it's not surprising, then, that a never-taken BRCA test wasn't going to slow me down.

Nor was an intervention from my friends. But that didn't stop them from trying.

◆ ◆ ◆

Not long after my aborted BRCA test, and at a time when I was up to my dilated pupils in the hug drug, ecstasy, and taking speed almost daily, my closest friends decided to act. Now, I'm not talking some *Oprah*-style arrangement filled with tears and trite affirmations and luxury rehab retreats. There was no five-step step-down program, no free tickets under my seat so I could go 'find myself' in the Aussie outback. And there sure as hell wasn't any public confession of guilt on my part, á la Lance Armstrong.

No, there was none of that.

This might have been an intervention but it was still suburban Manly in the early 2000s, and my friends were forced to use whatever options were available to them at the time. That's right: they dobbed on me to my mum.

'Krystal Anne Barter! You get your arse back home right this instant!' Mum's voice barrelled out of my mobile phone as I putted up the hill in my crappy Ford Laser. I was off to Katy's house and had spent the last few minutes trying to coax my powder-blue bomb up this hill; I was hardly going to turn back and head home now.

'What the hell?' I said to Mum.

'Don't you "what the hell?" me, young lady! That's my line!' she screamed at me. 'What the hell is going on with *you*, Krystal? I've just had your friend Bec on the phone telling me that she's worried about you because you're taking drugs all the time!'

Oh, shit. I couldn't believe we were finally having this conversation.

'*Drugs*, Krystal? Since when do you take drugs?' She was still screaming.

Now I *really* couldn't believe we were having this conversation. Was she serious? Had it actually escaped my parents' attention that I spent more time getting high than normal people spent at their nine-to-five? Apparently so.

'Krystal, you're my baby! How could you do this to me?' Mum was crying now. Great.

'Mum, she's lying,' I said flatly.

'Really?'

'Really,' I said. 'You know what Bec's like.' I paused for a moment here. Mum *did* know what Bec was like: loyal, lovely, one of my closest friends. There was no reason for Bec to lie to Mum and if Mum stopped and thought about it for too long she'd realise that. I changed tack.

'Look, I'm not taking drugs, Mum. You've got to believe me. I'm just not.'

'You're not?' There was a tentative note of hope in Mum's voice.

'I'm not.' I knew Mum desperately wanted to believe this; she wanted me to convince her.

'So you don't have to worry about a word Bec said,' I went on. 'But, hey, I've just arrived at Katy's so I've gotta go now.'

'But—'

I cut Mum off: 'I said, I've gotta go now, okay?'

'Okay,' Mum's voice sounded small now, with all the anger drained from it.

'I'll be home tomorrow sometime. And forget about the drugs, Mum. There are no drugs.' With this, I hung up the phone before she had a chance to reply.

I parked my car at Katy's, jumped out and raced to the front door. I couldn't wait to tell her about Bec dobbing; and take some of those non-existent drugs.

◆ ◆ ◆

Now, it might sound uncanny that *two* of my closest friends decided—independently—to address my drug habit on the same day. Uncanny, or downright unlucky, depending on whose side you're on. But when you consider just how far out of control my life had spun by now, it's probably *more* surprising that my friends had waited this long. It was becoming painfully obvious to everyone around me that there was some sort of screw loose in my brain when it came to illicit substances. It was no secret that when I was out partying I wasn't afraid to push

The Lucky One

myself one step further than everyone else, to take life faster or higher or wilder than everyone else. And the problem with always being one step ahead when it comes to drugs, of course, is that you're always one step closer to disaster, too. My friends recognised this and decided to act before it was too late. Which is why, fresh off the phone from my irate mother, I now walked slap-bang into Katy's own brand of tough love.

'Krystal, you've got to get your shit together.'

'What?' I stared at Katy, open-mouthed and stunned. The two of us were sitting crosslegged on her bed, planning our night out together. The small zip-lock bag of speed I'd just produced was lying on the quilt between us. Katy was not as much of a party girl as I was, but it wasn't like my plastic pouch didn't contain enough supplies for her, too. 'What do you mean?'

'I mean, you've got to get your shit together,' she repeated, indicating to the powder that lay in the (suddenly cavernous) space between us. 'You can't keep this up, not at this rate, or you'll kill yourself.'

Oh, that again. What the hell was wrong with everybody today? I wondered.

'Yeah, real funny, Katy,' I said and laughed. 'Now, let's get on with killing ourselves.'

Katy, however, wasn't laughing. 'I'm serious, Krystal, and I'm doing this for your own good.'

Doing what? I thought, bemused, as she stood up and walked out into the hallway.

'Muuuum!' she shouted. 'Can you come here a sec?'

Somewhere in the house the hum of a vacuum cleaner died, and then footsteps rapped across the parquetry floor. Katy hung in the doorway looking sheepish and righteous and slightly sickened, all at once, and suddenly I didn't like where this was heading. I swiped the bag of powder from the quilt cover and stuffed them into my pocket and, seconds later, Katy's mum, Anne, appeared and strode into the bedroom.

'Where are the drugs, Krystal?' This woman was taking no prisoners.

'Anne, I'm not sure what you're talking about …'

'The drugs,' she repeated, and I did my best to appear nonplussed.

'Have I done something wrong? Because if—' I began.

'Get the drugs out, Krystal—*all the drugs*—and show them to me.' She didn't raise her voice, in fact she appeared decidedly unfazed, and yet I was stunned this was happening. Behind her, down the hallway, I could hear Katy's little brother banging around in the kitchen. Next door, a lawnmower was starting up. It sounded like such a normal day.

'Anne, I think there's been some sort of mistake,' I said smoothly. 'I don't know what Katy's told you,' I shot a look towards the doorway and Katy actually flinched. 'But you should know that I would never—'

Anne cut me off again: 'C'mon, Krystal, I'm not buying it. Now, get the drugs out.' She held out her hand expectantly and I sighed.

'Look, I think I'll just head off, Anne. I've obviously come at a bad time …'

'Mum, you've got to get her sorted out.' At last Katy spoke, but her pleading tone surprised me.

'I know, I know—' her mum waved her away. 'C'mon, Krystal, let's get this over with.'

The Lucky One

For a moment I was derailed by Anne's words. Where else had I heard that recently? Oh yeah, that's right, my own mum said the exact same thing at my BRCA1 test. It seemed there was a lot in my life lately that required me to just grit my teeth and get it over with.

Then Anne said, 'I'll call your parents if I need to, Krystal,' and with that, she had my full attention.

'My parents? Are you serious? I don't think that's necessary. We're only talking about a couple of tabs of speed,' I said, beginning to panic now. I didn't really believe Katy's mum would call my parents, but then I would never have expected her to stage an intervention inside her daughter's room, either. Anne calling my parents was not a gamble I was prepared to take.

'Fine, I'll give you the drugs but only if you don't call my mum,' I said, cringeing at how pathetic that sounded but totally prepared to grovel on that front. I did not need Mum and Dad knowing about this. Not when I'd just had such a close shave with Mum on the phone, and not while I still enjoyed going out most nights without having to pass a sniffer-dog test first. If Mum and Dad had any inkling I was doing drugs, they would make my life unbearable.

I reached into my pocket and withdrew the plastic bag containing my precious white powder.

'Well, come on then,' Anne said. 'Follow me. And bring that.' She nodded sharply at the powder then strode off down the hallway. 'I won't have drugs in my house!' she called over her shoulder with all the authority a mother naturally assumes, even if she wasn't *my* mother.

I trudged behind her down the hall into the kitchen, where Anne already stood at the sink. Katy trailed and again hovered, unsure, in the doorway. Anne turned on the kitchen tap with force. 'Right, flush them.'

There was no point in arguing now. 'Fine,' I said and opened the bag and tipped the powder down the drain while Katy and her mum stood witness. 'Happy?'

'Very,' Anne said grimly. 'But don't make me have to do that ever again.'

◆ ◆ ◆

I can safely say that was the first and last time Katy's mum made me wash narcotics down her kitchen sink. Just like it was the first and last time two of my friends staged (separate) interventions on the very same day. Apparently, neither Bec nor Katy knew what the other had finally summoned the guts to do. Nor, then, could they have known about each other's timing. It was a case of 'At last!', rather than 'But why now?', when they learned what the other had done.

It was for me, too, I guess. I'm not going to pretend that I had any sort of epiphany that day in Anne's kitchen—there was no great bolt from the blue; no parting of clouds so that a piercing sunbeam could illuminate my (newly drug-free) face. There were no Disney blue birds twittering around my head and it certainly wasn't the end of my drug-taking or my drinking. Not by a long shot. But it was a wake-up call of sorts. Both Bec's call to my mum, and Katy's appeal to her mum, had the effect of making me stop and think, at least momentarily, about what it was I was doing. If my habit wasn't cool with my friends, then was it really cool with me? Their opinions hit home far more than the opinions of those *at* home (Mum and Dad, I'm looking at you).

The Lucky One

Then, there was the fact my friends cared so much about me. If you ever have a friend who's going through a tough time, or who's screwing up or acting out or generally just making a mess of things, don't underestimate how much your concern means to them, even if they don't show it at the time. I know; I've been there. That Bec and Katy cared about me enough to risk my wrath and jeopardise our friendships, well, it meant a huge amount to me. It still does. So much so, that I've remained friends with both of them. Until recently Katy had lived overseas and Bec is busy with her second baby, so we don't see each other as often as we'd like, but we're in touch as much as our lives allow and that's due, in no small part, to the amazing friendship they showed me back then.

After my interventions (and it feels so American to say that; like, I should have a therapist, and a dog-walker, and maybe a therapist for my dog-walker), I did ease up on the wild living a little. Don't get me wrong, partying was still my raison d'être—the promise of each night was the only thing that got me up and out of bed each morning—but I cut back a bit on the drink and the drugs, both in quantity and frequency. What stuck with me most from that day was the feeling of self-consciousness I had about my lifestyle. You mean most people don't swig vodka like it's H_2O? They don't take uppers on any day ending in 'y'? It's easy to lose perspective when you're stumbling around in a permanently drug-induced haze. And, like I said, I certainly didn't change overnight after that day; not by a long shot. But slowly, slowly, I did start to pull back on the drugs front. It's funny that, in the end, it was being confronted by my friends—the people I respected, the ones I partied *with*—that made me realise my behaviour wasn't normal, nor desirable.

Krystal Barter

♦ ♦ ♦

We all have the chance to learn from our mistakes in life and my teenage years certainly offered plenty of scope for that. Mistake after mistake after fuck-up after mistake; it feels like the only thing that was consistent about my adolescence (aside from my family's recurring cancer) was my ability to make the wrong choice. In hindsight, would I change things? Would I erase how I acted and what I put my parents through? In a heartbeat. But, unfortunately, I don't have that luxury. I can't hit 'rewind' followed by 'delete', and so I'm forced, probably for the rest of my life, to feel pained every time I think about the way I treated my family and my friends (and my body) when I was younger.

And yet, on some level, I don't regret any of the things I did as a teenager. They shaped the person I am today and I'm (finally) proud of who that person is. I believe everything happens for a reason and if I didn't take the path I did, I may never have met my husband and had my beautiful children. How can I regret the chain of decisions that got me here?

What I *can* say without hesitation is: I'm a better person for experiencing what I did. If I hadn't rebelled so much when I was younger, I might never have come to appreciate my life and my family in the way I do now. Maybe it's true that we *do* have to nearly lose the things that mean the most for us to realise just how important they are.

And even though I partied hard and fast, teenagers are known for that kind of behaviour so it wasn't like I was alone. I still see so many kids around the Northern Beaches today who are out of control and I fear for some of them. Not even the best parents, a great education and awesome friends could stop me from acting the way I did, and I know not all of the kids I see are so lucky. If my children ever come to me and tell me they're struggling with drugs, or they're in some other kind of trouble, I'll sure as hell feel empathy for them. Moreover, I'll be able to tell them that I know their pain can end and that it's possible for them to turn their lives around if they want to. I know; I've done it.

But perhaps the most important thing to come from all this is the realisation that my past doesn't have to define me. It's taken me a long time to get here but I've finally made peace with the fact that I was a pretty awful daughter (and sister and granddaughter and friend) when I was a teenager, but that doesn't mean I'm an awful person, full stop. No, I get to choose—fresh, new, each and every day—who I am now and how I'm going to live my life. Just like I chose to have a double mastectomy to try and avoid walking in the cancerous footsteps of my mother and my grandmother, I chose to stop wasting my life on drugs and then changed things for the better. Anyone who knew me as a drug-stuffed, out-of-control teenager would struggle to believe the wife and mother and businesswoman I've become today. But it was only when I realised I didn't *have* to be the person I was back then—that I hadn't signed anything to say 'this is who Krystal Anne Barter is now and so, therefore, who I will be for the rest of my natural life'—and accepted this, that I was finally able to change.

Well, that, *and* because I met a boy.

CHAPTER 6

Chris was everything I never went for in a guy. I liked the heroin-chic, skinny look; he was a body-builder. I sought the life 'n' soul of the party; Chris was quiet. I craved 'bad boy'; Chris was a never-done-drugs-before kinda boy. No one in their right mind would have pictured us together. Luckily, my friend Paul was nowhere near his right mind when he suggested that Chris and I should hook up.

'You've gotta meet my flatmate, Krystal. His name's Chris. And I think he's perfect for you.'

'Really?' My mind conjured up an image of Johnny Depp in his *21 Jump Street* years, perhaps with a dash of Gregory Peck from *Roman Holiday*. Dark, brooding, dangerous. In my daydream we were hopping from party to party, pausing just long enough to tear up the dance floor, *Dirty Dancing*-style, in front of our adoring crowd, before he whisked me off into a taxi and home for a night of wild and debauched passion.

'Yeah, he's the most boring guy I know,' Paul said.

Boring? 'Er, you're not really selling him to me, Paul.'

'Yeah, but he *needs* you, Krystal! If anyone can liven this guy up, then it's you.'

'Uh, thanks. But, no thanks.'

'Seriously, we're desperate!' According to Paul, all Chris did was go to work, go to the gym and then fall asleep in front of bad, prime-time TV. If they didn't introduce someone like me into his life, then their once-happy household might have to endure *Better Homes & Gardens* on TV every Friday night from now until eternity. 'So for the love of god, Krystal, *take him out!*'

And that's how my husband and I met.

◆ ◆ ◆

The first time I met Chris my salient impression was: muscles. Because, boy, were there a lot of them. Chris and I moved in similar social circles so I'd seen him around at various parties and nightclubs, but I'd never taken much notice of him. Those muscles had put me off. But now Paul had arranged for the two of us to 'meet' properly and so here I was having dinner in Charlie Bar in Manly, up close and personal with all that rippling flesh.

'How's your steak?' I began safely enough.

'Good,' Chris replied.

'Is it? That's good. That ragout with it looks delicious, too. I nearly wish I'd ordered the same as you instead of this pizza,' I said, fiddling nervously with the crust. 'Not that this pizza is bad!' I added hurriedly. 'I mean, you have to try pretty hard to make a pizza bad, right? It's just that your meat looks so good.' Oh god, *what did I just say?*

Chris smiled a slow, shy smile. 'Yeah, it's good,' he said.

I waited to see if further assessment was forthcoming. Nope, nothing. This was a man of few words. But wait—'Would you like some?' he added.

'Sure!' I said. He might be a man of few words but at least he was a *gentleman* of few words. Even if he did let me babble away incessantly. *Why can't I stop talking tonight?*

'You know, you remind me a lot of my mum,' he said quietly, putting his fork down and looking at me intently.

'Your mum?' I squeaked. 'That's a good thing, right?' I wished the butterflies in my stomach would just buzz off and I could, at least, act like I was a normal member of the human race.

'Sure,' he said. There was that smile again. 'My mum's a real cracker. Big personality.'

'And even bigger after a few drinks …,' he added, thoughtfully tapping his chin. 'But you'll love her.'

Now it was my turn to be silent. His mum was a 'cracker,' *Which is why I reminded him of her?* As first date compliments go, this wouldn't exactly make my top ten.

'Ah, good,' I said vaguely. 'That's good.'

'Yeah, good,' he repeated and smiled shyly at me again before turning his attention back to his steak.

◆ ◆ ◆

And yet somehow, amid the muscles and the fact I reminded him of his mother, I started to fall for Chris that night. He was quiet

The Lucky One

and softly spoken but he was thoughtful and considered in his opinions. He was also fun and upbeat and had a wicked sense of humour. And by the time the downlights were lowered and the bar staff were wiping out glasses, I already knew I really liked this guy. A lot. And as I watched him across the table I'm afraid to say I thought: 'I can't wait to introduce you to my parents. They're going to be so proud of me for once!' (Not just because Chris was a Kiwi, which was cause for celebration in my family as my mum and all her family were born and bred in New Zealand.) Mostly, though, I knew they'd be thrilled for me when they met Chris because he was articulate and intelligent and far gentler than any guy I'd ever met before. I don't know if it was because he was older than me (he was 26 to my very immature twenty), but he seemed incredibly self-assured and just so *calm*. We really couldn't have been more different if we tried.

As he walked me to the front door of my parents' house later that evening, my hand was trembling slightly in his. What was *wrong* with me? He's just a boy! I *never* get like this over a boy! And yet I felt like Frank Sinatra's polka dots and moonbeams were swirling around my head. I floated up the front path, like one of those cartoon characters whose feet hover centimetres above the ground. Then, at the front door, Chris turned to me and without warning kissed me firmly but very gently on the mouth and I swooned.

'So we're official?' he asked and the butterflies in my stomach took flight again.

'We're official,' I smiled coyly, and then I leaned into those muscly arms.

◆ ◆ ◆

Krystal Barter

After saying goodbye to Chris I did my cartoon-float into the house, closed the front door behind me, then rested my back against it and shut my eyes while I relived the last few minutes. *He kissed me! We're official!* I grinned to myself in the dark.

'That's it! This one's a keeper!' A disembodied voice screeched down the hallway, and my eyes snapped open in shock.

'Mum!' I admonished. 'You scared the hell out of me!'

She casually appeared out of the lounge room in her dressing gown. She must have been waiting up for me to get home.

'What are you doing up anyway?'

'Good night?' she asked, smugly, ignoring my question.

'Not bad,' I said, doing my best to appear nonchalant and not as though she'd just taken ten years off my life in fright.

'Not bad? This one's a keeper,' she forecast again.

I stared at her like she was a crazy woman. 'Mum, you're mad. Chris and I have only just met. You and he have *never* met,' I reminded her. 'So how can you possibly know he's the one.'

'And anyway,' I added, 'I'm only twenty! I'm not interested in getting too serious. You're being ridiculous, Mum.'

She continued to grin. 'Sure, sure, whatever you say. But I know love when I see it and you may as well hire a sky-writer with the news, the way it's written all over your face.'

I peered at her through the midnight darkness; her outline was barely discernible in the dim blue light of the flickering TV in the lounge. 'You can see love, can you, Mum? Well, I can hardly see you, let alone love, so I'm going to bed, you crazy woman.' And then I wandered off to my room, fumbling through the darkness and my crush.

◆ ◆ ◆

My Great Nan, Annie (left) on her wedding day, with Great Great Grandma (middle).

Mum and Dad on their wedding day in 1981, with Great Nan (right) in pink floral dress and gloves.

Mum (aged 22), with me at 10 months.

Me and Nanny Beryl – from my hairdressing days.

A pink bridesmaid (1991) and believe-it-or-not I still have the dress!

And a pink dinosaur ride too (aged 6). There is definitely a colour theme emerging.

At home with mum and dad and my brother Andrew (2001).

Dad and me (aged 16). Yep . . . I was a handful.

I was only 19. And lucky to have friends like Bec (left) and Katy (right).

And then there was Chris . . . the love of my life.

21st birthday with family and friends at Oceanworld, me and Chris at the front—and that gold dress.

Our engagement party, held 1½ months after finding out that I was pregnant.

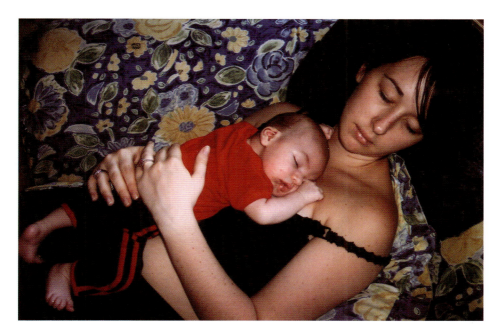
Asleep with Riley, just 6 weeks old.

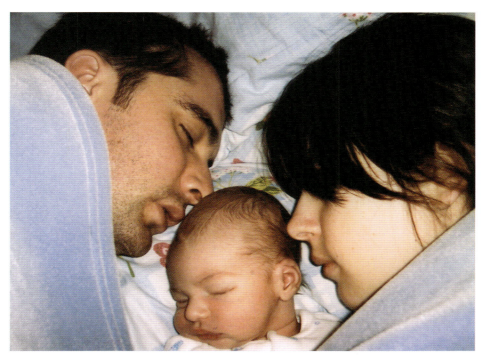
Me, Chris and Riley (3 weeks old).

Me and my bridesmaids.

After much searching, I found my perfect pink wedding dress.

The Lucky One

That was 9 January 2004. I can remember the date clearly because that was the day everything changed—markedly, and for the better. In the weeks following our first date, Chris and I spent almost every waking moment together. We hung out at Harbord Headland, overlooking Freshwater Beach, eating fish and chips; we went out for dinner, and we watched movies I can't remember the names of (and probably couldn't recall five minutes after the credits rolled, such was my new-crush delirium). We lost hours staring dopily into one another's eyes. In short, we did all the things that had been done by millions of other couples all over the world, and yet everything felt so new with Chris. For me, I guess it was.

Chris was unlike anyone I'd ever dated before and, on this score, my family and friends couldn't have been happier. 'He's such a nice guy' were the words I heard most often during those first few heady weeks of courtship as everyone around me fell hard for Chris, too.

'What a nice boy!' my mum exclaimed as he arrived to meet my parents bearing a bunch of beautiful blue irises for Mum.

'He's a nice guy this one, Krystal,' was Dad's assessment.

'He's just so *nice!*' said my girlfriends, and my guy friends, and our neighbours, and the kid at the DVD store, and pretty much everyone else that came into contact with him. *He's nice. Oh, he's nice. He's a really nice guy.*

Chris was my prince charming who'd ridden up on his white horse (hell, he even worked at a horse farm!). So it's no surprise, then, that barely two weeks after we'd met, I was in love with this nice guy myself.

The strangest thing was he felt the same about me.

Krystal Barter

One evening, when we were snuggled up on the couch watching some corny 1950s musical of my choosing—and when we'd still only been together for less than a month—Chris leaned over and tucked a strand of hair behind my ear and looked me in the eyes and told me he loved me.

He loved me? He *loved* me! Chris loved me and my heart soared. It did handstands. It did cartwheels. It did loop-the-loops until it made itself giddy. My heart was an all-singing, all-dancing musical tribute to Chris. Here I was, nuts about this guy, and it just so happened he loved me back.

But wait, he loved *me*?

On some level, I failed to understand how he could love the person that was me. Because at twenty years old I was, frankly, still a screw-up. I was still drinking excessively and I was still partying recklessly. I thought I was utterly unlovable. So how was it possible that this guy (this guy who was so *nice*) could see anything in me that he thought was worthy of love? It was a strange but wonderful mystery to me.

But not for long.

As it turned out Chris didn't find *everything* about me lovable. It wasn't long after our 'I love you' conversation that we had another that started with 'I love you, but ...' and it descended from there.

'Krystal,' he said, 'the drugs have to go.' As did the cigarettes and the self-destructive behaviour, he told me. Chris was a clean-living, body-conscious, health-conscious guy and he wasn't prepared to, as he put it, 'kiss an ashtray'. Choose me or choose drugs, was the basic gist of things.

Coming from anyone else, an ultimatum like this would barely have made a dent, but coming from Chris it cut me to my

The Lucky One

core. If the choice I faced was between Chris and hard living, well, then, I didn't need to phone a friend to help me decide. I chose Chris and, practically overnight, I stopped taking drugs. I was lucky that it wasn't something that was difficult for me to do; I simply chose to stop smoking pot and popping speed, and I did. No withdrawal symptoms, no struggle. In fact, I was surprised how little I missed getting high. Looking back now, with the clarity that comes with age and time (not to mention, the clarity that comes when you don't have drugs racing around your bloodstream), I can see that this decision no doubt saved my life. And I have Chris to thank for that.

So if we were close before, Chris and I were inseparable now. We took road trips to visit his mum on her farm at Five Day Creek, in the mountains halfway between Armidale and Kempsey in rural New South Wales. We dropped in on his dad at his beach house at Port Macquarie on the sunny mid-north coast. And somewhere between the two we decided we wanted to do more travelling together and so we booked a trip to Phuket, Thailand. The hitch? Both Chris and I were strapped for cash and struggling under the weight of our combined credit card debt. Hardly ideal for planning a holiday.

It was at this point that Mum and Dad (very kindly) offered for Chris to move in and live with me in the tiny front room at home. The house would be a little squashy, sure, what with Chris and I and Mum and Dad and my younger brother and a couple of dogs, too. But a good way to save, nonetheless. And that's how it came about that, after only about five months together, Chris turned up at my place in his little red Mazda, with his clothes on the back seat and his ironing board in the boot, and he simply never left.

Krystal Barter

◆ ◆ ◆

It was also around this time, though, that I started feeling unwell. Nothing major. It was just that sometimes I felt faint, and occasionally a little queasy; mostly I just felt a bit 'off colour'. Plus, I was gaining weight despite my efforts to lose it. And as anyone who has struggled with eating will tell you, a few extra kilos can be traumatic at the best of times, but right now the timing couldn't have been worse because my 21st birthday party was looming fast—and this was to be no ordinary party, people.

My parents had stepped up to the plate yet again and had hired out Oceanworld Manly, an underwater aquarium on the waterfront at Manly Cove, inviting one hundred guests to help me celebrate alongside the sharks and the stingrays and whatever else was floating on by as we sipped on champagne and marvelled at the marine life. The balloons were ordered and the menus selected but, most important of all, Mum and I had found the most amazing dress for me to wear. After scouring the shops for months and months we'd discovered the most incredible gown. Think: slinky, gold glomesh. It had a low, plunging neckline, clung perfectly at my hips and then finished dramatically just below the knee. It was *to die for*. I felt like a Bond girl when I slipped it on and (after only a few minor alterations made at the time of purchase back in April) it fit me like a glove. Or so I thought.

Now, in August, and just days before my big bash, I tried on my divine dress and discovered it was far too tight. *The horror!* Staring at the strangled, gold creature in the mirror I was mortified to see I had an enormous arse and a pot belly (and neither were figments of my hypercritical imagination).

The Lucky One

'Muuuum,' I wailed. 'I'm fat!'

I was standing in front of the full-length mirror in Mum and Dad's bedroom while Mum trawled through her jewellery box looking for a pair of earrings for me to wear. I turned and glanced back at myself over my shoulder, in case this new angle suddenly made me drop 5 kilograms. It didn't.

'How did this happen? I look like a *whale*!' All those gym sessions felt like a cruel joke.

'I thought the only marine life at the party was going to be on the other side of the aquarium glass,' Dad said dryly, but only once he was a safe distance away and exiting the room.

'Muuuum!' I sobbed and flung myself onto her bed.

'Shhh, don't listen to your father. You look beautiful,' she said. 'Although we might want to let that side seam out a little …' And she reached for the phone to dial the dressmaker.

◆ ◆ ◆

Several days later I was flitting among my guests, who were flitting among the tropical fish at Oceanworld: my party was underway. The room was packed, the place was jumping and I was positively *poured* into that gold dress. It rubbed raw under my arms, it was tight across my stomach and it threatened to split open along the seams at my hips at any moment. Eight hundred bucks worth of glomesh had never felt so uncomfortable.

'You look gorgeous, babe,' Chris assured me, as I tugged at a side seam that was stretched to within an inch of its life. I grimaced, embarrassed that he was seeing me like this.

And as I moved around the room that night in stiff, constricted movements I had that awful sensation that people were whispering behind my (helplessly exposed) back. *What is she wearing? Where's the rest of her dress? No more birthday cake for her!* Of course I knew they weren't saying these things—these were my closest friends and family, after all—but that's what it *felt* like everyone was saying as my dress chafed angrily against my thighs.

Perhaps, I pondered, now that I was 21, my metabolism simply wasn't what it used to be? Maybe this is what getting old felt like?

I slugged my champagne and itched at my glomesh. Happy birthday to me, I thought glumly. I was in danger of sliding into proper wallowing territory after this party was over, proper Bridget Jones-watching, Cadbury-eating, professional woe-is-me territory. But first, I was going to have a few champagnes and celebrate properly; at least, I would have, if I hadn't felt so damn sick.

CHAPTER 7

'Krystal Barter? The doctor will see you now.' I stood up too quickly and had to steady myself on Chris's arm as the surgery waiting-room walls danced dizzyingly in front of me. On the far wall, a poster for immunisation showed a bandaged teddy-bear waving a large needle rather too cheerfully. In the corner, daytime television blared out angrily from a battered television, lowering the IQs of all the patients sitting in its vicinity. The doctor's door gaped open, like a yawning, cavernous mouth, waiting to swallow me up. I hated medical waiting rooms. To me they just meant cancer.

'Do you want me to come with you?' Chris asked softly, standing and placing his hand at the small of my back.

'No; it's okay,' I said. If I was about to learn that I was dying, then there was nothing that Chris being there could do to change that. Because that's the thing. When you come from a family like mine, where people see their oncologist more regularly than they see their dentist, then suddenly any old symptom, no matter how small or how commonplace, is blown out of all reasonable proportion.

Prior to this appointment and back before my party, I'd had a blood test to find out why I might be feeling so rotten. Faint? Lethargic? Anaemia, was the answer! My doctor prescribed iron supplements and advised me to eat more red meat, satisfied that, like many young women, I simply wasn't getting enough protein from my diet. But the only thing my new steak diet seemed to do was cause me to stack on a load of unwanted weight. So here I was back at the doctor, more exhausted than ever and several kilograms heavier to boot, convinced that, in fact, I must be dying. I entered the surgery with trepidation.

◆ ◆ ◆

'Krystal? Take a seat please.' An unfamiliar doctor smiled at me, kindly, as she opened my file on her desk and explained that my usual GP, Dr Sally Beath, had been called away that afternoon. 'So I'm afraid you'll have to make do with me,' she said, introducing herself as Elana Roseth. 'Now, why don't you tell me what seems to be troubling you?'

I took a deep breath, held her gaze, and then blurted in panic: 'I think I have cancer!'

To her credit she didn't even flinch. The following conversation went something like this:

The Lucky One

Doctor: Cancer, you say? Well, why don't we start by running through some of your symptoms, Krystal, and then we can take things from there. Do you need to take a minute first?

Me: No, it's fine. The sooner we get this started, the sooner we can get the treatment underway. Okay, so firstly, I'm tired all the time.

Doctor: Tired? Alright. Are you working, Krystal? Or studying? Or both? Could it be that you're overdoing things? And are you looking after yourself and eating right?

Me: That's the problem! I'm eating better than ever but I just seem to be putting on weight around my stomach. And I feel faint.

Doctor: Okay, then.

Me: And I feel nauseous, like I want to vomit.

Doctor: Right.

Me: But only in the mornings.

Doctor: I see.

At this point, Dr Roseth put down her pen and regarded me closely before she spoke: 'Krystal, do you think it's possible that you might be pregnant?'

I stared at her as though she'd just spoken in Hindi, and she may as well have for all that I comprehended what she'd said.

'Preg—*what?*' I spluttered.

'Pregnant,' she said again. 'Are you sexually active, Krystal? Because it may be that you're pregnant.'

I laughed. 'Oh no, I don't think you understand. *There's something seriously wrong.*' I spoke these last words as you would to a small child. 'Besides, I'm on the pill—I never miss—there's no way I could be pregnant.' I laughed again, more generously now, as if it were impossible to stay straight-faced at such a silly suggestion.

'I see,' she said. 'But you know the pill isn't fail-safe, don't you? Are you supplementing it with any other form of contraception?'

I shook my head.

'Okay, well, just for my own peace of mind, would you mind doing a urine test and then we can rule out pregnancy conclusively?'

◆ ◆ ◆

Five minutes later I received the greatest shock of my life.

'Krystal, you're pregnant.' The doctor's words were kind but firm and with them I felt the world slipping out from underneath me.

Pregnant? I was pregnant? I felt like I would vomit. I felt like I would die.

'Krystal! Are you okay?' Dr Roseth leaned towards me in alarm. I could feel all the blood draining from my face and I gasped for air.

'That's it; deep breaths,' she said calmly. Then, satisfied I was alright, she leaned back into her chair.

I thought back over the past few weeks—the fatigue, the emotional upheaval and the constant churning of my stomach. I remembered how, just last month, Chris and I had planned a romantic night out to watch the musical *The Lion King* at the Capitol Theatre in Haymarket. Extravagantly, we'd hired a room at the nearby Sheraton on the Park hotel at Hyde Park so we only had a short taxi ride home after the show, but even that

The Lucky One

had left me exhausted and I'd collapsed on the plush, king-sized bed and fallen asleep before a single champagne cork could be popped. Then I thought back to my 21st birthday party and the way my dress had stretched taut over my belly. *My 21st!* My head snapped up.

'I'm 21!' I blurted and the doctor looked at me in bewilderment. 'I'm 21! So I can't be pregnant!' It was as if I couldn't hold both thoughts in my brain. Babies were for 30-somethings with husbands and houses and sagging boobs and no life. Babies were for those women who had done all the things that they ever wanted to do and so there was nothing for it but to get a store loyalty card for Pumpkin Patch and start stewing apples and mushy pears *and with them the twilight days of their long-forgotten youth!* I was 21 and I owned a gold dress, dammit. I was going to Phuket with my boyfriend at Christmas. I. Was. Not. Pregnant.

The doctor reached into her files and produced a piece of blue paper with 'Sydney Ultrasound for Women' plastered across the header. Just the sight of the word 'ultrasound' made me laugh, only this time, when I laughed, it was decidedly more maniacal than it had been earlier in the appointment. Until my laughter gave way to tears and suddenly I was bawling like the proverbial.

'I … can't … be … preg … preg … I can't have a baby!' I blubbed. 'I don't want a baby! Chris doesn't want a baby!'

I sobbed even more when I remembered Chris, who was sitting patiently in the waiting room, probably reading *Australian Geographic* magazines that were decades old. It wasn't true that Chris didn't want a baby. Or, at least, I didn't know if it was or not. We'd never, ever talked about it. It had simply never come up. Having known the guy for only eight months, and with both of us still determinedly in our twenties, why on earth would we discuss babies? Now, though, we were about to have that conversation and under the worst possible circumstances. I sobbed and hiccupped and sobbed some more. The doctor passed me a box of tissues and spoke in a calm and measured voice.

'Krystal, why don't we ascertain how far along you are? I'm writing you a referral for an ultrasound and you can book that in at any time you like.'

She printed the words 'UNWANTED PREGNANCY' in screaming capitals on the form. I blushed and looked away.

'Now, are you going to be alright after you've left the surgery today, Krystal?' she asked. 'Did anyone accompany you along this afternoon?'

I nodded. Oh, someone accompanied me here, alright. Only we hadn't realised there were three of us along for the ride.

◆ ◆ ◆

Back out in the waiting room, Chris sat calmly playing with his mobile phone, blissfully oblivious to the fact his life was about to be turned upside down. He stared at the screen, happily distracted. I took one look at him and I ran.

I couldn't help it; I just panicked and so I bolted straight for the car. I can't imagine what Chris must have thought when he saw me running, red-faced and crying, out of the surgery without pausing to see him. When he finally recovered from the surprise and chased me outside, he found me barricaded inside his little red Mazda that was parked opposite a primary school

The Lucky One

gate at 3.20 p.m. Home time. Around us a sea of shrieking, lunatic children began to rush past the car, free from school for another day. We weren't even an island, merely some flotsam, battered on both sides by the oncoming tide. Chris tapped on the glass to be admitted inside. I relented and unlocked the door. When he sat down beside me, I wordlessly passed him the ultrasound form.

It took him a full minute to work out what it meant. 'Ultrasound request … transabdominal/pelvic region … dating scan … nuchal translucency …' His eyes searched the text. And then: 'UNWANTED PREGNANCY' screamed from the bottom of the form.

'Whoa!' his eyes widened as he found the information he was looking for.

'I am so sorry,' I whispered, as I wiped my runny nose with the back of my hand. I braced myself for him to run, then, like I'd just bolted from him.

'Babe, it's okay,' were the first fully formed words out of his mouth. 'So you're having a baby. *We're* having a baby. Wow. Jeez!' He ran a hand through his hair and let out a long breath. Then he saw my panicked face: 'Krystal, we'll work this out. I promise we will.' How I desperately wanted to believe him.

Then Chris dropped the ultrasound form, letting it flutter to the floor of the car, and he picked up my hand that was streaked with snot and tears. He gripped it tightly in his and then he lifted it to his mouth and kissed it, once, twice, then a third time. And the tide of yahooing school kids flowed swiftly around us.

◆ ◆ ◆

Krystal Barter

My family's reaction to the news of my pregnancy was overwhelmingly positive. Once Mum realised we weren't making it up (*'Oh, good one, Chris! Pull the other one!'*) she threw her arms around Chris and I and hugged us tight, laughing and crying and excitedly making plans all at once. Nan was unsure whether to be outwardly happy for me or just reserved because she could see I was so obviously distressed. (But, on the inside, I just knew she was grinning from ear to ear at the prospect of becoming 'Great-Nan' for the first time.) And Dad? From amid all my hysterics and my protestations that I wasn't going to go through with the pregnancy, Dad simply grinned and said: 'What's with the tears, Krystal? This is the best news I've heard all year!'

I, however, was still baffled as to how I got pregnant in the first place. Sure, I know *how* I got pregnant. By 21 years old I was pretty much across the whole birds-and-bees thing. What I mean is: how did I get pregnant *despite being on the pill*? I'd been on it for years now and had never once forgotten to take my tablet, nor had I ever run into any complications. Several weeks prior to falling pregnant I had switched to a different pill, which had a slightly lower dosage of oestrogen but, I was assured, was no less effective as a contraceptive. And I followed all the rules associated with switching pills (that is, start the new pill on the day after the last one; don't miss a day; and wait one full cycle before having sex or else use additional contraception). Still, here we both were. Well, three of us now, apparently. This baby must have been pretty determined to enter the world to have made it out of the starter's blocks. And yet my gut reaction was to end the pregnancy.

◆ ◆ ◆

The Lucky One

On the day I went and had my first ultrasound—the ultrasound that would decide our baby's fate—my mind was made up *for* me. And not in the way I expected.

As the radiologist smeared cold gel on my stomach and began to move the ultrasound wand over the curve of my flesh, I turned to face the flat-screen TV on the wall. The grainy black and white image still showed the results of the last ultrasound that was held in this room and a large, fully formed baby floated in front of my eyes. It was curled up, contented, with its thumb in its mouth and its eyes firmly closed. One tiny hand had been raised, fingers splayed, at the moment the image had been captured and you could see every perfect finger in detail. And then it moved.

'Meet your little baby, Krystal,' the radiologist said happily.

I stared at the screen, and then I stared at her.

'That's—that's not my baby,' I stammered. 'That's someone else's baby. My baby isn't a baby, it's just a foetus, no, it's a *pre*-foetus.' I turned back to the screen in alarm.

'No, darling, that baby is yours. And going by the measurements here and here'—two small crosses appeared on the screen, marking the crown of the head and tip of the tailbone—'your baby is already fourteen weeks old. You're into your second trimester now.'

I gasped in shock. Fourteen weeks old? Second trimester? Our baby would be starting school soon. And needing help with university fees not long after that. We'd need a cot and a pram and a bunny rug and some Golden Books. And at that instant the 'pre-foetus' suddenly became our precious baby.

When I left the ultrasound clinic that day I phoned Chris to tell him I'd changed my mind; we were keeping the baby.

Krystal Barter

Chris deliberately hadn't come with me to the ultrasound as he wanted me to arrive at my own decision about termination, without any pressure from him. He would support me whatever I decided, he told me, but it was my body and my life and the decision had to be mine. And when I rang him on that Tuesday in September and told him I couldn't go through with an abortion, that there was a beautiful little baby growing inside of me and that we would keep and love and raise it as best we could, well, of course Chris agreed and we were parents from that moment onwards.

◆ ◆ ◆

That's not to say things ran smoothly from here. Chris and I were still very young and very broke and living out of my parents' front room. We were daunted and scared and frighteningly underprepared for a baby. We knew nothing about birthing or breast feeding or baby care. Hell, I'd never even held a real-life human baby before. In fact the only thing Chris and I *did* know was that we were hopelessly out of our depth. So we cancelled our trip to Thailand (I would be seven months pregnant then and too uncomfortable to fly, not to mention the fact we'd need that money now for other things), and we began to prepare for one of the biggest changes in our lives.

Towards the end of the year, when I was in my final trimester and feeling bloated and swollen and hormonal and dazed, my mum held a baby shower for me and, during that afternoon, someone wafted a squirming bundle in front of me and insisted I hold it. *It*. I didn't even ask if this baby was a boy or a girl. I just balanced the child precariously in my shaking arms until someone else took pity and rescued the poor bub from my grasp. It was almost Christmas and our baby was due in March. In a few short months, Chris and I would be face-to-face with our baby for the very first time. We had a helluva lot to learn before then.

◆ ◆ ◆

First though, Chris had a surprise for me. With a girlfriend who was heavily pregnant (and gaining weight by the day), Chris had decided it was time to propose. Being the kind of guy that he is, he did everything by the book, diligently ticking things off in the weeks leading up to the big day. He bought a ring (a stunning pink sapphire that I'd fallen in love with earlier in the year when I was out shopping with both of our mums); he asked my dad's permission (Dad said: 'Take her!'); and he'd devised a romantic plan in order to ask me to spend the rest of my life with him.

Only, he didn't count on me messing things up.

It was drizzling the day Chris planned to propose. A fine, misty rain, so slight it could almost be mistaken for the dank humidity that soaked the sagging Sydney air. Chris and I were off to Subway to pick up lunch, then onto Harbord Headland where we would sit and eat and watch the sets roll in at Freshwater Beach, like we did when we first began dating, and where Chris was going to astonish me by getting down on one knee. A Subway sandwich, a stunning vista and a sparkling sapphire: if there's one thing Chris knew, it was that the way to a (heavily pregnant) girl's heart was via her stomach. Well, that was the plan, anyway.

'Chicken teriyaki or meatball?' Chris fiddled nervously with the sandwich wrappers as he proffered them for selection. The drizzle on the windscreen built up into fine, trickling creeks now that the wipers had been switched off.

'What, are you on crack? Chicken teriyaki! I may be hormonal but I'm not completely mad, you know. Who in their right mind would choose meatball over teriyaki?' I held out my hand and Chris absentmindedly passed me the meatball sub.

'Uh, close,' I nagged him, picking up the correct sandwich myself. 'Where's your head at?'

'Huh? My head? Oh, nowhere, nowhere,' Chris said, acting more vague than was usual. 'C'mon, let's go sit on the bench.' And he went to open his driver's side door. The instant he did there was a crack of crazy-loud thunder, followed soon after by a blue flash of lightning that lit half the dismal sky. The noise of the thunder, plus its uncanny timing, made it seem like it had been scripted, like something out of a bad school play. Chris opened the car door anyway.

'What are you *doing*?' I said as the rain began to fall heavier now, pelting the windscreen and hammering on the roof. 'You can't go out there! You'll get soaked!' Chris ignored me and stepped outside and his hair and his clothes were instantly drenched. He started running, sandwich grimly in hand, around to my side of the car and I clocked where he was headed and slammed the lock on my passenger door.

'No way!' I laughed as he pounded on the window. 'There's no way you're getting me out there in that!'

I shrieked as he plastered his dripping face against the glass. 'C'mon, Krystal! C'mon! It's not that bad, just get out for

The Lucky One

a minute,' he begged me, the rain pouring down like only a Sydney storm can. 'Just get out for one second? Please?'

I laughed and shook my head vigorously. 'Got my Subway, got the radio, I'm going nowhere, baby!' I waved my sandwich in front of his pathetic eyes, then mimed unwrapping it in slow-motion as he watched in dismay from out in the rain. Eventually, he gave up and trudged back around to his side of the car, clambering in and drenching the driver's seat at the same time. His sandwich flopped limply inside its soggy wrapper.

'Oh, baby! You're soaked!' I laughed again, grabbing an old beach towel off the back seat and starting to tussle his hair dry. 'What were you thinking, going out in that storm?'

Chris shrugged, defeated, and started the engine to go home. 'Well, that didn't go so well,' was his only response.

◆ ◆ ◆

By the time we were back at my parents' house, the rain had eased off. Chris was still damp but the heat and the clearer weather meant we could have the windows wound down on the ride home and the salty Manly breeze had dried him quite a bit. We headed inside and to our front room 'retreat', where Chris grabbed my hand and pulled me down onto the bed.

'What the—' I began saying but Chris was having no interruptions this time.

'Krystal Anne Barter,' he said solemnly, 'I was planning to do this at Harbord Headland today.' Then he dropped onto one knee at the foot of our bed. My stomach dropped with him.

'Krystal,' he said again, clearing his throat nervously. 'Krystal—' He paused.

'Yes?' I prompted. He was taking his time now that we'd finally got this far.

'Krystal—you know that we're having a baby soon and that I'm one hundred per cent committed to you, and to our baby.'

I held my breath and waited for him to continue.

'Well, like I said, you know we're having a baby together,' he repeated, then stopped, and I wondered if I was going to have to help him. 'And that we're going to be together forever.' I still hadn't let that breath out.

'Well, if you're willing, then consider this the start of our new life together.' With that, he reached into his sodden pocket and pulled out a small, dark blue box, which he opened to reveal my dazzling pink ring.

'Chris!' I shrieked. 'Yes! Yes! Yes! Yes!' I jumped up and threw my arms around him, knocking the box (and the ring) onto the floor. 'Yes! Yes! Oh, I love you, Chris!'

'I love you, too, babe,' he said as he recovered the blue box from where I'd knocked it under the bed and slipped my engagement ring onto my finger.

My engagement ring! We were getting married! I was astonished. Laughing. Crying. Hugging him. Happier than I'd ever felt in my life.

'But I can't believe you wouldn't get out of the car for this!' he said accusingly.

'*I* can't believe you ate soggy Subway for this!'

'That's love, babe, that's love.' And then my fiancé (*fiancé!*) kissed me.

CHAPTER 8

On 26 December 2004, a magnitude 9.0 earthquake occurred off the west coast of Sumatra, causing a series of devastating tsunamis that killed more than 200 000 people, across more than twelve countries, throughout the Indian Ocean basin. It was one of the deadliest megadisasters in recorded history. And I should have been there.

The 'Boxing Day tsunami' hit Phuket particularly hard. The tourist mecca was battered by a 9.2-metre wall of water, killing more than 5000 people in the region, many of them tourists. As we sat on the couch at Mum and Dad's—me, seven months pregnant and sweltering in the heat—Chris and I watched the news in disbelief. There was Phuket, and then Ko Phi Phi Don, and then we saw scenes of the resort we'd picked for our holiday. Bloated and dismembered bodies floated up on the screen. Dead. Drowned. Decimated. At the very resort where Chris and I had been booked to stay at that week.

We had wanted to stay on the island from the Leonardo Di Caprio movie *The Beach*, which we learned was filmed mostly on Ko Phi Phi Lei, which forms part of the Phi Phi Islands. But it was so tiny there was no accommodation on the island so we booked into a resort on nearby Ko Phi Phi Don, that is, until we found out I was pregnant; then we cancelled our holiday. Chris's mum and stepdad were supposed to be there with us, too. The four of us had planned to have Christmas together in Phuket, before splitting up to do our own thing for New Year, and then on to Chang Mai after that. Only, when we were forced to cancel they'd downgraded their plans and just popped across to Bali instead (which is where they were, safe from harm, thank goodness, when the tsunami hit). I remember talking to Mum about our trip and asking her if it was alright if Chris and I missed Christmas at home that year because I'd never skipped spending that day with the family before. Mum, of course, had said it was fine. So Chris and I were looking forward to Christmas Day on Phuket Beach, before heading off to the Phi Phi Islands and then into the mountains to Chang Mai to explore.

Now, though, we were sitting safe and untouched back on our couch in Sydney while all these poor, poor people washed up in wave after wave after wave of death. It was horrifying.

I'm not an overly spiritual or religious person (my good Catholic education fell down a little there). But I do believe things happen for a reason. I think that everyone has a path in life but that there are many different versions of this path available to us, so every time we make a decision, we're choosing a path and choosing our fate. When Chris and I chose not to travel to Thailand that Christmas, it was one of the luckiest decisions we ever made.

I seem to have faced a freakish number of life-changing decisions already in my short existence (I am, as I write this, only 29 years old). At each of these points—at each pivotal moment when my life came to a cross-road—I chose the right path, and it was always thanks to someone who was close to me. It was Chris who saved me from drugs when I chose to ditch them in favour of our relationship. It was Mum who saved me from that car accident back in high school. And now it was little Riley James, our beautiful, healthy baby boy, who was born at 4.28 a.m. on 12 March 2005, who saved Chris and I from the Boxing Day tsunami, and probably saved our lives.

◆ ◆ ◆

Riley was born at Royal North Shore Hospital after a relatively smooth eight-hour labour. I'm told it was a quiet birth by usual standards. But I did have a small haemorrhage and I lost quite a lot of blood in the process. Still, every drop was worth it the instant I met Riley and held him in my arms for the first time.

Even though we knew already we were having a boy, Chris and I still hadn't settled on a name by the time he was born. We'd agreed on 'James' as the middle name (after my brother, Andrew James, and Chris's father, Alan James) but we were tossing up between 'Riley' and 'Jye' for the first name until the last minute. But the instant Riley was born—all scrunched up and red-faced and quite simply perfect—Chris took one look at him and said: 'That's Riley.' And so Riley he was. And our friend, Paul, who had introduced Chris and me just over a year ago, kindly agreed to be Riley's godfather.

Life with Riley was remarkably easy. He was a gorgeously happy baby who slept well, breastfed well and was generally pretty cruisey as long as his mummy or daddy was close by. He slept through the night from the time he was about four months old, causing my friends to joke about what an 'earth-mother' I must be to have produced such a contented baby. (Laughable, really, when you consider how I felt about motherhood just a few months earlier.) Yet now Riley was my entire world. I adored him and I adored being a mother. I used to dress the poor kid in sailor stripes from head to toe (matching hat, jumpsuit, socks and shoes), until he looked like some sort of nautical-themed clown. I'd push him in the stroller and be lost in such a new-motherhood-fog (that's two parts adoration to one part sleep-deprivation) that I'd run the stroller into doorways or into unsuspecting pedestrians. Mine was a love so deep no Huggies advert could ever have prepared me. Overnight, I had transformed into this incredibly maternal, incredibly protective mother lion who lived each day simply to look after her family. So for the first few months of Riley's life the three of us lived in a blissful bubble, safe from the world in our teeny-tiny front room at my parents' house. And throughout it all we never forgot that the only reason Chris and I were there at all was because of Riley.

Riley was our guardian angel from the day he arrived. Before that, even. It was to be a while yet before I had the opportunity to try and save my own life via a double mastectomy. Until then? I was more than happy to be surrounded by wonderful family who would do it for me: first Chris and Mum, and now little Riley. Only, for a newborn baby, Riley really stepped up to the plate. You see, he wasn't content with just saving his parents' lives when he was in utero by causing us to miss the tsunami. No, the second time Riley saved my life was when he was eighteen months old.

◆ ◆ ◆

'Chris?'

'Mmmmf?'

'I'm going to do it.'

'Mmmmf.'

'I'm going to do it, Chris; I've decided.'

'That's great, babe,' Chris drawled into his pillow. 'Do what?'

I rolled over and propped my hands behind my head so I could see Riley's bassinet from where I lay in bed. He was asleep with his thumb pressed into his mouth and his fat, ruddy cheeks were illuminated by the early morning sunshine. I never loved him so much as when he was sleeping.

'I'm going to get genetic testing.' The room was still, with that delicious new-day feeling, before real life intruded and rudely woke everybody up.

'You're gunna *wha—? Are you serious!*' Chris said and he sat bolt upright in bed. He looked at me in surprise and at the same time I tried to shush him, but it was too late and Riley stirred and began to whimper. Good morning, real life.

'Really? You're gunna go and get tested? Babe, that's *great!*' Chris grabbed me now and swept me up in an enormous bear-hug. In his bassinet, Riley began to cry.

'You're totally making the right decision, Krystal,' Chris said. 'You know I'm behind you one hundred per cent. When are we gunna go? Do you wanna go today? You know it's gunna be okay. We'll work it out together. *It's about bloody time!*'

Chris's monologue was always going to end here. For years now, ever since my first failed attempt at taking the BRCA genetic test when I was eighteen, Chris and Mum had been waiting in quiet support for me to decide to go back and take the test for real. They were very patient. Chris, in particular, very rarely raised the issue with me, preferring instead to wait for me to want to talk about it, in the hope that one day I would arrive at my own, independent decision to take the test again. He realised it wasn't something I could be pushed into. And there was a lot to consider. For instance, what would it mean for me if I tested positive for a genetic fault? How would I react? What would it mean for our marriage and my life as a mother? Was there anything I could do to stop from getting cancer anyway? Or, was I just sentencing myself to a life of agony while I waited for cancer to strike?

Or, what if I *didn't* test positive? I would be overjoyed, of course, but what would that mean for my mum and my nan, who'd had to suffer so much because of cancer? And what would it mean for our relationships? Would I experience some sort of strange survivor guilt?

Plus, there was the fact that Mum and Nan had both tested positive for the BRCA1 gene fault, which meant it was unlikely that my results would come back inconclusive. Doctors were confident they would arrive at a conclusive result. And while it might sound obvious (I mean, why else am I doing the test if it's not to get a conclusive result?), it was an eventuality I had to prepare myself for. I couldn't just go along to have the test taken on the assumption it might not tell us anything.

Then, there was the minefield of insurance to negotiate. My parents had organised life insurance for me back when Mum tested positive for BRCA1. (They locked in my insurance and healthcare prior to my gene test because they had heard lots of stories about insurance being difficult to obtain if you are BRCA mutation positive). But if I did test gene positive could my health insurance company renege? Might they alter my coverage in future? I couldn't imagine any insurer would want to touch me if they knew I carried a genetic fault. All these questions swirled around in my head, mostly unanswered. This was new scientific ground we were breaking with genetic testing and, back in 2005, there weren't many people who had trod this path before me and so I had no one to turn to with my barrage of fears and worries and my long list of questions.

Of course, top of the list loomed the biggie, the one which was up to my own DNA to answer: *Was I, or wasn't I, BRCA1 positive?*

On paper my odds looked pretty good. While one in nine Australian women will develop breast cancer by the time they're 85 years old, only 10 per cent of these cases will be classified as belonging to a high risk family, with 40 per cent of these families harbouring cancer genetic mutations (15 per cent for ovarian cancer). As my mother was a confirmed carrier of a BRCA1 gene mutation, I had a 50 per cent chance of inheriting that gene fault from her. How bad were my odds? It's not like there were thousands of women walking around out there with the breast cancer gene fault. If you surveyed people wandering down Pitt Street in Sydney, you'd have to be pretty unlucky to bump into many that were BRCA1 mutation positive. It wasn't like brown hair or being right-handed or having a propensity for being okay at ball sports. This thing wasn't *common*, not by a long shot. And yet, no matter how many times I convinced myself of this, I only had to picture my family tree and my heart sank. There, on every branch, on every leaf in some places, hung the skull-and-cross-bones symbol of death. Breast cancer. It was like ringbark or borers or root rot; it was the elm disease of our family tree. There were a hell of a lot more women (and men) in our family suffering and dying from breast and ovarian cancer than there seemed to be among the general population, and I knew that couldn't be just a coincidence. We *had* to be carrying some sort of gene mutation and it terrified me to think I would find out for sure.

What's more, it was only four years since I tried to take the BRCA test and fled the doctor's surgery in a flood of tears. Yet here I was, choosing to go back again. Was I really that much more mature now and any better equipped to cope? Would I crumble at the last minute and react the same way again? I would be *mortified* if, when faced with that needle, I became hysterical again and had to back down. Would I go through with it? *Could* I go through with it? Why should things be any different this time around?

The answer, quite simply, was Riley.

As I scooped him up out of his cot that morning and soothed his crying and waited for his big crocodile tears to stop and make way for his even bigger, gurgling laugh, I thought, for the millionth time lately, that I had to get tested for Riley's sake. While I was breastfeeding Riley I'd suffered mastitis about ten times. Each instance was incredibly painful and my sensitive

The Lucky One

swollen nipples felt as though they had red-hot pokers applied to them every time Riley wrapped his little mouth around them. Then, there were the throbbing lumps in my breast tissue as my milk hardened and got blocked in my milk ducts. *Oh, the agony!* The only thing worse than the pain was the heart-stopping fear I felt each time I touched one of my tender breasts and found a new lump there. Was it congealed milk or was it cancer? Were we talking mastitis or mastectomy? My sleep-deprived mind would race. Sitting in the near-darkness of those 5 a.m. feeds, blue light seeping into the cold horizon, I would imagine, terrified, that this was it. This was the dawning of the day I had been expecting all along, this would be the day I discovered I had cancer.

The fear I had felt so acutely as a teenager had never gone away, I'd simply pushed it to the back of my mind. But throughout the last few years when I'd met Chris and fallen in love and gotten engaged, I had never once forgotten that, beneath it all, I was a woman who was most likely doomed.

Then, as soon as I had Riley my life took on a completely different direction and, with it, a new gravitas. Now, I had a real reason to live, and a real reason to stay healthy, not to mention a responsibility to this amazing little person to stick around and look after him for as long as I possibly could. And if a genetic test could give me the information I needed to do this? Well, maybe it was about time I got tested, after all. Suddenly, the decision about whether or not to undergo genetic testing was no longer mine alone; it affected people beyond me, and those people were the ones I loved the most. I couldn't bear the thought of looking into Riley's eyes one day and telling him that Mummy had breast cancer and, worse, that I might once have been able to do something to prevent it but I chose not to educate myself. I couldn't bear to hear him say to me: 'But, Mum, you could have *found out* about this. I don't understand why you didn't just take that blood test. *You could have known.*'

◆ ◆ ◆

Which is why I decided it was time to stop burying my head in the sand and pretending this cancer threat didn't really exist. Instead of viewing genetic testing as my misfortune, I needed to start seeing it as my gift: a gift of knowledge that might allow me to save my own life and so be there to see more of Riley's. My story could have been so different if I didn't accidentally get pregnant with Riley when I was 21. I might still be ignoring the bleeding obvious that was my family history and putting off that genetic test every time I went to see my GP. I could still be living each day as though I was guaranteed to have thousands more just like it; and so why waste a gorgeous morning like this doing something as depressing as getting a blood test when I could be at the beach or going for lunch or getting my nails done or watching paint dry or just about anything you can think of other than facing up to my genetic destiny?

Riley, that's why. Riley was the reason I finally decided to bite the bullet and take a genetic test for breast cancer and I'm so lucky I did. My future could have taken a completely different path if it hadn't been for my little guardian angel. For the second time in his short life, my son saved me.

◆ ◆ ◆

The Lucky One

I had a blood test for the BRCA genetic fault in August 2006 when I was 22 years old. The test took place at my local GP's surgery and was just like any other blood test. They could have been testing me for the flu or for my glucose levels or for a niggling vitamin D deficiency, for all I cared. After all my agonising for so many years about whether or not to get tested, when I finally did it, it was an anti-climax. Like, *that was it? That's what all the sleepless nights were about?* I was in and out of the clinic in less than twenty minutes and as I wandered back to my car I couldn't help but feel strangely disappointed. I'm not sure exactly what it was I had expected. A certificate? A plaque on the wall? Perhaps an overhead fireworks display? (The doctor, it must be said, had congratulated me on my brave choice and on being so proactive about my health.) But still the enormity of deciding to take a genetic test and the simple act of giving blood in order to do so were ridiculously incongruous.

Of course, the sleepless nights weren't over the test itself; they were over the *results*. Chris and I had talked about these at length and he showed such unbelievable support, always saying things like, 'Babe, I knew when I got engaged to you what I was getting myself in for. Cancer gene, or no cancer gene—I'm not going anywhere. I'm right by your side no matter what.'

One of the things we did discuss was how I might approach the news: what my mental state should be when I went in to get my results and how I could best prepare myself for the worst. I was like an elite athlete psyching myself up for competition and this was my macabre Olympics. But, unlike most athletes, the strategy Chris and I came up with was: think negative.

'Look at it this way,' Chris reasoned, 'if you go into this expecting to learn you've got the breast cancer gene, then you'll be as ready as you'll ever be to hear the bad news. Whereas, if you blindly hope right up until the last minute, then there's a good chance you're going to be disappointed.'

'And the shock will be hell,' he added quietly.

I closed my eyes and physically braced at the thought.

'But if you expect the worst and you get the all-clear,' he continued, 'then you're laughing.'

I tried to imagine a scenario, any scenario, where laughing might be in order. The idea seemed so foreign to me at the time. I knew when I took the test that it could be up to six months before I had the results. But having spent years deliberating over whether or not to take the test, now that I'd done it I wondered how I could possibly wait that long for the outcome. Could I really get on with life as normal while elsewhere, off in some lab somewhere, a technician was scrolling through my DNA to see if I might die an early death from cancer? Could I really wake up every day for six agonising months and feed Riley his Weet-Bix and mashed banana and wave Chris off to work and pretend like it might not all be about to come crashing down like a house of cards?

It turns out, I didn't have to.

Three weeks after I took the blood test I received a phone call telling me my results were available and that I was welcome to come in and meet with my genetic counsellor. *Already? And, genetic counsellor?*

'Genetic counsellor!' I exclaimed to Chris as soon as I hung up the phone. 'I've got my own genetic counsellor. That can't be a good sign. And what does it mean that my results are in

The Lucky One

so quickly? Was it really that painfully obvious that I'm going to get cancer?' So much for all the sports-psychology stuff that Chris and I had been practising. Here I was panicking and before the starter's gun had gone off.

'Just breathe, sweetie,' Chris said, sweeping me into one of his enormous bear hugs. 'I'm sure these days they're required to get genetic counsellors in to deliver this sort of news regardless of the results. Plus, surely it's a good thing we don't have to wait any longer? And, anyway, what happened to "thinking positive"?'

Chris and I had nicknamed our approach 'thinking positive', as in testing 'BRCA1 positive' (meaning cancer-prone) and not 'thinking on the bright side'. Although our strategy was to plan for the worst and to expect to hear the words 'BRCA1 positive', we somehow felt that by referring to it as 'thinking positive' we were taking charge of the situation and not just being victims.

But the situation now felt like it was sliding out my control *and fast*. Sure, I wanted to know my genetic test results—I was desperate to end the worrying and the wondering and the biting my nails to the quick—but was I really ready to hear what my genetic counsellor had to tell me? *Was I ready to even have a genetic counsellor in the first place?* Sure, just minutes ago I thought I had months to prepare for this news and now I was only going to get a few weeks. But if I was freaking out this much at only a slight hiccup in my plan (and a good hiccup at that; I mean, three weeks of waiting is better than six months, right?), then how on earth would I cope if my test results were not what I expected? And what did I expect anyway? I *thought* I expected to learn I was BRCA1 positive, but was I really prepared for that eventuality? Really? Deep down? And, if so, was I ready to hear it or did I just *think* I was ready? Maybe I was trying to convince myself I was fine when I wasn't? Maybe I wasn't even close to being fine? Hell, could *anyone* really be fine with hearing that they're highly likely to develop cancer, and soon? I was infinitely unsure the day Chris and I travelled to the Hereditary Cancer Clinic at Prince of Wales Hospital in Randwick, in Sydney's eastern suburbs, to meet my genetic counsellor.

◆ ◆ ◆

'Krystal? It's good to see you!' An intelligent-looking woman smiled at me from the far side of her desk. This was no genetic counsellor; this was Dr Kathy Tucker, head of Hereditary Cancer at Prince of Wales and a long-time friend of the family. I'd known Kathy since Mum and Nan first tested positive for the BRCA1 gene, back when I was only eighteen years old, and she'd been part of our lives since.

'How could I not meet with you today?' she asked me, seeing my confused face. 'I'm afraid I hijacked your meeting as soon as I heard you were coming in here.'

I was immediately relieved that Kathy, someone I knew so well and trusted, would be the person delivering my test results.

'As you were told over the phone, the results of your recent genetic test are now available, Krystal. But we'll get to those in a minute. First, I'd like to ask you, are you ready to receive your results today?' Kathy asked.

In just about any other situation I could think of (exam results, driving test results, the final week of *Masterchef*), this would be a redundant question. *Of course* I'm ready! Don't leave me in suspense! But not this time.

The Lucky One

'Yes, I'm ready,' I said and I reached out for Chris's hand. Then I baulked. 'At least, I think I'm ready. I'm trying to be ready! How do I know? Can you take a test to see if you're ready to get your test results?' I joked lamely. I wasn't sounding like someone who was anywhere near ready.

'Think positive,' Chris said in a low, steady voice as he gripped my outstretched hand.

Kathy smiled at both of us patiently. In front of her sat a single sheet of A4 paper covered in an intimidating set of numbers and medical hieroglyphics. It was staggering to think that my puny vial of black-red blood had been transformed into this impressive sheet of numbers, and that this impressive sheet of numbers was about to dictate my whole future.

'Yes, I'm ready,' I said again, lying, but not prepared to wait any longer.

'Well, then,' Kathy said. 'Krystal?'

'Yes?'

'Krystal, you're positive for BRCA1.'

I let my breath out and felt the strange sense of relief that comes from knowing you've arrived at rock bottom. *Positive. I was positive. I had the breast cancer gene.*

Chris squeezed my hand.

'Krystal?' In front of me Kathy was trying to get my attention. 'Krystal, I know what you've just heard is a shock but I want you to believe me when I say that your journey starts here.' She smiled gently again and paused while she let me digest this.

'Your test results revealed the same genetic fault as is present in your mum and in your nan but your journey will be different to theirs.' I think I actually smiled at this.

Krystal Barter

'You're not going to tread the same path as they did,' Kathy went on, 'because you have valuable information about your genes that wasn't available to your mum and your nan before they developed cancer. So there's simply no way that your story won't be different.'

Truly, I don't know how she did it but Kathy managed to raise my hopes about my future that day as she delivered the very worst news. If you are ever unlucky enough to hear the words 'BRCA1 positive' then I can only hope you are lucky enough to hear them from Dr Tucker. She was truly amazing that day and has held my hand for so much of my journey since. In fact, I now consider her to be so much more than a doctor to me; I consider her a friend.

But she wasn't finished yet.

'So, Krystal, by being proactive and constantly monitoring your breast health, there are ways you can catch breast cancer early. It takes patience and vigilance—'

'Wait, *what?*' I interrupted. 'Patience and vigilance?'

I was incredulous. Was she telling me that—having just found out I had an insanely high chance of getting cancer before I hit 30 years old—the best course of action was to sit around and wait? *To wait!* I could no more wait to be struck down with cancer than I could lie down in the middle of Military Road in Manly and wait for a semitrailer to come hurtling along! And at what point do they consider I've waited enough? When I've watched my mum and my nan nearly die of this bloody disease? When I've undergone genetic testing and discovered the odds are stacked against me so high that I can barely see the sky? When I'm diagnosed with my first bout of cancer? Or when I'm dying from it? Or when I'm no longer here at all but just a case study in some medical textbook about the severity of hereditary cancer? Would Riley want me to wait until I was sick and dying and too riddled with cancerous tumours to be able to bend down and pick him up anymore? There was no way in hell I was prepared to wait.

'Surely there's something I can *do*?' I asked Kathy.

'What we recommend for someone in your position, Krystal, is to register for high-risk screening. This is offered through our family cancer clinics and involves going for six-monthly ultrasounds and yearly mammograms in order to monitor any changes in your breast tissue.'

'Okay. Thank you,' I said, and I really was grateful. 'But surely there's something a little more proactive I can do? Like actively actually *do*, rather than just watching and waiting? Can you get pre-emptive chemotherapy? To kill any cancer before it even hits?'

Kathy looked sympathetic. 'I understand your frustration, Krystal, I really do. But until we have evidence of changes in your breast tissue, or until you're a little older and more firmly within the high-risk zone age-wise, I'd be loathe to recommend anything too drastic.'

'You've had a big shock today,' Kathy continued. 'You've received some huge news and it's a lot to take in, no matter how much you might have been expecting to hear it. I'm not surprised that you're feeling anxious or angry or scared or all of these things. It's perfectly understandable. But the best thing for you to do right now is to go home and talk things over with Chris and have a really good long think before you start planning your next step.'

'After all,' she added brightly, 'what you've received today is *not* a cancer diagnosis.'

Krystal Barter

Sure, I thought. But there's an 80 per cent chance I'll get one eventually.

◆ ◆ ◆

Over the next few weeks and months I experienced nothing but overwhelming love and support from my family and close friends. I only told a handful of people outside of my immediate family but everyone I told was incredibly positive. And not in the 'think positive' way Chris and I had been in the lead-up to my test results. Mum actually said she would rather I had this genetic flaw than not, because at least it meant I would be well looked after. Anyone can get breast cancer, as our family is painfully aware, but knowing that I was BRCA1 positive now meant my breast health would be closely monitored and any changes to my breast tissue should be picked up immediately.

And while I was so lucky to have such incredible support, I did feel a certain amount of pressure to deserve it. I mean, here were my mum and my nan, who had gone through breast cancer themselves and come out the other side (sans breasts) and who were still so indefatigably positive about my prospects. If they could experience cancer firsthand and still summon up such joie de vivre when talking about me and my future and my BRCA1 status and how I would beat this thing—then, dammit, I would. I could hardly curl up in a ball and wave the white flag, could I? I didn't actually *have* cancer, and they'd both been through it at least once, so I could hardly complain. In fact, if anything, I owed it to them to put on a brave face and get on with life.

The Lucky One

Not to mention the fact that my diagnosis brought with it all sorts of baggage for my family by way of stress and worry and, that old chestnut, guilt. By coming up BRCA1 positive, I caused my family untold distress. Chris and Dad felt enormous anxiety and that sense of overprotectiveness that men feel for the women they care about the most. Mum was devastated yet so very determined not to show it. And, at the same time, she was racked with guilt at having passed her genetic mutation on to me. And if Mum was racked with guilt then Nan was near-crippled with it. Nan had hoped that my brother and I might have been the first generation to escape the breast cancer gene in our family but now, because of my news, she knew it could survive for more generations and she blamed herself. Double-guilt. Guilt with a side order of guilt. Guilt of truly Catholic proportions. Nan blamed herself for passing her genes on to Mum, and then again for the fact that Mum had passed her genes on to me. It was a viscous pass-the-parcel that no number of Hail Mary's could interrupt. So the only thing left for me to do was to assure everyone else I would be okay.

And it worked, too. My nan has since told me that my positive attitude was what helped her deal with my diagnosis. By staring down my BRCA1 status and saying, 'I have a lovely baby and I'm planning a wedding; good times are ahead', I was able to focus my attention, and the attention of those around me, on all the positive things we had going for us.

On the inside, however, I was starting to unravel. I felt scared and lost and hopelessly alone. For all my family's demonstrations of love and support, ultimately it was me that had to face the high probability of cancer. Mum and Nan might have been there and done it all before, but this time *I* was the one that had to fight. I was the one that had to steel myself for regular mammograms and ultrasounds and lose my breath every time I felt a lump in my breast. I was the one that may well have to undergo chemo or breast-removal surgery or face a shortened life expectancy (although, I couldn't bear to think about that yet). I was the one that had to steel myself to do these things and there was no one else that could step in for me, much as they would have done so if given the chance. Right now, I was more encouraged by family and friends than ever before and yet I'd never felt so alone.

And so, each evening, when everyone else went to bed, I'd make myself a strong cup of tea and sit up into the night with the only person I felt I could turn to: Dr Google. Desperate for information and hungry for answers, I trawled cyberspace. Information was a little thin on the ground at the time. (It's amazing how much things have improved in just the past few years. Now you can access everything, from checklists of questions to take with you when you receive your genetic test results, to Pinterest sites that offer hairstyle ideas for each stage of growing out your post-chemo 'do'.) Back then, things were a little more basic but this is some of what I learned:

- Breast cancer is the most common cancer among Australian women: 14 940 women were diagnosed with breast cancer last year (2013), which is about 40 per day.
- One in nine women will be diagnosed with breast cancer before the age of 85 and it is the most common cause of cancer deaths in women.
- For those who test positive to the BRCA1 gene fault, in most cases the lifetime risk of developing breast cancer is between 60 and 80 per cent up to the age of 70; or approximately five

The Lucky One

times greater than for a woman with no family history of breast cancer. And the risk is somewhere between 10 and 60 per cent for ovarian cancer. (To be told I had up to an 80 per cent chance of developing breast cancer put me in the 'extremely unfortunate' bracket.)

- About 5 per cent of breast cancers are due to inherited 'faulty' genes. These faults or mutations take place in the 'cancer protection' genes (which, in my case, was in the BRCA1 gene).
- Most people are born with two working copies of each of the different 'cancer protection' genes in their cells; these are growth-control genes that regulate orderly growth and division of cells. A small number of people inherit a change in one of the copies of one of their 'cancer protection' genes—that is, they are susceptible to uncontrolled cell division and growth—which means a higher than average risk of developing cancer at some point in their lifetime. (Why, hello there, that would be me.)
- About 12 000 Australians are believed to be carrying the BRCA1 or BRCA2 gene fault (mutation) and research shows that 17 per cent of Australian women who test positive for the faults choose to have a mastectomy. (A sobering statistic.)
- If these faults do lead to cancer developing, it may tend to do so earlier in life. Similarly, new cancers can develop in more than one place in the body. (I was seriously tempted to stop researching right then and there.)
- In particular, BRCA1 mutations may increase a woman's risk of developing ovarian and pancreatic cancer. (Okay, okay, enough already!)

Then, just as I'd decided it was about time me and Dr Google parted ways, I stumbled upon this: Anyone who tests positive to the BRCA1 gene mutation, whether they go on to develop cancer or not, can pass their mutation on to their sons or daughters. And I realised, as I read it, that I may have already passed my faulty genetic makeup on to Riley. In reply to his saving my life (twice), I may have destroyed his.

CHAPTER 9

Since my BRCA1 diagnosis, I've met many (amazing) women who have faced the same fate as I have and each and every one has reacted differently. Some women like to keep the information to themselves, finding strength from sharing it with only their closest family and friends and priding themselves on the fact that the rest of the world would never know what they're going through. Others are more public in their response, opening their arms wide to include everyone, even relative strangers, in their journey towards dealing with their BRCA1 status. I fell somewhere between the two. I leant on my family and close friends and thrived on their support; I needed it some days just as much as I needed air to breathe. But among my wider circle of friends and acquaintances, I kept the news of my cancer-courting status to myself. It wasn't that I deliberately wanted to shut people out, or that I was being stoic in doing so. It was more that I relished those times when I didn't have to think or talk about cancer and I could be plain old Krystal Barter, BC (Before Cancer-loomed-large-in-my-life).

And yet I didn't shut *everybody* out. What stopped me from falling completely into that first, more private, camp (and also the way in which I differed from that second group who opened up to their family and friends) was that I chose a third option: I went very, very public. That is, I went to the media with my BRCA1 status.

At the time I was deciding whether or not to undergo genetic testing, my mum had agreed to an interview with the *New Zealand Woman's Weekly*. It was to be a profile piece on Mum, written by journalist Wendy Colville, but one which told the broader story of our family's cancer curse. To write the article Wendy had spoken at length with Mum over the phone about her battle with cancer and she'd been to visit Nan in Matamata to record her journey, too. (In the article, Wendy described Nan as 'a warm and generous woman, a former farmer with grace and typical country hospitality. On the day I visit her in Matamata she whips up a packed lunch of asparagus rolls and homemade cake for my trip back to Auckland.' We joked within the family that Wendy only included Nan in the article as an excuse to sample her amazing butter cake.) The only person missing from the article was me.

So when Wendy phoned, just 24 hours after I'd received my BRCA1 diagnosis, I agreed to take part in her story. It might seem like a strange thing to do, especially for someone who couldn't face telling the girls in her netball team, nor most of

The Lucky One

the people she invited to her 21st birthday only a year or so earlier. Yet, for me, sharing my story with the media was the most positive thing I could think of to do. It allowed me to take the devastating news of my BRCA1-positive mutation status and transform it into something life affirming by (hopefully) encouraging other people who were in similar situations. Or, at the very least, letting them know that they weren't the only ones going through this and that they didn't have to do it alone.

I'd just like to add here that this attitude was definitely inherited from my mum. Shortly after Mum recovered from her double mastectomy in the 1990s, she began volunteering for the National Breast Cancer Foundation. She made me volunteer, too, much to my initial dismay, but I gradually grew to love my work there (although I never admitted that to Mum when I was a moody 14-year-old). We were featured in an article in *New Idea* magazine for our work and I was wildly embarrassed at the exposure. However, I eventually grew to be proud of what we'd done after I had strangers recognising me in public and telling me what a brave family we were and what a worthy cause we were helping. In this way, Mum taught me the power of harnessing the media for a good cause.

When Wendy's article went to print in *New Zealand Woman's Weekly*, it did much to raise awareness about hereditary breast cancer. It explained the medical science behind the BRCA1 gene and revealed how I, too, carried this flawed (mutation) gene, just like my mother and my grandmother. Wendy wrote: 'Twenty-four hours after the diagnosis Krystal sounds cheerful and upbeat, and says she won't dwell on the result.'

'At the moment I have too much going on in my life. I don't really have time to sit down and think about it, which is a good thing,' I was quoted as saying. 'It just makes you want to live every day as if it's your last. We've always had that motto. Even though you've got to make sure you can pay your bills, you've still got to enjoy yourself, because you might get hit by a car tomorrow. You've just got to enjoy life …'

I don't remember saying this to Wendy. In fact, five minutes after our conversation I couldn't have told you *anything* I said to her during the hour-long interview. I think I was still in a daze after my diagnosis. But the final article captured exactly the message I wanted to send. Being BRCA1 mutation positive was *not* going to ruin our lives; it was *not* going to stop us from enjoying ourselves—because we wouldn't let it.

It was at this point that I decided: 'You know what? If I can help just one other person, especially a person affected by hereditary breast cancer, by opening my life up to the media, well, then, it's worth it.'

That's not to say talking to the media is the right thing for everyone to do. Becoming a pin-up girl for BRCA1 mutation status (as I inadvertently did) is not for everyone. Plus, of course, this meant that all my family and friends would soon know about my situation. Even total strangers would recognise me from media interviews and come up to chat to me as if they'd known me all my life.

About a year after we'd spoken with *New Zealand Woman's Weekly*, Mum and Nan and I agreed to an interview with Australia's (now-defunct) *Madison* magazine. It was a similar sort of piece to the *Woman's Weekly* story, but the fact it was published locally made for a much greater impact on us. I remember one day a woman tapped me on the shoulder as I waited in the express checkout lane with my barbecue chicken

The Lucky One

at the supermarket in Manly. She'd read my interview with *Madison* (and recognised my face from the accompanying photo shoot) and she wanted to tell me how heartbreaking my story was and what a brave thing I was doing by sharing my story so publicly. Incidents like these were hugely inspiring for me but, at the same time, incredibly surreal. I had never had a public profile of any description before now—never sought one—and so to have people recognise me at the supermarket as I bought a chook for dinner was a strange new experience for me.

◆ ◆ ◆

The other thing that I did at this time was to contact my local family cancer clinic to ask to be added to their register for high-risk screening. Family cancer clinics are run by the government and are usually located within public hospitals. They provide surveillance and treatment information, as well as counselling for families with a strong history of cancer. They also coordinate a register of at-risk individuals which allows family members to undergo medical tests, such as mammograms and, more recently, MRIs, much more regularly than a person with no history of cancer in their family, and at no or minimal cost. This was the list I needed to be on. My local clinic, the Hereditary Cancer Clinic, was located at the Prince of Wales Hospital (where I saw Dr Kathy Tucker and received my BRCA1 gene mutation diagnosis). Kathy had said that I wouldn't even have to attend the clinic to be put on their register; it was simply a matter of phoning them. It sounded easy enough.

◆ ◆ ◆

'Good morning, Hereditary Cancer Clinic.'

'Hello, I'm phoning to self-refer for your register for high-risk individuals,' I said, putting on my best telephone voice. 'Dr Kathy Tucker recommended I contact you.'

'Okay,' said the voice down the line. 'Can I start with your name and family history, please?'

'Sure. My name is Krystal Barter and I'm BRCA1 mutation positive.' It felt like a line from an Alcoholics Anonymous meeting, but I pressed on and explained the history of hereditary breast cancer in my family. In particular, I pointed out that my great-grandmother, my grandmother and my mother have all had breast cancer. 'Now I've just tested positive to the family gene fault, which is why I'd like to register for advanced screening, please. I don't plan on getting breast cancer any time soon!' I tried to make light of my dark family tree but there was no need; the woman at the cancer clinic had obviously heard it all before because she didn't miss a beat.

'Well, you're taking a great first step towards avoiding cancer, Krystal,' she said encouragingly. 'If I can just get a few more details from you, then we'll get you onto the register straightaway. How old did you say you were, Krystal?'

'Oh, I didn't,' I replied. 'I'm 22.'

There was a momentary silence from the other end of the phone line.

'Twenty-two? Krystal, I'm afraid it's a little early to be adding you to the register. Our statistics show that the incidence of breast cancer doesn't spike until women are well into their 30s. If you'd like to phone back then, we'll be more than happy to add your name to the register.'

Now it was my turn to pause. *My 30s?*

The Lucky One

'But my test results show that I'm likely to have cancer by the time I'm 30!' I blurted.

'Well, that will show up with screening, if you do.'

'But I want to do something *before* I get cancer. That's the whole point!'

'But you can't detect cancer before it's occurred,' was the calm reply. 'That's not how screening works.'

'So you're saying I have to wait to get cancer before you'll help me?'

'No, I'm saying we don't start screening until you're 30 because that's the point at which most high-risk people begin to develop pre-cancerous changes in their breasts. Changes that can be detected by screening.'

I felt like I had slipped down a rabbit hole into Wonderland for all the sense this conversation was making.

'But I've already told you: my situation is *different*. Thirty could well be too late for me. I might have cancer by then!'

'Well, if you do, then the screening will pick that up.'

Argh! This really was Wonderland! And I was the white rabbit running around in circles shouting, 'Too late! Too late! For a very important date!'

I took a deep breath and tried again: 'Look, I appreciate you have rules and procedures around these things. But I've just learned I may have cancer by the time I'm 30—I'm more than likely to—and I can't sit around and do nothing about it. I just can't. Is there *any* way you can make an exception and add me to the register even though I'm only 22? I may not be here for you to add me in eight years time.'

◆ ◆ ◆

And that's how I was added to the family cancer clinic register. I started my screening program several weeks later and this involved a routine of six-monthly ultrasounds and annual mammograms. (This was in addition to my own self-examinations at home, which I was undertaking with grim determination). There was also the option of MRI (magnetic resonance imaging) technology, which is often used in conjunction with mammograms as MRIs are able to pick up even the most minute abnormality in very dense breasts. MRIs are particularly useful for younger breasts (like my 22-year-old boobs) where the tissue can be far denser. At the time, however, MRIs were the only option on the high-risk register that *weren't* free. And, at a cost of around $600 a pop, they were well beyond what Chris and I could afford, even from our lap of luxury that was the front room of Mum and Dad's house. (There now exists a high-risk rebate for MRIs but this wasn't even mooted at the time.)

So I stuck to my ultrasounds and mammograms, undertaken at the formidable red-brick Royal North Shore Hospital at St Leonards. The ultrasounds use the same technology as pregnancy ultrasounds, although the equipment is specific to breast tissue, and the images are generally considered complementary to mammogram results. They were quick, pain-free and hardly an ordeal, considering that they could save my life.

The mammograms, on the other hand, were less fun. Although I only had to have a mammogram once a year, anyone who has ever had one will tell you there are more enjoyable ways to spend your time than with your boob squashed between two metal plates. Even though the women at Royal North Shore Hospital were always as gentle as possible, and even though I knew mammograms were one of the best screening tools available for breast cancer (along with self-examination), I always dreaded seeing the friendly reminder letter with my name on it. Worse, though, than the brief discomfort, was the dread that going for a mammogram brought on. *Would this be the test that showed a tumour was growing? Would this be when I learned I had cancer?*

Each time I made the trip to Royal North Shore it was with a heavy heart. That the journey to the hospital was so similar to the way that we used to drive to Nanny Beryl's in Frenchs Forest when I was a kid seemed like an especially cruel joke. We even drove past the turnoff for Frenchs Forest, in fact. It seemed impossible to me that these two buildings—the hospital and my beloved Nanny Beryl's house—could exist in the same universe, let alone be separated by just a few road arteries and less than twenty minutes of driving. But they were. And I was making a very different journey now to the ones I used to make to Nanny's.

CHAPTER 10

As my world morphed into a dizzying merry-go-round of monitoring and mammograms and medical jargon, I had another, much more welcome 'M word' to distract me: marriage. Chris and I had set our wedding date for 10 March 2007 and this was now less than six months away. We'd chosen St Andrew's Presbyterian Church in Manly for our fairytale wedding, followed by a reception at the International Tourism College in Manly (where Nicole Kidman famously married Keith Urban just a year before). Ours was to be a beautifully classic affair (think: a 14-member bridal party and a four-tiered wedding cake) but with one major exception: the colour. Billy Idol had it all wrong because, as far as I was concerned, it was a nice day for a *pink* wedding.

The Lucky One

I can't quite remember when I decided to forgo a white wedding in favour of a pink one, but once I'd had the idea it seemed impossible that I'd ever choose anything else. After all, not only is pink my favourite colour but it's the colour of my family. Whenever I think of my family's tainted history, I see this colour which has become associated with breast cancer: pink. And later, when I set up my charity, Pink Hope, it would come to symbolise my family's future, too. (Plus, I'd never been a white kinda girl; I have fair skin, so wearing anything too pale drowns me out. And a fake tan just wasn't me.)

I wanted to wear pink at my wedding to honour all those wonderful women in my family who had fought long and hard against breast cancer. And I wanted to wear pink in honour of Chris. Chris, who was agreeing to marry me even though he knew I was BRCA1 mutation positive; Chris, who was standing by my side despite the fact I was probably going to get cancer one day or, at the very least, lose my breasts; Chris, who was unflinching and unfailing in his love for me. By walking down the aisle wearing pink, I wanted to show Chris that I was bringing with me my family's medical history, as well as my (and potentially our children's) genetically flawed future. But, most importantly, I wanted to show the world that, in agreeing to marry me, Chris was taking on a helluva lot and that I couldn't have loved him more because of it.

I decided not to tell Chris of my plans for a pink wedding; instead I wanted to surprise him by walking down the aisle decked out in my favourite shade. So began my hunt for the perfect pink wedding dress. As you can imagine, there isn't a huge demand for wedding dresses in any colour much beyond the spectrum of whitest-white through to ivory, and Mum and

I soon realised that I'd need a bespoke gown. We trawled bridal boutiques and specialist websites in the hope of finding a design we could turn pink, but all to no avail. Nothing seemed quite right. And we soon got bored of explaining to snooty bridal store assistants why we wanted pink in the first place.

Of course, my gown dilemmas were nothing when compared to my mum's journey down the aisle. During our mornings scouring the Northern Beaches' bridal stores, and our evenings at home pouring over *Real Weddings* magazine, Mum gradually told me the story of her own wedding preparation. And it wasn't pretty.

♦ ♦ ♦

Mum had left her family home in New Zealand and was living in Melbourne when she met my dad and got engaged. She was young (just twenty years old), giddy with the freedom of big-smoke Melbourne after small-town Matamata and madly in love. And so on the day she bought her wedding dress, Mum phoned home in a rush of excitement to tell her parents all about it. Only she didn't bank on them having news of their own. Her dad answered the phone and, after letting her gush about the wedding gown that lay pristine in its glossy white box on the bed beside the phone, he said he had something 'sad' to tell her: 'Julie, your mother has just had her breast removed.'

Mum was devastated. And floored! She had no idea that Nan was even *sick*, let alone undergoing a mastectomy. *Was it cancer? How serious was it? How long had they known? Why on earth hadn't they told her about it?* Mum struggled to focus as Grandad told her that Nan was in intensive care because she was having breathing difficulties after the operation. Mum's wedding dress lay gaudily on the bed. 'Where did this come from?' Mum managed to say eventually. 'I didn't know there was anything wrong with her! Why didn't you tell me there was something wrong with her?'

'Do you think you could come over?' was all Grandad said. And Mum was on the next plane home.

It turned out that, when Mum and Dad had flown to New Zealand for their engagement party only weeks earlier, Nan already knew she had a 50-cent-sized lump in her breast. But she'd kept the knowledge from them because she didn't want to ruin their holiday. When Mum returned to Matamata this time (with her wedding dress in tow), she found Nan in a hospice. *She's dying*, was Mum's first thought. Nan, however, had other ideas. No matter how sick the chemotherapy was making her (and it was making her mighty sick), Nan's only concern was for the other patients in the hospice. 'See that gentlemen over there, Julie-Ann?' she'd say to Mum. 'He's really ill. It's so terribly sad.' And so while Mum had been back in Melbourne, blissfully worrying about her wedding dress, Nan had been worrying about everyone else in the hospice. *Was nobody thinking about Nan!*

Mum stayed with Nan for three weeks before returning to Melbourne and to Dad and to their (now somewhat relegated) wedding plans. Grandad would ring Mum with regular updates but, more often than not, Nan would be unable to talk because the chemotherapy would render her unable to lift her head off the pillow enough to speak on the phone. Chemotherapy was a vastly different prospect back in 1970s New Zealand and each bout would leave Nan bedridden for up to ten days at a time. Grandad said that every time he had to drive her to the hospital for her next round of treatment, Nan would cry all the way in the car just knowing what pain and sickness lay ahead of her. Mum, of course, felt terribly guilty at being in Australia and being in love while Nan was suffering so much on the other side of the Tasman. She felt that, as a daughter, she should have been there to support Nan when she needed it most. And the fact she was having such a wonderful time with my dad didn't help.

However, by the time Mum and Dad and all of Dad's family travelled to New Zealand for the wedding, Nan's health was starting to improve. Slowly but surely, her body began to regain strength. It was as if Mum's wedding lifted her and gave her a reason to fight on. So much so that Nan had somehow managed to drag herself out of bed and to the dining room table, where she'd put together her salient contribution to her only daughter's wedding: the flowers. Now, Mum was pretty laissez-faire about the whole wedding thing. Remember, this was in an era before wedding planners and bridal magazines and Kim Kardashian's wedding extravaganza. In fact, the only thing that Mum really cared about (and I mean really, *really* cared about), aside from the groom, of course, was the flowers at the wedding. And Mum wanted fresh. So when she arrived back in her family home in Matamata to find Nan had lovingly made bouquet after bouquet after bouquet of stiff, artificial flowers, her heart sank.

'I hated them!' Mum laughed as she recounted this to me in yet another changeroom of yet another bridal boutique one day. 'Your nan had tied each bunch with a garish satin ribbon and then wrapped every bouquet individually in tissue paper to protect it. And I absolutely loathed the lot of them! But all I said to Nan was: "They're beautiful. Thank you." Because how could I possibly say anything else? After everything the poor woman had been through to make them for me?'

'That wasn't what worried me the most, though,' Mum added, still laughing. 'No; what worried me more was the cake. Because your nan had ordered that, too. And if the flowers turned out this bad, then what on earth was the cake going to look like?'

◆ ◆ ◆

What was obvious to both of us was how much joy Nan got from being involved in Mum's wedding. This was something I wanted to do for *my* mum, now, with my own wedding. (Especially given that, after our wedding, Chris and I would finally be leaving the family nest and moving into a place of our own. Mum was doing her best to be supportive and to suppress her disappointment at our leaving—buoyed, no doubt, by the fact that we had bought the house next door to her and were moving in there!)

But, what I didn't expect was for Mum's involvement in our wedding to be such a treat for me, too. With the wedding date fast approaching, and with my dress no closer to being found, Mum surprised me with a weekend shopping trip to Melbourne to visit the boutique of renowned Australian bridal designer Mariana Hardwick.

Anyone who has been to Mariana Hardwick's flagship store knows what I'm talking about when I say it's divine. Housed in the heritage-listed Hardwick building in Melbourne's throbbing

Brunswick, somehow this innocuous store (which combines Hardwick's couture bridal house and the actual atelier where her lavish gowns are sewn on site) is a haven of cream and gold serenity among the cafes and hipster bars of achingly cool Brunswick. Climbing the grand oak staircase, with its elaborate *MH* crest emblazoned at the pinnacle, I was Scarlett O'Hara off to choose a gown to marry Rhett in. I felt fated to find my dream dress here.

Unfortunately, fate didn't get the memo. Or, at least, not entirely. Technically, I *did* find my dream dress at Mariana's that day. I fell in love with a stunning satin gown that had a strapless fitted bodice, complete with beading and hand-dyed lace, and that flared into a flattering A-line skirt. Classic yet modern, pretty yet sexy. That the dress of my dreams didn't come in pink wasn't a problem, either, because the lovely girls at Mariana's had been collecting pink material samples for me for weeks in the hope of finding one that was just the right shade. Only each and every single one of them was *awful*.

'What about this one?' asked the sales assistant called Candy (I kid you not). She held a heinous Barbie-pink swatch against my décolletage.

'Er, it's sweet but …' I looked at Mum imploringly for help.

'It's not you, darling,' Mum said decisively and Candy put the swatch onto the (rapidly growing) 'no' pile on the counter.

'Or this?' she tried, holding up a sickly sweet one.

'Uh-uh.' I shook my head and grimaced apologetically. 'Sorry.' I wanted to be a pink bride, not a musk stick.

Too peach; too rich; too saccharine; was that magenta? These colour swatches were giving me a sugar headache. I thanked Candy but explained we couldn't order a Mariana Hardwick design, as much as I wanted one, if we couldn't find the material to have it designed *in* and so we started to leave. Then just as Mum and I were descending, disappointedly, down the grand staircase, Candy came bounding after us with a brown paper package in her hand.

'Wait, Krystal!' she called out. 'This sample just came by courier. It's another pink swatch—maybe this one's the one? Do you want to open it?'

Reluctantly, dubiously, I did. And there, inside the package, was the most beautiful strip of material I had ever laid eyes on. Soft but somehow striking, this scrap of pink satin with its ragged edges looked like a petal torn straight from a rose. You could almost smell its old-world fragrance.

'I love it!' I said to Candy. 'You've found the perfect pink!'

And so Mariana Hardwick's seamstresses worked their magic and my dream pink wedding dress was stitched into reality.

♦ ♦ ♦

Less than four months out from the Big Day, I was beginning to feel like my life had turned a corner. I was 23 years old and as-yet cancer-free. I had kicked the drugs, I was off all booze and I had survived an unwanted pregnancy only to discover I adored being a mum. I was soon to marry the love of my life while our gorgeous toddler, Riley, stood by our side. So to find my perfect (pink!) wedding dress really was the icing on the cake. I couldn't believe my luck.

So you can imagine my surprise, then, when one lazy Sunday afternoon in November—the sort of lazy afternoon when the jacaranda trees in Sydney are just starting to explode into a dreamy purple haze and the first strains of summer are wafting over backyard fences along with the smell of burnt sausages—Mum phoned me in tears.

'Krystal?'

'Mum?' I said, sitting up fast from where I was sprawled on the couch on the back patio.

'Mum? What's wrong? Why are you crying? *Is it cancer?*' This was a ridiculous question, given that Mum was phoning me from Eden, on the New South Wales far south coast, where she and Dad had gone away for the weekend and where, I was pretty sure, the township was known for its fish (it was historically a whaling village) and its chips (it now exports woodchips) but not so much for its malignant tumours. And yet, with our family's track record, I was always on cancer alert.

Mum sobbed even harder.

'Mum? What's happened? Are you okay?' I was becoming frantic now but I could hear her taking some deep breaths and steadying herself on the other end of the line.

'I'm okay, I'm okay,' she assured me.

And then she paused before adding: 'But, yes; it looks like cancer.'

I was stunned.

◆ ◆ ◆

It took a few agonising minutes, and much 'tag-teaming' as Mum and Dad passed the phone back and forth between themselves, taking it in turns to talk as Mum succumbed to fresh tears; but I eventually got the story out of them. Mum had been for her first screening test on Friday as part of a high-risk program for ovarian cancer, they told me. Dr Kathy Tucker (my genetic specialist for hereditary cancer but also Mum's specialist) had been phoning Mum at three-monthly intervals for years now, advising her to remove her ovaries because the risk of ovarian cancer associated with our BRCA1 gene mutation was just too high for someone my mum's age. But each time Kathy phoned, Mum had a new excuse—work, grandchild, my wedding to plan—why it wasn't a good time for a prophylactic oophorectomy. Now, though, it looked like she didn't have a choice.

When Mum went in for her test (a test she said was a bit uncomfortable, a bit embarrassing but *not*, as she now regretted, worth postponing for so long), she chatted idly about her weekend away to the doctor wielding the probe. Next, she was sent to see Dr Kathy Tucker to receive her results. Then, as Mum and Dad sat in the waiting room, flicking through out-of-date magazines and planning what time they should head off down the coast in the morning to beat the weekend traffic, Kathy walked out of her surgery and addressed them— the only patients present—with urgency: 'Julie-Ann, there's something wrong. There's something wrong with your results.'

Something's wrong?

Kathy explained that she needed to confirm some more details and would be back again shortly but, in the meantime, she gave my parents strict instructions not to leave the surgery.

Something's wrong? Something's wrong? I can't imagine what Mum felt as she heard those words uttered yet again. How many times would our family be shocked with the news that there was 'something wrong' with our results? How many times would we have to remain in the waiting room for further tests or more bad news or another dire diagnosis? Dad began to fidget; he can't keep still when he's nervous.

After what must have seemed like an age, Kathy emerged again and called Mum and Dad into her consulting room. There she told them that the ultrasound had revealed some very suspicious-looking abnormalities in the region in and around Mum's ovaries. Suspicious enough to warrant an appointment with a surgeon first thing Monday morning. Suspicious enough that it must surely mean cancer.

'But I'm going away for the weekend,' Mum had blurted, clearly unable to process what she'd just been told. 'And then it's only sixteen weeks till Krystal's wedding! I've already told you I don't have time to have my ovaries removed!'

Kathy leaned across the table and gripped Mum's hand. 'Julie-Ann, this is important. I need you to see the surgeon on Monday morning and to take whatever course of action he recommends. In light of what we've found today, I don't expect you'll be able to keep your ovaries.'

And with that, Mum and Dad were released back into the waiting room, back to the tattered magazines, back to their tattered weekend plans and back to their tattered, shattered lives.

◆ ◆ ◆

Mum told me all this over the phone from Eden because she said she couldn't bear to see my face if she told me in person. For the same reason I passed the phone wordlessly to my nan, who was staying with us in Manly, so that she could hear the news from Mum in just the same way. When Mum and Dad got home that night, our household was eerily calm as we braced for the storm that was ahead of us. Then on Monday morning Mum did as instructed and went to see the surgeon.

His opening line was brutal but at least it was unambiguous. 'I have to tell you,' he said, peering at her ultrasound images, 'Julie-Ann, this doesn't look great.'

'How bad are we talking?' Mum said. 'Will there be chemo?'

'I don't think so,' was his reply. 'If it's as bad as it looks there will be no chemo.'

The surgeon explained that he wanted to operate. Tomorrow. (Which, as the first Tuesday in November, was Melbourne Cup day in Australia.) Everything was happening at a terrifying pace. Just last Friday Mum was going in to have her first ovarian scan as a high-risk patient. By Tuesday she would undergo surgery, possibly *life-changing* cancer surgery. It was breakneck and breathtaking and, despite everything our family had already been through, incredibly shocking. Mum, understandably, was absolutely terrified. Even now, she wells up when she remembers this time in her life.

On the day of the surgery our family went through that strange process whereby everyday life refuses to take a back seat even though there are much (*much*) greater things going down. The minutia was worse than usual, in fact, because we'd had so little time to prepare. Toothbrushes had to be packed into hospital bags; washing had to be brought in off the clothes line; cars still had to be filled with petrol even though we were driving to hospital for what was shaping up to be cancer surgery. As my parents sat nervously waiting for Mum to be wheeled off to the anaesthetist, Dad rattled through his 'to do' list. 'I've phoned your boss, I've phoned my mother; your mum and the kids are driving over in Andrew's car to be here when you wake up. I've cancelled the vet, I'm going to go and move our car in an hour so our parking ticket doesn't expire ...' And on it went.

I can't imagine poor Mum heard a word of it, though, as she contemplated what lay ahead of her. The surgeon had warned her that if she woke up from the surgery with a large cut to her abdomen that this would be a bad sign as it meant the tumour was extensive and much more likely to be malignant. A small incision, however, would mean that the surgery was keyhole and therefore whatever tumour was detected hadn't spread far.

The very first thing Mum did when she woke up from the anaesthetic that day was to slide a shaking hand up the length of her belly to survey the damage. It was horrific. As her palm felt higher and higher up her distended stomach, the bandages wound on and on. She was sliced all the way from her vagina to past her belly button. Well over 15 centimetres in total. *It's over. It's all over,* she repeated to herself and tears streamed down her cheeks. In that moment she knew she had ovarian cancer.

As the orderlies wheeled Mum back to her room to meet with her surgeon (and to have her worst fears confirmed), she cried the whole way. Soundlessly, there was no dramatic sobbing; just a silent, constant flow of tears. Tears of fatigue and defeat. Cancer finally had her beat.

When they reached Mum's ward, the orderlies negotiated the maze of identical white corridors with proficiency, the only sound the faint rattle of the trolley wheels on the linoleum floor. But as they got closer to her room Mum heard another noise; the noise of shrieking, wailing women. Women screaming at the top of their lungs with—what? Sorrow? Joy? Had someone

The Lucky One

died? Mum couldn't make it out. Then a boy called out 'Yessss!' and Mum heard something that sounded like the sound of flat hands slapping the concrete walls all along the corridor. 'It's not cancer! It's not cancer!' somebody was shouting. There was laughter and confusion and the sound of people running up and down the corridor, slapping the walls in ecstasy, their feet skidding on the plastic floor. 'It's not cancer! It's not cancer!' they whooped again and again and again, their shouts bouncing off the hospital walls. *Who was this crazy family?*

Us.

When Mum got close enough she realised it was *our* crazy family, going berserk because her surgery had just revealed the most beautiful news in the world: it wasn't cancer.

Mum's surgeon had delivered her results to us just moments before Mum arrived. Somehow, he said, against all the odds, the tumour on her right ovary was benign. In addition to the tumour, Mum was suffering severe endometriosis; so severe that when they opened her up in theatre the horrid stuff had came bubbling up and out of her wound and this was why her initial ultrasound looked so grim. Mum had had the tumour removed, as well as the masses of endometriosis, plus some damaged sections of her bowel. Hence the extensive bandages. But what none of us could believe—including the surgeon who was so astounded he'd asked for Mum's biopsy to be tested twice—was that there was no cancer present.

The surgeon told us that they'd cheered in theatre when the result of the biopsies came back. But that was nothing compared to the cheering our family was doing now. We were all so certain that this dreaded cancer had come for one of us again that we didn't dare think that Mum's surgery would show her ovaries to be cancer free. The best any of us had hoped for was that they'd caught the cancer early enough for the tumour to be contained and maybe even possibly removed. We were thinking in terms of: *How much chemo would Mum have to have?* And, *what would her life expectancy be now that she had secondary cancer?* Not: *How long till Mum can come home and get back to planning my wedding?* It was one of the best days of all our lives.

Mum, however, was trying desperately to quieten us all down. In her usual style (and just like her own mother), Mum was more concerned about everyone else around her and right now she was worried we might be disturbing the other patients on the ward. 'Shhh!' she hissed at us, trying uselessly to wipe the smile from her face. 'What if there are other patients around who haven't had good news today?'

But we couldn't help ourselves. Mum didn't have cancer, that's all we cared about right now, and who could blame us for wanting to tell the world?

◆ ◆ ◆

Several weeks later, Mum was at home again and recuperating well. As Dad and I sat chatting over a cup of tea one evening, he turned to me and said: 'You know, when I went to move the car on the day of your mum's surgery, the strangest thing happened …' He placed his mug down on the table and fiddled with it, looking slightly embarrassed about what he was about to tell me. 'When I opened the driver's side door to get out and head back to the hospital, I found two $2 coins on the ground and they were stacked perfectly on top of one another.'

The Lucky One

This, Dad claimed, was the instant he knew Mum didn't have cancer.

'It was a sign, Krystal!' he said. 'These coins were a sign that me and your mum were meant to be together. No cancer was going to separate us that day!'

As he finished saying this he fished into the pocket of his jeans and withdrew a scrap of tissue paper and inside were wrapped two $2 coins. He still had them! It was so uncharacteristic of Dad to be getting all voodoo on me over a couple of coins he found on the pavement, yet they clearly meant so much to him that I couldn't help but share in his enthusiasm.

Those coins have since become folklore within our family. They're still wrapped in the same piece of tissue paper but they're tucked away in Dad's bedside drawer where they're keeping Mum and Dad safely together forever. It may only be four bucks, but to us it's worth two lives, still entwined, against all the odds.

CHAPTER 11

As for Chris and I, the day for entwining our lives (at least legally) soon arrived. Mum's surgery was in November and our wedding was in early March and the time in between seemed to vanish. Chris still knew nothing about my secret plans to whitewash our wedding pink so Mum and I had our work cut out plotting and planning and making my rose-tinted dreams come true. Thankfully, following her surgery Mum's health had improved rapidly, so she was able to throw herself back into her role of wedding planner extraordinaire with gusto. (The change in her—post-surgery—showed just how sick the endometriosis had been making her beforehand, although we hadn't realised it at the time.)

The big day finally arrived. On our wedding day, I carried a lace handkerchief that once belonged to my great-grandmother, Annie, as my 'something old'. My 'something new' was my precious pink Mariana Hardwick dress (that fitted me perfectly, unlike the disastrous gold dress from my 21st birthday). Chris and I signed the wedding register with the same pen my parents used to sign their wedding certificate 25 years earlier as our 'something borrowed'. And for 'something blue' I had a small blue bow woven through the (pink) garter I wore. But it was my 'something old' lace handkerchief from Granny Annie that meant the most. To me, it was more than just a token to satisfy some sweet old rhyme. By carrying this precious scrap of lace with me I felt like I was somehow honouring all the brave women who'd gone before me in our family and who'd fought so valiantly against our family's curse. If the shadow of breast and ovarian cancer was going to hang over our wedding then I wanted it to be in a positive way for once, and this set the tone for so much of our wedding.

During the service, for instance, our minister said a special prayer for all the women in our family who couldn't be with us that day because of cancer. And our bonbonniere (handmade by Mum) consisted of gift boxes, wrapped in pink silk and vintage lace, which housed pink lollies and a National Breast Cancer Foundation ribbon signifying that a donation was made to the foundation on behalf of every guest. Then there was the fact that our reception was a sea of pale-pink perfection, with pink organza draped from floor to ceiling, pink David Austen roses adorning every table, rose petals and pink lollies scattered across every surface, a four-tiered pastel pink cake covered in frosted pink flowers as our centrepiece and all of this illuminated by hundreds of twinkling soft pink fairy lights. Plus, of course, I was a blushing bride in my pink satin wedding dress (which would later be sold to raise funds for KConFab, the Kathleen Cuningham Foundation Consortium for research into familial breast cancer). Our entire day was reflected through a prism of breast cancer pink and for once I couldn't be happier. (By the way, Chris loved the fact our wedding was pink. It didn't take him long to get over the initial shock of seeing me in a pink bridal gown—he knows to expect the unexpected with me. Plus, he's a man who's comfortably in touch with his feminine side, so an all-pink affair was no problem for him (in so far as it was me, and not him, who was dressed in head-to-toe pink!)

As I walked down the aisle on Dad's arm that day we were surrounded by all of our loving family and friends. My mum and my nan were standing proudly in the front pew, blubbing away. Riley, our beautiful son, was happily ensconced with his Matchbox cars at the feet of the bridal party having been carried down the aisle by my brother. And here, at the head of the aisle, was my gorgeous, calm, faithful Chris (albeit, looking a little surprised at seeing me in pink!). A million thoughts raced through my mind as I made my journey up the aisle: *Who would have thought, sixteen weeks ago, that Mum would be here to see this today? And Nan! I can't believe Nan is happy and healthy and standing here, too! Oh, I'm so thankful for Riley, my little guardian angel. And, most of all, aren't I lucky to have Chris to stand by me through it all?*

Mum, though, said she only had one thought in her head: *Finally my letter can be tossed away!* All Mum could think about was the letter she'd written to me—way back when she was first diagnosed with cancer, when I was only 14—begging me not to mourn her death on my wedding day. It seemed inconceivable to her back then that she would ever survive to see me walk down the aisle and now, even as I went sashaying past in a blur of smiling pink satin, Mum couldn't quite believe what she was seeing.

My standout memory of our wedding day, however, was Riley. As a part of our wedding service Mum had organised an opera singer to sing *Ave Maria* while we signed the registry. She had the most amazing voice and had stunned everyone in the church into silent awe from the moment she first opened her mouth. Everyone except Riley.

During our wedding rehearsal, Riley had made me and Chris nervous by spending the entire evening running around the church shouting and demanding attention and banging the polished wooden pews with his metal toy cars. *Oh well,* we reasoned, *he's a two-year-old. Surely, our guests will understand that it's hard for him to sit still for a full 40-minute church service…*

But on the day of our wedding, Riley was an absolute angel. He sat quietly at Chris's feet and played happily with his Matchbox cars, completely oblivious to what was going on around him, until the moment the opera singer took to the pulpit. Suddenly, Riley came to life and for the whole time she sang Bach's masterpiece, Riley was rapt. He sang along in a series of 'ahhh's' and 'laaaa's', his tiny voice well and truly drowned out by her powerful soprano, until she arrived at the last line and he continued on without her, performing a high-pitched solo for the enchanted congregation. As his last happy 'laaaaaa' echoed around the church, Chris and I grinned at each other proudly—having Riley share our wedding day with us was so very special. Little did we know, exactly nine months later to the day, we would be welcoming Riley's younger brother into the family. I fell pregnant on my wedding night.

CHAPTER 12

Jye Andrew was born 10 December 2007 in a flurry of panic and drama. He spent the first five days of his life in intensive care, among a mass of tubes and beeping machines, his tiny hands and feet a disturbing shade of blue due to fluid on his lungs that he'd swallowed during his birth. By some miracle he pulled through it unscathed and, after a further week spent in hospital, our blond-haired, blue-eyed boy was allowed to come home with us. But even before this—before his traumatic birth and before his time in intensive care—Jye's ride had been a rough one.

One day when I was less than six months pregnant with Jye, I was hanging the clothes on the line in the backyard when I began to bleed. Really bleed. I felt no warning and had no pain but suddenly my jeans were wet with blood. I was terrified. Convinced I was having a miscarriage, I raced inside and phoned Chris but there was no response as, by now, he was working as an electrician and had a job on in Wollongong that day and mobile reception there was patchy at best. Frantically, I tried Mum. Again, I got no response and the patch of blood on my jeans was growing by the minute. By the time I managed to reach Dad on the phone I was near-hysterical and my jeans were soaked.

'Dad, Dad! I'm bleeding, I'm bleeding!' was all I could manage.

'I'm coming straight over,' he said and he was there within minutes, striding down the front hallway, shouting: 'Where are you? Where's the cut? I've bought band-aids.'

When Dad saw me standing in the middle of the lounge room that day, with Riley in my arms and a dark stain of blood between my legs, he froze. 'Oh god. Get in the car,' he instructed. 'We're going straight to the hospital.'

◆ ◆ ◆

By the time we reached Royal North Shore Hospital's emergency department, the bleeding had blessedly stopped. On my arrival, doctors ran a number of tests but no one could determine where the bleeding was coming from, nor what was causing it. All they knew was that a miscarriage had been averted.

'I'm afraid we don't yet understand what just happened to you, Krystal,' one doctor explained to me, 'but I *can* tell you that there doesn't appear to be any harm done to your baby. He looks just fine according to all our tests. Still, we'd like to keep you here for a few days to monitor you further and we'll be checking your iron levels ...' He continued speaking but my mind was already elsewhere.

My baby was fine! He was going to be okay! I leaned back into my pillow as relief overwhelmed me. My little baby was fine and our little family was safe. I felt like I'd just found out all over again that we were going to have a baby, my joy was that immense. *We're having a baby and our baby was fine!* I grinned at Dad and at Riley, who was struggling in Dad's arms, trying to escape down onto the hospital floor. *Our little baby was fine!*

'You've got a tough one there, Krystal,' Dad said after the doctor had left, indicating towards my stomach. 'A real Barter-fighter.'

I ran a fatigued hand over my rounded belly. 'We sure do,' I said and smiled. A Barter-fighter, a Codlin-warrior; and of course there was Chris's strong genes, too. Our little boy was going to be okay, I thought.

◆ ◆ ◆

Moments later, after Dad had left to take Riley home for a sleep, a nurse appeared by my bedside armed with a clipboard and asking me to sign a declaration form. 'What's this?' I asked warily. I was in no frame of mind to be making executive decisions just then.

'It's a consent form,' she explained diligently. 'Because you're not yet 23 weeks pregnant, if you go into pre-term labour now, our doctors won't attempt to revive your baby. I need you to sign here to say you understand this.'

Pre-term—what? What do you mean you won't revive my baby? What the hell was she on about? I began to panic. *I thought the doctor just told me that my baby was fine!*

'But—my baby's okay. The doctor told me he's fine. Why would you need to revive him if he's fine?' I was confused and looked around for the doctor who'd just been in to see me. 'Can you call the doctor back in here?' I asked, my voice rising several octaves in distress. 'He told me my baby's fine. He told me!'

'It's alright,' soothed the nurse. 'This is just a standard permission form. I'm sure you won't need it; I'm sure your baby *will* be fine.' She proffered the clipboard for me to take.

He's already fine! I thought. I was getting agitated now. *If you would just call the doctor back in here, he'll tell you—my baby is fine!*

❖ ❖ ❖

Eventually, the medical staff determined it was a mistake that I'd been asked to sign a non-revival consent form. For whatever reason, this paperwork was given to me when it shouldn't have been. It was a simple mix-up. 'So sorry, wrong bed!' My baby *was* fine and there was no reason to think that he might need reviving; not now, not ever. The form was removed, as was, apparently, the nurse who gave it to me, because I didn't see her again at any point during my time on the ward. The hospital was very apologetic and over the next four days, while I remained there on bed rest, the staff did everything they could to reassure me that Jye would be alright. But it was too late by then. Anxiety had set in.

The Lucky One

Anxiety that was made worse by the fact that the medical staff at the hospital still had no idea why I had bled in the first place. This terrified me. I was convinced I would start bleeding again without warning and this time I would miscarry. Or that Jye would be born with some terrible disability or illness. Or that something would happen to Mum or Nan or just about anybody I could think of that I cared about. Or that my own cancer scare was just around the corner and that I'd be giving birth one day and having my breasts removed the next. I was a walking doomsayer and there seemed to be nothing I could do to control it. My mind ran riot, conjuring up worst-case scenario after worst-case scenario, each more horrifying than the last and all of them frighteningly real in my head.

❖ ❖ ❖

I'd like to be able to tell you that things turned around after Jye was born that Christmas, but it wouldn't be true. After it had been touch and go for our precious boy after his birth, and enduring those agonising few days when he was in intensive care, watching him struggle to breathe and being unable to reach out and hold him or even touch him through the plastic wall of the humidicrib, life seemed to get darker, not lighter. At a time when I had so much to be thankful for—an (eventually) healthy baby; a delightful toddler; an amazing new husband; my own health (at least for the time being)—I was struggling to haul myself up and out of bed each day.

Rationally, sensibly, I knew there were many other people out there who were far worse off than I was and so I was doggedly determined not to curl up into a ball of 'poor me's'.

Krystal Barter

Instead I lived at a manic pace, worrying, fretting and generally obsessing over everyday things. *Which jumpsuit should I put Jye in today? Is this one warm enough? Too warm? Will he need a singlet underneath or might he get too hot? Oh god, what if he's already overheated? What if he's dehydrated? Should I wake him for a feed? I should wake him for a feed* ... On and on it went.

Then, when I wasn't busy agonising over my children's wardrobe dilemmas, I invented a positive *Gray's Anatomy* of ailments that struck me down at all hours of the day and night. Chris and I would be in the middle of watching some Hollywood blockbuster on the couch in the evening when I'd suddenly turn to him, stricken and clutching my chest. 'Chris! Chris, take me to the hospital! I'm having a heart attack!' And I honestly believed I was. Real and excruciating pain would crush my chest and I'd be gasping for air as my left arm began tingling and my jaw started to ache. Time and time again, Chris dutifully put down his popcorn and bundled me into the car and drove me to our local medical centre, where an angiogram would reveal no actual threat to my heart. Or an MRI would suggest there was nothing wrong with my spine. Or a CAT scan would show my brain wasn't haemorrhaging.

My mum always jokes that *she's* a patchwork quilt—front and back—given she's had 28 surgical procedures during her life, pulling her apart and stitching her back together again, patchwork square by patchwork square, until she only vaguely resembles her original form. (She keeps a list of her operations in her wallet because she's given up trying to remember them all and there's a special section on this list dedicated to what she affectionately calls her 'disctomies': her double mastectomy

The Lucky One

(removal of both breasts), hysterectomy (uterus), lumbar discectomy (spinal disc) and oopherectomy (ovaries).)

Now, though, I was doing my darndest to catch up with her. I inflicted any and every heinous disease I could think of (malaria, anyone?) onto my poor, confused body and then put it through the medical-test-wringer as doctors went about proving me wrong. It wasn't as if I *wanted* to be sick; far from it. I just couldn't get my head around the fact that I wasn't. And so I lurched from medical crisis to medical crisis, dragging my poor husband with me, and consequently our first few years of marriage were far more dramatic than anything Chris and I might have been watching on the small screen.

◆ ◆ ◆

Funnily enough, it never occurred to me at the time that my hysterical fears about my health might have anything to do with being BRCA1 mutation positive. I mean, even a pop psychologist could have a pretty good stab at linking: a) my absolute conviction that I was dying of *something*, with b) the fact that my genes dictated I was at a high risk of developing breast and/or ovarian cancer. (Who knows, maybe my subconscious was just trying to help me out? Like: *Hey, don't you worry your pretty head about breast cancer. This stroke is going to kill you first ...*)

It should have been a dead giveaway, though, that my panic attacks got infinitely worse every time I researched my BRCA1 mutation status. Whenever Dr Google and I had a little late night rendezvous looking into 'genetic mutation' or 'breast cancer/statistics' or, heaven forbid, 'risk-reducing mastectomy/images', my anxiety and my nightmares and my phantom coronaries would go through the roof again. I can see now that my very real, very physical pain was a symptom of the total lack of control I felt over my health and my future.

And, although I didn't know it at the time, this is apparently a common response from people who find out they are BRCA1 mutation positive. I've met girls just like me who, after being told they're up to 80 per cent likely to develop breast cancer, convince themselves that they're dying of lung cancer or a brain tumour or heart disease. Something, *anything*; it doesn't matter what. We're convincing ourselves that we're doomed to die of anything other than 'old age' and so get to work doing just that. The worst part is that this mentality isn't something that can be 'fixed' in the same way that genetic predisposition can be managed or cancer risk can be reduced. Even after taking dramatic action to avoid cancer, like having your breasts removed, so often the fear of cancer and of dying remains. All that can be done is to try and keep it under control. At the time, though, I felt like I was going crazy.

❖ ❖ ❖

I guess it's to my credit (or, more accurately, to the credit of my supportive family and friends) that I didn't return to drugs or alcohol at this time. Because it could have been tempting. But since I had my beautiful babies it never crossed my mind. The strongest thing I 'used' now, though, was herbal tea and I became a chamomile junkie, downing three or more cups of tea per night in an effort to try and get some sleep. I refused to touch sleeping tablets, having left my pill-popping days behind me. But as such, and as a result of having two boys under the

The Lucky One

age of three, I wasn't getting anywhere near the recommended eight hours of sleep in those days and this did nothing to help my mental state. Anyone who's ever had sleeping problems (or who's ever had young children—the two seem to be one and the same) knows the completely debilitating effect that a lack of sleep can have. It's no wonder they use sleep deprivation as a form of torture treatment. You'd give away state secrets, too, just for a little golden slumber.

So, between my lack of sleep and the anxious dread of my waking hours, between my invented diseases and my very real threat of cancer, those were dark days for me. And it wasn't a quiet, menacing shadow of depression I suffered from, either. It was a wild, shrieking panic that woke me in the night; that stabbed red-hot pokers of fear into my eyes and blinded me from all rationality. It gripped me tight and fast and shook me till I was left cowering in a corner, begging to be left alone. And, in the end, the only relief I got came in the form of a most unlikely friendship, forged with a Jewish girl from the opposite side of the globe.

CHAPTER 13

Dear Lindsay,

I am a young mum from Australia with a BRCA1 mutation and I'm emailing to say how inspired I am by your story and by your charity, Bright Pink.

I feel like I have been searching for someone like you to chat to for a long time.

Our family history is very similar. Just like you, my grandma and my great-grandma both had breast cancer. And just like you, I've watched my mum battle breast cancer, too. I'm in the midst of researching my options as a young woman who is likely to face breast cancer but there's no charity like Bright Pink here in Australia to provide support or information.

The Lucky One

I understand you must be incredibly busy but I would love to ask you a few questions, if that's okay?
Many thanks,
Krystal Barter

Lindsay Avner was a fellow BRCA mutation carrier from Chicago, Illinois, and I first stumbled upon her during one of my late night Google-athons. Initially, I was drawn to Lindsay because our stories were so similar. As I said in my email to her, our great-grandmothers, grandmothers and mothers had all suffered breast cancer, plus Lindsay and I both tested positive to the BRCA gene mutation when we were 22 years old. Amazingly, Lindsay had then gone on to become the youngest patient in the United States to opt for a preventative double mastectomy (she was just 23 when she had the surgery). This, I reasoned, must be why this brown-haired, brown-eyed, all-American-girl with the toothpaste-ad smile seemed to fill my search engine whenever I entered 'BRCA' and 'USA'.

But there was more to her than that. As I sat at my computer, sipping chamomile tea like a junkie and intending to go to bed in just five more minutes, I gradually uncovered Lindsay Avner's story. After she learned she was BRCA mutation positive, and faced with the prospect of a risk-reducing mastectomy, Lindsay discovered an absolute dearth of resources for young women in her situation. (By now my interest was piqued; this was a very familiar-sounding story.) As Lindsay explained it, there was plenty of guidance out there for women who *had* breast or ovarian cancer but nothing for girls like us who were 'high-risk' and who wanted to take a proactive approach to their health. So Lindsay created 'Bright Pink', an online community offering support and education to high-risk women. When I first learned about Lindsay in 2008, Bright Pink was in its infancy; now it's one of the USA's fastest-growing non-profit organisations. I was hooked. The moment I opened the Bright Pink homepage, with its explosion of hot pink and the glossy-haired 'Team Bright Pink'—girls who looked more like glamorous homecoming queens than potential cancer victims—I felt like I had found a home.

I immediately emailed Lindsay in what was to be, as they say in *Casablanca*, the beginning of a beautiful friendship.

Lindsay and I just clicked. Over email, she shared her family history with me and explained how she'd arrived at the difficult decision to remove her breasts. I confessed to her that I wasn't sure I would *ever* reach that point, but knowing there was someone else out there who had been in the same situation as me and who had shown the courage to undertake a preventative mastectomy, well, that gave me infinite inspiration. Nothing was off-limits during our conversations on cancer and Lindsay patiently waded through even my most bizarre questions, giving me advice that no doctor or specialist ever could.

Do you miss your real boobs? Do you ever regret your mastectomy? How did you know you were making the right decision? How bad *was* the pain? What do your breast implants feel like to touch? Do you have any sensation in your boobs? Do guys *really* like them or are they put off by the thought of fake boobs on their own partner? Do you have much scarring? Did you get nipples with your breast reconstruction or did you not bother? The list was endless. Yet through her emails (and later the occasional Skype conversation) Lindsay managed to answer them all. (For the record: Any guy that has ogled the

The Lucky One

rack on a Playboy bunny at some point in his life is never going to turn down fake boobs in the bedroom. Oh, and there's still plenty of sensation there, too. It's your own skin holding the implants in place, after all.)

Over the following months Lindsay became the sister I never had. She gave me unending support and encouragement, and just knowing what she'd achieved with Bright Pink helped me to find the positives that could be drawn from being high-risk. Lindsay changed my perception of my BRCA1 mutation status—changed my future, really—and while I was so thankful I stumbled across her and Bright Pink I was also sad that one of my closest confidantes on my BRCA journey had to come from the other side of the world.

Where were all the Lindsays in Australia? Where was our Bright Pink community bringing together all the high-risk young women that must exist here? Whenever I bemoaned this fact to Lindsay, she gave me the same answer: go and create a local online community myself; that's what she did. Sure, I would laugh and retaliate, is that before or after I look after two toddler boys? How on earth would I find the time to do it? Plus, I could hardly go about setting up a support network to help high-risk women navigate their journey when I was barely out of the starting blocks myself. Still, there was no denying that everyone in my position needed a Lindsay in their life. I just hoped that someone in Australia would come up with a Bright Pink equivalent here, and soon.

In fact, I raised the idea at a National Breast Cancer Foundation breakfast event at Dee Why at this time. Mum and I were both speaking at the event and so I thought it was a good opportunity to test the water and see if there was much interest in starting an online community like Bright Pink in Sydney. While the response was overwhelmingly positive—someone at the event even offered for his company to provide free web support services and gave me his details so I could follow-up with him after the event—the underlying message was loud and clear: *you* do it. But I wasn't able to. I couldn't. Not with everything else that was going on right then.

◆ ◆ ◆

It was around the time of my newfound friendship with my 'sister', Lindsay, that I started to wonder if Riley and Jye would like one of their own. A sister, that is. It was no secret that Chris and I adored being parents and, despite the fact that Jye was less than twelve months old and that I wasn't coping as well as I could be (with my high-risk cancer status), I was becoming increasingly obsessed with the idea of having another baby. And not just any baby—the perfect baby. Alongside 'BRCA', 'preventative mastectomy' and 'Bright Pink', one of the top searches on my computer was 'PGD' or pre-implantation genetic diagnosis. You see, in vitro fertilisation was so advanced by then that it was possible to screen embryos prior to implantation to check for all kinds of specific genetic diseases. Genetic diseases such as BRCA mutation carriers.

I wanted to have a breast cancer-free baby.

My family was, understandably, a little apprehensive about the idea.

'Really? Another baby already?' Chris asked tentatively, as he stood at the kitchen sink rinsing the Mount Kosciuszko of baby bottles.

The Lucky One

'A designer baby?' my mum queried, although she didn't press me further. If anyone understood the complex emotions tied up with our flawed family genetics, it was Mum.

'Yes, a new baby!' I enthused. 'A little girl who will grow up never having to worry about her breasts.'

The more I researched the idea, the more fanatical I became. 'Did you know there are about one hundred babies born every year in Australia through PGD? The technology is amazing,' I raved to Chris. 'Imagine if one day they could completely eradicate the BRCA1 gene mutation just by screening embryos? The high-risk cancer community needs to know about this!'

I was so excited about what I was learning that I got in contact with a friend of a friend, Kirsty, who was a producer on the Nine Network's current affairs program *60 Minutes*, to see if she would be interested in following our PGD journey and sharing it with her viewers. 'It would be an Australian first,' I explained to Kirsty over the phone. 'No other couple in the country has successfully screened embryos to select a girl who is free of the BRCA1 gene fault before, so we'd be pioneers.'

Unsurprisingly, Kirsty jumped at the story and we agreed to stay in close contact as I continued researching our PGD options on the long road to implantation.

In my head, though, I was much further down the PGD path. I'd already dreamed us up a future where both our attempts at implantation and IVF were wildly successful and Chris and I were the proud parents of a healthy baby girl. I'd even gone as far as to name our daughter 'Bonnie', after Bonnie Blue in *Gone with the Wind*. My imaginary Bonnie, along with my real-life but geographically distant Lindsay, were the two bright spots in my life right then and I talked incessantly to one (Lindsay) about my plans for the other (Bonnie). The rest of the time, however, I was still constantly anxious and perpetually sleep-deprived (not to mention still self-diagnosing terminal illnesses at an alarming rate). It didn't take a medical professional to see that I needed help and that's exactly what Mum prescribed for me.

'Krystal, I've booked you an appointment with a psychologist in North Sydney this morning,' Mum announced as I opened my front door to her one morning in the spring of 2008. I gawped at her, a triangle of Vegemite toast hanging precariously out of my mouth. Behind me Jye screamed passionately from his bassinet while Riley was apparently dismantling my kitchen, one very loud stainless steel saucepan at a time, and *Bob the Builder* blared out of the television. I was still in my pyjamas.

'A psychologist?' I echoed. 'You mean a shrink?'

'A psychologist,' Mum said. 'Bronwyn. In Chatswood. She's very good apparently.' Mum thrust a piece of paper with a scrawled address on it into my hand as she bustled past me and into the house. 'I'll look after the boys!' She called over her shoulder, as if I should go and jump in the car as I was.

'But I don't need a psychologist,' I protested. 'A housekeeper, maybe.' I scooped up a pair of Riley's Spiderman undies that were lying in the hallway with my toe. 'But not a psychologist.'

'Yes, you do,' Mum corrected me. 'You're suffering anxiety. I'm suffering anxiety just looking at you. Now go and get in the shower, you've got to be in Chatswood in an hour.'

❖ ❖ ❖

The Lucky One

My new shrink kept an immaculate but welcoming office. It was all burnt copper and caramel tones with the occasional, well-placed statement piece of artwork. Nothing too provocative but pieces that were interesting enough to stimulate conversation, I guess, if things ran a little dry. In all, it was just as you'd hope a psychologist's office might look: warm, neutral, relaxing. There were no Spiderman undies littering the hallway.

'Krystal, why don't you start by telling me why you're here today?' Bronwyn said when I sat down and I was momentarily flummoxed by the simplicity of her question.

Because I can't sleep? Because I have two very small boys and I'm tired all the time? Because my mum marched into my house this morning and made me get in the car and drive here? None of those answers sounded worthy of requiring a shrink.

Bronwyn smiled. 'I understand you've got something of a complicated medical history? Would you rather we started there?'

I nodded. This was familiar territory; I could do this patter in my sleep. 'I'm BRCA1 mutation positive,' I began, 'which means I have an 80 per cent chance of developing breast cancer and at a much younger age than most women would. My mum had the disease and my nan had the disease. In fact more than 25 women in my family have had breast or ovarian cancer at some point so the apple's not falling far from our family tree,' I joked lamely.

'I see,' Bronwyn smiled again and nodded for me to continue. And so for the next 45 minutes we discussed my genetic cancer inheritance. *How did I feel about it? Was I scared? Angry? What did it mean for my relationship with my family? With my kids? Was I considering preventative surgery? What were the factors for and against this in my mind? Was I scared of having a mastectomy because of my children? Was I scared not to have a mastectomy because of my children? Did I feel guilty about the possibility I may have passed this genetic mutation on to them?*

'Of course I do!' I said when Bronwyn asked this. 'More than anything I wish I could protect my kids from this.'

Then I told Bronwyn of my plans for PGD and how I wanted to have a baby that I could offer a cancer-free existence.

'So it's important to you that your children are sheltered as much as possible from cancer?' Bronwyn asked.

'Well, yes.' This seemed obvious to me. 'It would kill me to see my kids go through what my mum and my nan have been through.'

'I see. And what about you? What about what you've been through?'

I thought back to my teenage years and to watching Mum slump to the floor in horror when she took that phone call and learned she had cancer; back to her surgeries and the time she collapsed; back to her vomiting and her weight loss and to the fear and the dread and the heartache and the waiting. I thought back to my drinking and my drug-taking and all the times I'd fought with my mum; back to the way that I hated her for being sick and hated her for being different and the way I hated her for having cancer when she should have been busy being my mum. I thought back to my nan with her eunuch-like chest and to her scars and her guilt and to her always-missing breasts. There was no way I was going to put Bonnie through that.

'I'd do anything to protect my baby,' I said quietly. 'That's why I want to screen my embryos for this gene mutation—to make sure she doesn't have to live through that.'

'And your boys,' Bronwyn prompted gently. 'You want to protect them from cancer, too?'

I frowned and paused because I wasn't quite sure what she was getting at. Of course I wanted to protect Riley and Jye. The thought that I might have passed my gene fault on to them was devastating. Did she even need to ask? Besides, hadn't I said that just a few moments ago? 'Yes, I'd do anything to protect my boys from cancer. But there's nothing I can do now—they've either got the BRCA1 gene mutation or they haven't.'

'True. But I'm not just talking about protecting them from their *own* cancer. There's the possibility of you getting cancer in the future, too, and if you were to develop breast cancer then that could affect their lives just as much as if they had cancer themselves. More so, while they're young and they need their mother. So by undergoing PGD and having another baby now—albeit a baby that's sheltered from cancer—aren't you putting off the chance to have preventative surgery and maybe the chance to protect your *existing* children from cancer? Your cancer.'

I was floored.

'And what about the fact that having PGD and IVF, while both are tremendous undertakings, are possibly more attractive options right now than having a risk-reducing mastectomy?'

'Like a band-aid solution?' I said and swallowed slowly.

'That's interesting you put it that way,' Bronwyn replied. 'I meant that I can see how the prospect of creating a beautiful new life might be infinitely more appealing than choosing to remove your breasts, but perhaps you're on to something. A band-aid solution, you called it? Well, certainly by choosing PGD at the moment you're making yourself unavailable to have breast surgery. You can hardly have a mastectomy when you're pregnant, can you? Maybe you're right to realise that's why you're attracted to the idea?'

◆ ◆ ◆

And that's how Bronwyn helped me to see I was in denial. Without directly saying it, in fact by letting me come to the realisation myself, Bronwyn showed me how my reasons for wanting another baby had more to do with my fear of a mastectomy than any desire for another child so soon. It's true that Chris and I hoped to have more children in the future, and I wasn't prepared to entirely give up on the idea of a genetically screened embryo. But it was also true that I was hiding behind PGD so I didn't have to face up to what I *knew* I needed to do: I needed to have my breasts removed.

When I walked out of Bronwyn's clinic that day it was with my mind made up. To be fair to my kids, and to be fair to myself, I had to do all that I could to prevent myself from getting breast cancer. And that meant preventative surgery. I went home and told Mum and Chris my decision. Then I phoned Dr Kathy Tucker that afternoon and asked her to recommend some breast surgeons for me. I was *not* looking forward to this— hell, I wasn't even sure I could really go through with it—but I realised now that this was about many more people than just me and so I had to try.

CHAPTER 14

For as long as I'd known him, Chris claimed he was not a 'boobs man'.

'I like your boobs, I really do,' he'd tell me earnestly. 'The trouble is you've got this incredible, bootylicious, Latino-style bum! For me? It's all about your bum, babe.'

Coming from anyone else, this might not sound as sweet as it did coming from Chris. The problem was, I was about to put his words to the test.

I was booked in to have my breasts removed in five months time, on 20 March 2009. My healthy, 25-year-old, cancer-free breasts. At the recommendation of my surgeon—breast and endocrine specialist Dr Mark Sywak—I was to have bilateral (double) skin-sparing total mastectomies which would remove my nipples, areolas and all possible breast tissue from both breasts. The only things left behind were to be my underarm lymph nodes and my chest muscles, which would help hold my implants in place once my new breasts were implanted, if implants were what I opted for. (The alternative was to have a subcutaneous mastectomy, where the breast tissue is extracted but the nipples are left behind. But I could see no point going through the pain of having my breasts removed without removing all possible chances of cancer, and this is what leaving my nipples intact would mean, in my case.)

During my mastectomy operation, doctors would also begin the (long, slow) process of reconstructing my breasts. My plastic surgeon, Dr Megan Hassall, would be on hand to insert tissue expanders into the cavity where Dr Sywak had removed all the breast tissue. These were a temporary measure—inserted to stretch the muscle and tissue to make way for implants further down the track—but they were the first crucial step towards re-creating a new set of breasts for me.

And, oh, it all sounded so easy and methodical! The way the information pamphlets described it, you'd think we were knocking up a piece of Ikea furniture. *Simply remove A from B, insert C and, presto, you've got D! Throw me an allen key and let's get started!* Don't get me wrong; I understood that, for the medical team, they *were* knocking up a piece of Ikea furniture in that this was their job and they needed to have a certain amount of professional detachment in order to do the amazing things they did every day. And I have nothing but the highest, highest praise for all of the medical treatment I received at the (very skilful) hands of Dr Sywak and Dr Hassall and just about everybody else I came across during my BRCA journey. No, it wasn't that simple at all.

The Lucky One

It was just that medical terminology such as 'subcutaneous mastectomy' seemed a world away from what we were actually talking about here. We were talking about *cutting off my breasts*. My boobs. Pieces of my own skin and tissue and membranes that, at this moment, still had my blood pumping through them. Breasts that were *mine* and had been mine since I hit puberty. These were breasts that had filled my bras since my training bra days. Breasts that been felt up by my boyfriends and admired by my husband; breasts that had held up my wedding dress and that had fed my children. Breasts that had, despite it all, been handed down to me by my family line. I was choosing to surgically remove my breasts even though they were young and healthy and free of all cancer.

Deep down I was terrified I was making the wrong decision.

◆ ◆ ◆

Where I knew I'd made the right decision, however, was in choosing Dr Mark Sywak as my surgeon. Of all the breast and endocrine specialists I met, when considering who should perform my mastectomy, Dr Sywak was easily the best looking. He was vaguely reminiscent of Keanu Reeves, circa *The Matrix* films in the late 1990s/early 2000s. And if I was going to have someone fondle my breasts in the name of science then, dammit, I wanted that someone to be hot!

Of course, it only added to Dr Keanu's—sorry, Dr Sywak's—appeal that he was so delightfully prim and proper in his bedside manner. A true professional. During one of my first appointments with him, when he was poking and prodding and assessing my naked breasts, I joked to the top of his head:

'You know, this would be a lot less awkward if you weren't so good looking.' He was so surprised I thought he might actually go through the floor.

But the greatest thing Dr Sywak gave me (aside from peace of mind about his surgical skills, and something to look at during my pre-surgery appointments) was kindness. I walked out of his surgery knowing I was making the right decision. For once in my journey I was confident. I still remember the day he put a hand on my shoulder and said: 'I can't say that you'll *definitely* get cancer in your lifetime – no doctor could – but with your family history and with your BRCA gene fault, you're in the high risk group.' It was the greatest thing he could have done for me because, at that stage, I was still so terribly unsure.

◆ ◆ ◆

And yet I pressed on. As part of my preparation for surgery, I had to continue my routine of regular ultrasounds and mammograms in order to monitor my breast health.

'Gotta keep abreast of my health,' I joked to Dr Megan Hassall and, generously, she had laughed. Megan has a wicked sense of humour and has developed quite a rapport with our family over the years. She was the plastic surgeon who performed Mum's bilateral breast reconstruction and so she must have felt some sense of déjà vu at seeing me walk into her surgery and request a recon twelve years later.

My appointment with Megan that day was to discuss the reconstruction process and to run through my options in terms of my new breasts. Silicone versus saline implants? Teardrop-shaped versus round implants? Or avoid implants altogether and opt for reconstruction using my own skin and fat (known as tissue flap reconstruction)? And, if so, attached flaps or free flaps? And where to get the fat from? My back? My bum? My abdomen? (Now, there's a thought.) And what about nipples versus no-nipples? The choices were mind-boggling. Who knew, for instance, that if I opted for nipples with my reconstruction I could have them tattooed on (to match the colour of my original areola) or attached via a nipple prosthesis (which attaches the nipple *using glue*)?

All of this was a world away from the options faced by earlier generations of women in my family. That is: they had no options.

As I've mentioned, when my nan had her mastectomy, breast reconstruction simply didn't exist so she went into hospital with breasts and came home with a barren chest and a packet of rubbery prostheses that she had to slip into her bra each day. (As time went on Nan's chest collapsed inwards to her ribs on one side, leaving her horribly disfigured and lopsided.) And for *her* mother it was even worse. Great-grandma Annie had to make her own DIY breast prosthesis, which she did by filling flesh-coloured stockings with *bird seed* then tying them off and sticking them into her bra to pad the cups out. Can you imagine what it would feel like to have spiky bird seed rubbing against your (scarred) chest all day? Not to mention the fact that, when she sweated, the bird seed started to sprout, sending out little green shoots like fingers. It would be comical if it wasn't so terribly sad.

I was lucky my greatest dilemma was deciding which exact shape of highly developed silicone implant I wanted (if, indeed, I wanted silicone at all). But, even so, I was relieved I had Megan and my mum on hand to help guide me through it.

What I *didn't* have, though, was anyone my own age (aside from Lindsay, half a world away) that I could turn to.

In her surgery, Megan had an impressive black, leather-bound portfolio of images of the successful surgeries she'd carried out over the years. This book was full to bursting point with the images of hundreds of women, all at various stages of breast reconstruction, showcasing the different options available to me. There were women with artificial implants and women who'd obviously had single-side lumpectomies and women who'd had complete bilateral mastectomies; women with minimal scarring and women whose breasts looked like a war zone before Megan got to them. *But wait—*

'Where are all the younger women?' I asked her, flicking through the pages looking for the section I couldn't find.

'There *are* no younger women, Krystal,' Megan said gently. 'Breast cancer is quite uncommon in women less than 30 years of age.'

'Oh, sure.' If I'd learned one thing from the family cancer clinic and their 30-plus screening regime, it was this. What I meant to say was: where are the images of women my age who were getting *preventative* surgery? I was specifically looking for pics of girls like me who had opted for a pre-emptive double mastectomy, rather than pics of those who'd had surgery because they'd already contracted cancer, because the end results could look vastly different. A woman who has had a lumpectomy to remove a tumour, for instance, might have significantly more scarring than I could hope to expect. Not only was I trying to get the most accurate idea of what I might look like post-surgery; the one thing I *didn't* want to do was look at any post-cancer-breast-recon horror stories. As if I wasn't scared enough!

The Lucky One

But when I explained this to Megan, she looked momentarily confused.

'No, I don't think you understand, Krystal. There are no younger women, *full stop*. Women your age aren't commonly having this surgery in Australia yet. It's still considered radical.'

I was so surprised that it took me a while to decipher what she was saying.

'Are you saying, for my age, I'm one of the first?'

'You're one of the first.'

I shut the book in my lap. Up until now I guess I had *known*, rationally, that risk-reduction breast removal surgery was unusual. Aside from anything else, the bewildered reaction I got whenever I mentioned to anyone that I was choosing to remove my healthy breasts was enough to tell me it was pretty extreme. Then there was the fact that I'd had to look outside Australia just to find someone else my age (Lindsay) who'd already been through it. Hell, Medicare doesn't even have an item number for the BRCA gene test so preventative breast surgery is hardly going to be high on its list. It was that rare in Australia. In fact, when my mum and my nan were both tested for the BRCA gene mutation back in 1999 and 2000 respectively, they were two of the first people in Australia to undergo such genetic testing. The gene itself was only discovered as recently as 1994, at the University of Utah, and so in 2008 in Australia, BRCA testing, and the associated medical response, were still only developing.

But knowing something and really *getting it* are two different things and, leafing through Megan's portfolio that day, suddenly *I got it*. I was out on a limb with this surgery and feeling very, very alone.

Krystal Barter

I handed Megan's book back to her. There was no point leafing through it if all the before-and-after photos were of middle-aged women (most of them post-cancer-surgery and all of them post-40). Sure, I'd breastfed two children so my boobs were hardly the perkiest in my peer group. But at 25, all of my girlfriends and I had some way to go before we were as saggy and well-loved as the women in Megan's book. I was hardly going to find the breasts I wanted in there.

And still, it seemed bizarre to me that—in an era when the media is saturated with images of bright young things flashing their boobs (have you ever watched music videos on TV on a Saturday morning?) and when Hollywood gives women a use-by date of about 40—I couldn't find a naked photograph of a 20-something woman who'd had a breast reconstruction. But that was the reality. Back when I was having my preventative surgery (and we're talking 2008 here, people; not exactly the dark ages), it was radical for a woman under 35 to choose to remove her breasts in Australia. No one was doing it, no one was talking about it and certainly no one was taking any photos of it. It was happening quietly, if at all.

I wanted to open up Megan's book and see other girls my age; girls who'd had this surgery and who'd come out the other side unscathed. But I couldn't even get that small comfort. Yet again, this was a journey I had to navigate on my own and, yet again, I felt incredibly isolated.

Megan was hugely sympathetic and said she wished there was someone—anyone—she knew who was my age and had undergone risk-reducing surgery so that she might put me in touch with them just to have a chat. But there simply wasn't anyone she knew. (These days I've given Megan strict

The Lucky One

instructions that any of her younger patients can call me if they're in the same situation and they want to talk to me. I left her a stack of business cards with my contact details on them and I've had numerous phone calls as a result. Every conversation starts the same way: 'Hello? Is that Krystal? I know this is random but Dr Hassall gave me your name and I just wanted to ask you ...' It's such a little thing to be able to do for someone but I would have killed to have received support like that.)

In the end I opted for teardrop-shaped silicone implants. I was told I didn't have enough fat on my abdomen for it to be used in a TRAM (transverse rectus abdominus myocutaneous) flap reconstruction (and what woman wouldn't pay to hear that!) so implants were my only realistic option. Where I did have a choice, though, was size. And just like Oliver Twist: *please, sir, I want more!* After much discussion Megan agreed to upgrade me from a 12B to a 12C, so that I would come out of my reconstruction one size bigger than my natural breast size. Finally, having lived under the dark cloud of cancer all my life, here at last I had found a silver lining.

♦ ♦ ♦

New breasts selected, Mum and I were back at Royal North Shore Hospital the following week for a routine mammogram on my original models. It was now November and, in accordance with the high-risk screening program, mammograms were carried out annually so this was the last screening I had to have before my breasts were removed in March.

'This is the final time you'll be seeing me,' I said to the mammographer, chatting away blithely while she concentrated on the screen in front of her. I've always found it impossible not to be friendly to people when they're helping me out in some way, like cutting my hair or packing my groceries or fixing my car or handling my boobs. 'I'm having a preventative double mastectomy next year so you won't see me back here any time soon!'

The radiographer baulked momentarily at the shock of what I'd just said. I guess it's not every day she saw girls my age come in for a mammogram, let alone announce they're lopping their breasts off. Then she smiled. 'Really? That's great news. I'd be happy if nobody needed a mammogram—even if it would put me out of business!'

Minutes later, I was fully dressed and back in the waiting room with Mum, ready to head on up to see my breast surgeon from the high risk clinic, who was responsible for monitoring my progress through the family cancer clinic. But before I could, the radiographer appeared and motioned for me to return to the imaging room.

'Krystal, do you mind popping back in for a few more quick images for me? It won't take a minute.' This had never happened to me before. I frowned at Mum.

'Sure,' I shrugged. 'Is everything okay?' I could feel my heart beginning to race even before the words left my mouth. I was discovering that 'Is everything okay?' was not a question I generally liked the answer to.

'Of course,' she assured me. 'I just thought that given this is your last screening before your surgery, it would be prudent of me to take some extra images.' The radiographer wouldn't, I noticed, meet my eyes when she said this.

So I returned to the imaging room and removed my top and dutifully lined up to have my breasts photographed some more.

The Lucky One

Then back out into the waiting room before Mum and I were released upstairs, in order to see my doctor for a debrief. But again things didn't go according to plan. Although we were running late by the time I got to her rooms, the doctor was running later still. 'She won't be much longer,' her receptionist assured us as she caught me checking and rechecking the time on my phone at obsessive intervals.

'I'm sorry,' I explained. 'It's just that we've got to pick up my sons from preschool shortly, so we're really going to have to go. Would you mind telling the doctor that we stayed as long as we could?'

The receptionist shook her head. 'There's a note on your file here that says she really wants to see you.'

Must be because of my preventative surgery, I thought optimistically, glancing at the clock on my phone yet again. Riley and Jye would be waiting for me to arrive at preschool soon and, if I was late, I could picture the scene in my mind. The boys would be hanging around by the front fence near the sandpit, backpacks on and artworks in hand, forlornly watching on as everyone else's mums arrived to pick their kids up and wondering if their own mum was ever coming back.

'What if I rebook for another time ahead of my surgery?' I suggested. If we didn't get on the road soon, I'd have the preschool director on the phone asking where I was.

'I don't think—' began the receptionist but she was interrupted by the blonde doctor bustling out of her room. Usually, she was a confident straight-shooter, and I liked that about her. But today she seemed flustered.

'Krystal! Julie! I'm so sorry I've kept you both waiting. Come in, please, and grab a seat.' She shut the door behind us with unintended force and it had the effect of feeling like she was locking us in.

'Doctor, I'm afraid we can't stay—' I started to say but she cut me off with the flick of her hand.

'Krystal, I've got news. We've found something …' Even before she finished her sentence, I knew she meant cancer.

'Your mammogram just now has shown up linear lines of calcification. The calcification is inconclusive but it looks like the preliminary stages of breast cancer.' Then she added sadly, 'In fact, it looks just like yours did Julie.'

She paused for a moment here while this news sunk in. With it, every single cell in my body felt like it slumped to the floor. Beside me, Mum was white.

'Krystal? Do you understand what I've just said?' the doctor asked gently. I nodded self-consciously. I felt like I was standing outside of my body, like I was watching myself in a movie. This wasn't happening to me.

'You should remember that one single mammogram is hardly conclusive.'

I nodded again.

'But with your family history, well, we have reason to be concerned.'

I opened my mouth to speak but nothing came out. Just air and terror.

'So what I'd like to do,' she went on, 'is to get you upstairs now for a biopsy to confirm these results. Then we can decide the best course of action from there.'

A biopsy? Stick a needle in me right now? Poke and prod and turn me into a pincushion like my mum and my nan? And for what? To double-check I had breast cancer when all the signs were screaming at that conclusion? Did I need a biopsy to detect the big red neon sign flashing above my head that read: CANCER, PLEASE STOP HERE! No, thank you, I did not.

'No; no biopsy, thanks.' At last my speech had returned to me. 'I won't be needing a biopsy, thanks. But I am prepared to do whatever else you recommend.'

'Alright,' she swallowed hard. 'Then I'd like to bring your mastectomy forward, Krystal.'

'Done,' I said. 'How soon do you want it?'

'Next week. You need to have your breasts removed next week.'

◆ ◆ ◆

When we left the doctor's surgery that afternoon I was a mess. Tears streamed down my cheeks and I sobbed and hiccupped loudly. My doctor didn't want me to leave while I was so visibly upset but I assured her I'd be fine; we really needed to get moving to pick up my boys. Back in the waiting room the receptionist took one look at me and Mum and wordlessly reached over and handed us a box of tissues. This only set me off worse than before and I howled even louder at this small kindness.

'Thank you,' I snivelled, as I tried to pass the box back across the desk to her.

'You keep them.' She smiled and then waved the tissues away, even though she looked in danger of needing them herself.

So we took the tissues and started walking back to my car, in what was perhaps the worst part of my afternoon. And on an afternoon when you're told it looks like you have cancer, that's pretty bloody bad. In order to get to where my car was parked in Royal North Shore's multistorey parking lot, we had no choice but to walk through Ward 12B: the oncology ward.

Now, an oncology ward is not a fun place at the best of times but having just learned you could soon be a patient, it's the worst place on earth. Stumbling down the corridor with Mum, my tissue box tucked comically under my arm, I tried not to see the various states of illness all around me. Sick, sicker, dying. Everyone in oncology was suffering some form of cancer and undergoing some form of cancer treatment and—even if they were in remission right now—it seemed impossible to me that this heinous disease wouldn't get them in the end. *Somehow, somewhere, even if it was in a secondary form or in a completely unrelated site on your body; even if it was years after your first diagnosis,* I thought bitterly, *once cancer came into your life, it never, ever left. Not until you did.*

This thought made me cry even harder. And for the first time in my life—in the middle of Royal North Shore oncology ward of all places, where I was surrounded by people who were suffering much more than I was at that point—I let self-pity take over and I wallowed in my wretched misfortune. *Why do I have to get cancer?* I sobbed. *Why weren't my family, with my beautiful husband and my gorgeous little boys, going to be spared?* I'd always managed to keep it together whenever I was surrounded by my friends (with their bright, shiny futures lying ahead of them) or in front of my young family; but here in the oncology ward, amid all this cancer-related suffering, it was as if I didn't have to pretend anymore. Like I could finally let my guard down and cry for myself. And so I bawled.

The hardest part was I had always believed I was beating this thing. Like I was one canny step ahead of cancer. I thought

The Lucky One

I could duck and dive and dodge my way out of a breast cancer diagnosis if only I could get enough genetic information and take enough screening tests and be proactive enough and vigilant enough and all those other things I was supposed to do. But now it was as if all that control had been taken away from me.

In many ways I'd already been battling cancer for years, even though I'd never faced diagnosis. Now, it looked like my fight might begin for real. And it was only as I walked through the oncology ward that day that the unfairness of it all finally hit me. *But I'm only 25*, I kept thinking. *I'm only 25 ...*

CHAPTER 15

The week that pre-cancerous changes were detected in my breast tissue was the defining week of my life. After months of acute anxiety, and years of deep-seated fear, I was finally faced with the very thing I had dreaded all along: cancer.

Still, I felt ambushed.

Where I thought I had a good five to ten years before my cancer gene kicked in, suddenly my breasts were changing now (and more than a decade earlier than my mum's had). And where I thought I had five months to prepare for surgery, suddenly I was looking at just over one week. Which is not a lot of time to say goodbye to your breasts forever.

It was an incredibly poignant time, and one I get goosebumps just writing about. It was so emotional; a gut-wrenching,

The Lucky One

heartbreaking, soul-searching time, when my whole world felt like it had been stripped raw and I clung to those closest to me for dear life. It was a time of dwelling and of hoping and of praying and of wishing.

But mostly it was plain old frenetic. I didn't catch my breath.

As soon as I got home from my appointment with the doctor, I went into overdrive. I told my family and my closest friends, who rallied around me with amazing support. I phoned Lindsay in Chicago and spent many, many hours talking with her. I began to make arrangements to have Riley and Jye looked after while I was away and then, with dread, I pulled out the bag I usually reserve for holidays and started to plan what to pack for hospital.

Then, in the hope that I might be able to prevent other women from suffering alone like me, I decided to take my story public. I reasoned that if opening up my life for observation encouraged just one woman to go out and have a mammogram or just one high-risk person to see their doctor and ask a few pertinent questions about preventative mastectomies, then my experience wouldn't be in vain. So on the day after I learned of the calcification in my breast, I phoned up *60 Minutes* and invited them along to follow my surgery.

I had been in ongoing discussions with *60 Minutes* about appearing on the program for a while now. Producer Kirsty was still interested in covering my (now-forgotten) journey through IVF and PGD and we had been in semi-regular contact about the story. Now, though, I phoned her up and suggested she send a camera crew along to film my experiences of surgery and (I nearly choked getting the words out here) to capture the moment when surgeons told me whether I had cancer or not.

Kirsty immediately agreed. A crew was organised to follow me and my family, starting in two days time, in order to capture our back-story before I was admitted to hospital. They would also follow the story of Stacey Gadd, a fellow BRCA1 mutation-carrier from the Adelaide Hills in South Australia. Although I didn't know it at the time, Stacey's breast surgery was scheduled for the same month as mine (we've met since then but I wish I'd known her in the lead-up to our mastectomies when we both could have used the shoulder to cry on). Importantly, neither of us got paid by the Nine Network. Neither of us was telling our story for profit; just in the hope it might help viewers in some way. Kinda like Angelina Jolie telling all to the *New York Times* when she underwent a preventative mastectomy. (In fact, we can't be sure Stace and I didn't give her the idea in the first place ...)

But, in all seriousness, I was worried what sort of story we might be giving Channel Nine's viewers. Because that week prior to surgery was a hell of a week.

◆ ◆ ◆

For starters, I had to undergo a process of lymph node mapping. This involved yet another visit to Royal North Shore Hospital, this time so doctors could inject royal blue ink into both my breasts in order to find my sentinel lymph node. From this small node, about the size and the shape of a baked bean, doctors would decide whether it was necessary to undertake a full auxiliary lymph node dissection during my mastectomy,

The Lucky One

or if the nodes were negative and could safely stay. Having your lymph nodes removed is not something to be entered into lightly, as this can cause pain, swelling paresthesias (abnormal sensations) or even permanent numbness in the arm and armpit region. Mapping the lymph nodes, however, is generally a quick 'n' dirty procedure that takes less than an hour in total.

Except in my case, when my mapping experience was complicated by the fact the doctors hit a nerve. This is ridiculously easy to do, as the lymph nodes near your armpits are a mass of nerves and ganglions, but it's also ridiculously painful. My body involuntarily contracted the instant the needle hit the nerve and I writhed in agony, tears popping out of my eyes.

'I'm so sorry!' exclaimed the doctor. 'We have no way of knowing where the nerves are placed so sometimes we hit one.'

I tried furiously to blink away my tears and to assure him it wasn't his fault but the pain was so intense it took everything I had just to get through it. And then gradually, eventually, the pain began to subside and the room came back into focus and I could begin to breathe again.

◆ ◆ ◆

Far worse than any physical pain, however, was the pain I felt for my nan. Nan flew over from New Zealand to be with us and, while I was infinitely glad to have her around, a small part of me wished she didn't have to witness this. If only for her sake. Having watched her mother and her only daughter go through this process (not to mention her own bilateral surgery), Nan found it nearly impossible to accept that her only granddaughter was having a mastectomy, too. She'd always hoped things might be different for me and I felt very sad for my nan that week.

Of course, among the tears and the medical tests and the planning and the packing, we had a film crew in our midst to distract us. Each morning an iconic blue-and-white Channel Nine minivan would roll into our driveway like the circus rolling into town, and from there the bedlam would begin.

'Is there any way we can fit a six-foot boom in here?' (Cameraman #1, peering optimistically into our living room with its five-foot ceilings.)

'How does it feel to put yourself through this surgery knowing that, without it, you might never get cancer anyway?' I was being asked.

'Can we get a shot of your naked breasts pre-surgery?' (Cameraman #1)

'Just act natural.' (Cameraman #2)

'Act natural? Topless? On national TV?' (Me, hiding behind a bath towel.)

♦ ♦ ♦

But somehow my *how-did-I-get-myself-into-this* moment didn't come until Kirsty, as producer, suggested we get some footage of me walking along Manly beachfront. In a bikini.

'A *bikini*?' I repeated, as if she had suggested a spacesuit, or perhaps a cowboy costume, for my sojourn down the Manly promenade.

'Yeah!' she enthused. 'It'll make for great TV. Young Aussie mum, strolling along one of our most iconic beachfronts, looking like she doesn't have a care in the world when really she

Four generations: Nan Val, Mum, me and my beautiful daughter Bonnie (aged 6 months).

Stacey Gadd and I were on *60 Minutes* together.

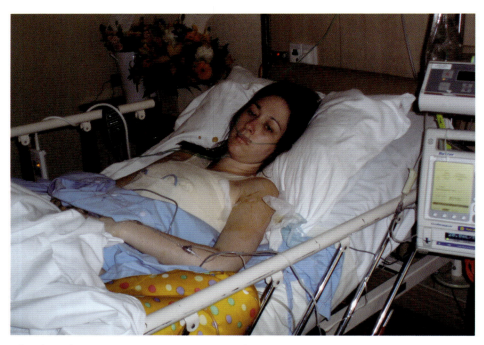

The day after my mastectomy in 2009 – definitely not my best angle.

With Jye on his 1st birthday, just after my surgery, with a pillow for protection.

Speaking at a *Harper's Bazaar* event in conjunction with Women of Influence award win in 2011.

Bumped into Joel Madden … yes! We have the sign with us at all times.

Leaving Australia for the first time, headed for the Big Apple!

Meeting Lindsay, who inspired me to found Pink Hope.

In Central Park.

Me and Lindsay, with Giuliana Rancic, at the FabFest conference in Chicago.

Stacey Gadd, Karl Stefanovic and Rachael Rogan at the 2012 Bright Pink Lipstick Day Launch.

Me with the beautiful Sarah-Jane.

On *Australia's Next Top Model* with Sarah Murdoch (I was a foot too short to be a contestant).

A finalist at the Young Australian of the Year awards, with Premier Barry O'Farrell.

Become a Pink Hope ambassador! A fun photoshoot for a cause that is close to heart.

Our beautiful children: Bonnie (2), Jye (4), and Riley (7).

has the weight of her entire family's genetic history on her, um, chest. Plus, you'll look hot.'

I laughed, long and hard.

'Sorry, Kirsty, but there's just no way. My boobs are one thing. But I just can't see how exposing my thighs on prime-time television is going to help anyone in their battle against hereditary breast cancer.' And so the idea was abandoned.

Instead, they took some shots of me and Mum and Nan walking along the waterfront at Clontarf (about ten minutes drive from our house in North Manly), and then of me and Chris and the boys in the playground there. Chris was nervous about the filming. He's an incredibly private person and felt totally unnatural in front of a camera and so it was a big concession for him to do this for me. And yet he didn't think twice about it. If sharing my story on *60 Minutes* was what I needed to do, then Chris would support me in that. Just like he had supported me for each step of my BRCA journey so far, and just like he was supporting me now as I headed to hospital to have my breasts removed and to begin my showdown with cancer.

CHAPTER 16

My mum often recalls the moment she learned she *didn't* have ovarian cancer. Her surgeon arrived to discuss the results of her ovarian operation, and to personally confirm it *wasn't* cancer, just as the mid-morning news was starting on TV. (This was right about the time our family was running up and down the hospital corridors, shouting in ecstasy, like crazy people.) At that very instant, when my 46-year-old mum looked up at her surgeon and was officially given the all-clear, the television on the wall behind him quietly announced that Australian actress, Belinda Emmett, had just lost her tragic battle with breast cancer. Belinda Emmett was just 32 years old.

And that's the thing about cancer: it's so damn unfair.

The Lucky One

I felt this acutely in the hours leading up to my surgery. As I lay waiting to go under the knife, I was scared about the pain and I was petrified of a bad diagnosis, but mostly what I felt was rage: rage at the injustice of it all. At the thought of all the other beautiful young women out there fighting for their lives.

Just beyond my hospital room I could hear *60 Minutes* journalist, Ellen Fanning, out in the corridor recording what was to be the opening salvo of her report. (As it turns out, this was eventually filmed in-studio. The initial recording out in the corridor must have been discarded, probably for sound reasons.)

'It's a family curse,' she declared in television-perfect pitch. 'Handed down from generation to generation and there's only one radical way to stop it.'

At this point, I glanced down at the plastic bracelet on my wrist announcing 'KRYSTAL BARTER: BILATERAL MASTECTOMY'. *This sure was pretty radical, Ellen,* I agreed.

Ellen went on: 'The two young women you're about to meet are just starting out in life but there's a huge shadow hanging over them. Stacey Gadd's only 22 and Krystal Barter is 25. They've watched their mothers and grandmothers fight breast cancer and they know they could be next. Both have inherited a genetic flaw which is likely, sooner or later, to cause cancer.'

Now my mind flashed, involuntarily, back to the moment last week when Dr Moore told me they had detected changes in my breast tissue.

'But Stacey and Krystal aren't going to wait,' Ellen was wrapping it up now. 'Rather than wait for cancer to come and get them, both girls have decided to act now.'

Have we? I wondered. *Have we really decided to* act?

I couldn't speak for Stacey who, at this stage, I'd never met, but what I was doing right now—lying here in my insipid blue hospital gown, willing the clock to stop, willing the orderlies not to come and get me, willing anything, *anything* to happen that might prevent me from having to go through with this—felt like the furthest possible thing from 'acting now'. I felt like I had no choice but to be here and that there was nothing remotely proactive about my 'proactive breast surgery'. *I have cancer in my DNA*, I thought bitterly, *and my whole life has been marching, inexorably, to this point. We are cursed. My whole family is cursed. And there is nothing I or anyone else can do about it.*

I could hear the orderlies now, shuffling up the corridor past Ellen and her film crew, until they arrived in my doorway to take me to theatre. No amount of genetic information or proactive mammograms or screening or counselling or anything else could save me now. I tried everything I could and yet here I was, only 25 years old, and about to lose my breasts anyway.

Truly, I was cursed.

◆ ◆ ◆

When I woke up from surgery a hippopotamus was sitting on my chest (that one from Riley and Jye's picture book). It flattened my chest and constricted my breathing, but at least by feeling that hippopotamus I knew I was still alive.

'I want Chris!' I blurted. 'Where's Chris? I want Chris!' And I strained to try and sit up and see where he was. 'Where's my husband?' I said again, more loudly this time.

'Krystal, you're in recovery,' said a disembodied voice from somewhere nearby. It wasn't a voice I recognised. 'You've just

The Lucky One

woken up from your surgery and you're doing fine. We'll have you up to your room and back to your husband in no time.'

I sank back onto the bed and tried to focus on my surroundings but the film of anaesthetic still veiled my eyes and this, combined with the glare of the overhead ceiling lights, made the world swim before me. *I would see Chris soon. I was doing fine. My surgery was over.* I tried to process each of these thoughts in turn but they kept skidding into one another inside my foggy brain. Giving up, I shut my eyes and let the recovery ward hum and clang and bustle along without me.

◆ ◆ ◆

The next time I woke up I was safely back in my hospital room with Chris and Mum keeping vigil. The hippopotamus was there, too. But somehow, under my warm woven blanket, and the watch of my family, the weight on my chest seemed to have lifted a little.

'Welcome back, babe,' Chris said and smiled.

'You did it!' Mum enthused.

I tried to smile back but I felt like I was bandaged so tight around my chest that I might pop open if I attempted to move even the muscles on my face. Besides, a grimace was probably the best I could summon right now. I wasn't in any pain—the anaesthetic hadn't worn off enough for that—but I certainly wasn't feeling jubilant, either. Aside from my mummified torso, I had four surgical drains attached to me (two inserted into either breast), collecting blood and lymphatic fluid. Each drain had a tube with a bulb at the end of it and the tubes were held in place with stitches. The whole effect was massively uncomfortable, as was the knowledge they could be there for days. I felt as if I might never move freely again.

Still, all this was nothing compared to the dread that was gripping me. As, one by one, the thoughts swimming around in my pea-soup brain began to coalesce (*my surgery was over; Chris was here*), my one fear remained: *Did I have cancer?*

'Has Dr Sywak been?' I tried to turn and face Chris and Mum as I asked this so that I could gauge their expressions, but my body was having none of it. The *Titanic* would have swung around more easily than this.

'No, not yet, sweetie.' Mum patted my hand. 'Remember, it might be a while before we know your results. The main thing for you right now, is to focus on getting better.'

◆ ◆ ◆

And so for four agonising days I waited to learn if I had cancer. For the first three days, the pain kicked in and the-site-formerly-known-as-my-breasts gave me hell. Initially, I was hooked up to Fentanyl (which is roughly one hundred times more potent than morphine) and the relief it brought was not just physical—it also let me exist in a permanently woozy state where the minutes melted into hours and the hours into days. Three days in fact. I have vague memories of Mum bathing me at this time and she tells me she did this every day (sometimes twice a day), in order to save me the ignominy of having the nursing staff do it. I also remember missing my boys terribly. Chris and I had decided before I came in for surgery that we didn't want Riley or Jye to see me in hospital like this, with drains and drips and beeping machines. It would be too distressing for them. Instead my family had made a wall of photos of the two of them beside my bed that was intended to inspire me (but, in reality, only made me more homesick for them both). More than anything, though, I remember Mum coming in each morning—she was always my first visitor—and throwing open my curtains and declaring: 'Every day is a new day, Krystal, and it *will* get better. I promise.'

I only hoped she was right.

◆ ◆ ◆

When Dr Sywak finally arrived with my test results, the *60 Minutes* crew were back onboard. Having given our family some time to recoup after my surgery (and me some time to look *slightly* less heinous post-op), Ellen and her film crew were now perched around my tiny hospital room, balancing preciously among drips and heart-rate monitors and bunches of flowers, waiting to learn if I had cancer. The mood was tense and falsely upbeat.

And Dr Sywak was uncharacteristically inarticulate as he delivered my results that day. 'Um,' he stumbled as he started, and the hippo returned then, plonking himself down on my chest and causing me to suck in air fast.

'Your pathology results arrived this morning ...' he continued and I strained to hear him over the blood pounding in my ears. This was it. This was the moment I had feared my whole life.

'The results were very good. As we suspected, there was evidence of *atypical ductal hyperplasia* there ...'

I held my breath.

'This is an abnormal pattern of cell growth in the breast tissue ...'

I couldn't breathe.

'But there was no evidence of any cancer at all.'

I didn't blink. I couldn't move. Did he just say, *no cancer*?

Around me, the room erupted into cheering.

'So, doctor, does this mean that Krystal will never have anyone say to her in her life: "You have breast cancer?"' Ellen got straight to the point but I was too numb to even register the question. I couldn't have told you my own name just then if you'd asked me.

Dr Sywak smiled. 'You've probably spent enough time with doctors to know they will never give you a 100 per cent guarantee but the chances of her developing breast cancer in future are less than 1 per cent.'

When the *60 Minutes* episode went to air, the footage of this moment cut to a montage of our reactions to the news: Chris hugging me; Mum crying quietly on the couch beside my bed; Ellen laughing happily with her crew. And throughout it all I am propped up in bed in my pale-pink peasant top, looking dazed and smiling vaguely.

Ellen's voiceover narrated the scene for the viewers at home: 'Krystal will almost certainly be the first woman in four generations to avoid the family curse. News that is almost too good to believe.'

What Ellen said in real life, though, was: 'He just told you, you have virtually no chance of getting breast cancer!' She was grinning at me in such genuine excitement that it was as if *she'd* just been told she didn't have cancer. My own response must have been something of a letdown.

The Lucky One

'It's good,' I said. 'It's good. It's great!' It was like confetti swirling around me that I couldn't lay a finger on.

'My mum had to sit there when she was 36 years old and be told that she had breast cancer and I'm 25 and I've beaten it,' I said slowly for the camera, and I was trying to make sense of it all as I said it. I was the first woman in my family to beat breast cancer.

I turned back to Dr Sywak and I felt a rush of gratitude. I had a lot to thank him and his surgical team for. 'This is the best feeling,' I grinned at him eventually. 'The *best* feeling.'

At last I felt lucky.

◆ ◆ ◆

When you stop and think about it, you realise my cancer scare was a blessing.

If doctors *hadn't* detected pre-cancerous changes in my breast that November then I would certainly have postponed my breast-removal surgery at least once. I'm sure of it. I was that scared of going through with it. (Or, imagine if I'd gone down the path of trying for a genetically perfect baby? I could have been nursing a newborn *and* advanced cancer right now …) The truth was, I had been so frightened and so unprepared to remove my breasts that there's no way I would have had the scheduled surgery in March if the decision had been left up to me. I needed a push and it just so happens that push was cancer. So it was a blessing in a way, this early-stage cancer detection. Without it my story might have had a much worse ending. In fact, I may not have been here to tell it at all.

Instead, my life post-surgery was something of a new beginning.

I always tell people that, the instant I discovered I had beaten breast cancer, I felt like an enormous weight was lifted off me—a weight that I'd been carrying around since I was a kid. And, hell, it wasn't like it was the physical burden of my breasts I was missing. Because those 12Bs were never heavy to begin with! They were pretty average, in fact, or at least they were after having breastfed two boys. But once my breasts were removed I was astonished at just how much they'd weighed me down. Post-mastectomy and cancer-free, I felt like I'd got a load off my chest—literally. Moreover, I felt like I could finally plan my future. I could think about travelling and about having another baby. I could plan a career, for the very first time in my life. I could dream of growing old and of watching my boys grow up and of seeing them get married and even, one day, of holding grandbabies of my own!

Before surgery, cancer loomed large over my life. I had lived in the shadow of breast cancer since my mum was first diagnosed back when I was fourteen. Longer, if you count my family history. But if cancer was my dark cloud (and bigger, better breasts the silver lining), then being cancer-free was like stepping into glorious light.

Finally, my life had colour.

CHAPTER 17

Naturally, that colour was pink. When I emerged from hospital and out into the world of saturated technicolour, I felt like my beloved Judy Garland entering the wizard's world of Oz. Everything glittered. On my slow, frail walk through the car park I spotted a patch of windswept dandelion flowers growing through the cracks in the bitumen and the sight of those pathetic weeds straining to reach the sunshine gave me a disproportionate amount of hope. Life, it seems, will battle against anything.

Years ago my mum and her friends set up a cancer-support group for women on the Northern Beaches called 'Active Women Touched by Cancer'. It's nothing formal, just a bunch of ordinary women, all waging their own war against cancer (or bearing the scars from earlier battles), who do whatever they can to make the load easier for each other. They do each other's washing and make cups of tea and ferry one another to medical appointments and proffer boxes of tissues and a shoulder to cry on as needed. Mum, in particular, seemed to be called on most often whenever one of these women was in the final stages of terminal cancer and wanted someone physically by their side as they lay dying. Over the years I've drawn so much inspiration from watching Mum and the others in Active Women support one another. But one story in particular will always stay with me.

I'll never forget Mum telling me about the stunning blonde woman in their group, Christina, who fought a long, valiant but ultimately unsuccessful battle against breast cancer. Christina was the stepmother of world surfing champion Layne Beachley, and was a glamorous woman who was always beautifully put together. Christina's last wish, in the final hours of her life, was to have Mum paint her toenails with fiery red nail polish. This final touch of glamour was her one last indulgence and her one last act of defiance. Christina never stopped fighting till the very end.

And so now, as I left hospital bruised and battered and bent-over with pain, I thought about Christina—an actual cancer sufferer—and was inspired to fight on.

But before I was discharged I'd had something of an epiphany on the idea of starting a local version of Lindsay's cancer charity, Bright Pink. Well, not so much an epiphany as the dull realisation: *If I don't do something, who on earth will?* Both Lindsay Avner and Stacey Gadd (my new mastectomy buddy from *60 Minutes*) were instrumental at this point.

Stacey urged me to try and set up a Bright Pink equivalent here, saying, 'Everyone like us needs a home to go to, a place to feel safe.'

The Lucky One

Lindsay was more succinct: 'Just do it,' she instructed. 'How do you think Bright Pink got started?'

And so, four days after I'd had my breasts removed—while I was still whacked out on painkillers and I was unable to raise my arms higher than my belly button without assistance—I had the nurses take out my laptop for me and prop it up against my knees while I lay in my hospital bed. And there, surrounded by drips and drains and drugs and doctors, I launched 'Pink Hope'.

At first, Pink Hope was an incredibly modest website. I looked up that guy from the Breast Cancer Foundation breakfast at Dee Why all those months ago and, to my surprise, he remembered who I was and was willing to get onboard and provide pro bono tech support for us. He did an amazing job (given he was working with a budget of nothing) and within weeks of my leaving hospital, Pink Hope was a fully functioning online community where women at high-risk of breast and ovarian cancer could find support and encouragement and information and, most importantly, other women just like themselves to chat to. I was stoked.

Of course, for the first two years of its existence, Pink Hope didn't make a cent. I learnt an awful lot about the charity sector during this time and about the in's and out's of securing philanthropic donations. I learnt about intellectual property law and about garnering and crediting reputable medical information to post on our website. And I learnt more than any girl with barely a passing interest in technology should *ever* have to know about 'back-end' website procedures. But I loved every minute of it.

After years of being at the mercy of cancer, finally I felt like I was in control. I'd played the victim for a very long time as a teenager; back then I barely knew how to do anything else. But as I pieced myself back together again in the wake of my mastectomy, when my life was arguably the lowest it had ever been, I found strength in getting on with the business of doing something for others. Don't get me wrong, I'm not a big fan of self-righteous posturing and that's not where this is headed. In fact, in the years since I founded Pink Hope, the charity has given me so much more than I ever expected. I've made some amazing friends, met some inspiring families and learned from some really incredible medical professionals. But at the time I set it up, Pink Hope gave me just one thing, and the very thing I needed most: it gave me hope.

Now, I was a woman on a mission to share that hope with others.

♦ ♦ ♦

That's not to say my life was rosy from the instant Pink Hope was born.

In the weeks following my surgery, I was mightily sore and sorry. To begin with, I was bandaged impossibly tight, from my stomach to my décolletage, and those bandages remained in place for seven days after I left hospital. Then came the dressings which had to be cleaned and replaced daily. Plus, I had drains attached on either side of me for ten days following my surgery and then, after they'd been removed, I developed a nasty seroma (or fluid build-up) that had to be drained manually by my doctor. I couldn't hold my babies, couldn't even cuddle them, which was the most awful part for me, and Jye was so frightened of how I looked now that he wouldn't come near his 'Mama' for the first week after I left hospital.

Chris, as ever, was a saint during this time. He was patient and sympathetic, and he did an amazing job of being both mum and dad for our boys. He took time off work to ferry me to and from my medical appointments and, perhaps most important of all, he told me I looked beautiful when the mirror was saying otherwise.

And if Chris was a saint, then Lindsay was divine intervention. Post-surgery, we were in touch often with Lindsay sending me all kinds of inspirational quotes and stories and filling my inbox with new and special pep-talks to help get me up and out of bed and somehow able to face the day. In particular, I was struggling with the fact that I was 50 per cent likely to pass my gene fault on to my boys. It was a flip of a coin, those odds, a simple 'yes or no' answer. And to think that *I* was the reason Riley and Jye faced such a half-and-half chance ... It was enough to make me physically hurt at the thought.

I still had baths with my boys after my surgery (they were four years old and eleven months old), but every time Jye saw my bruised and swollen breasts with their train tracks of stitches down each side he gave that sharp intake of breath that kids make whenever they know something is sore or hot.

'Ooh-ooh,' he would utter breathily, waggling his fat fingers and wincing in sympathy.

'It's okay,' Riley would instruct him. 'Mummy's had an operation on her boobies so they don't make her sick.'

This was the line Chris and I had taught Riley and, although he could parrot it, we couldn't be sure just how much it actually meant to him. I mean, *I* sure as hell still struggled to make sense of the whole hereditary cancer thing, and most adults couldn't comprehend the idea of a preventative mastectomy; so how could we honestly expect a child to? Still, kids are amazingly resilient and we felt we had to tell Riley something to reassure him that his mummy was safe.

While we tried to prevent the boys from worrying about me, I was still tormented with fear for them. What would I do if I found out they were carriers of the gene mutation? Would they avoid all the BRCA-associated cancers for men (such as male breast cancer, pancreatic cancer, and prostate cancer)? I hoped beyond all hope that they would dodge the BRCA bullet and live long and cancer-free lives.

Their fifty/fifty odds weighed heavily on me until Lindsay sent me this simple quote from author Mary Anne Radmacher: *Courage doesn't always roar, courage is sometimes the little voice at the end of the day that says, 'I will try again tomorrow'*. Seems pretty innocuous, right? Wrong.

When I opened up the email from Lindsay that contained this one single sentence, I suddenly realised how I could help my boys: I could be brave for them. If I wanted Riley and Jye to live bold, courageous lives, despite the threat of cancer, then I had to show them how. And not in a big, loud, *ta-da-here-it-is!* kinda way. But just quietly and consistently, day-in and day-out; I needed to be doggedly determined not to let this thing beat us so that they would do the same. I couldn't get depressed, couldn't be defeated, couldn't live in fear—I had to think and plan and act and embrace life in a way that says: 'You know what, Cancer? I won't play by your rules. I've got too much living to do.' Then, hopefully, my boys would do the same.

The Lucky One

And this idea all stemmed from one short email from Lindsay. Honestly, I don't know what I would have done without her.

◆ ◆ ◆

Closer to home, my three best friends couldn't have been more split in their reactions to my surgery. My lovely friend, Erin, who I'd known since school days, had cried at the foot of my bed every day I was in hospital. She would stand there, struggling to hold her composure, repeating the words 'You are just so brave' as if it were some kind of yogic mantra. Erin bought me a book and flowers and called me during the times she was unable to visit. She really was very sweet about the whole thing. So was Jaime, who I have been best friends with since we were seventeen. Although, unlike Erin, Jaime could hardly bear to look at me when she visited me in hospital (she said it made her feel a little faint), but she was so heartbroken over the whole situation and so desperate to support me that she forced herself to keep coming back every day to see me.

Then, there was Bec. Bec is two years older than me and has always been a—generally much-needed—second mum to me. (This is the same Bec who phoned my *actual* mum about my drug-taking back when I was a teenager.) Bec always looked out for me, always supported me and always had my back no matter what I did. When it came to my breasts, though, Bec was angry.

'I don't understand why you're doing this. You don't have cancer!' she said to me, matter-of-factly, when I first told her I'd decided to have surgery. Bec couldn't accept that a normal, healthy, rational person would cut off their breasts *just in case* they got cancer, and nothing I could say could convince her otherwise.

'Just Google it,' I'd argued. 'Go home and Google "BRCA-mutation-positive-slash-now-what?" and then tell me you wouldn't do exactly the same.'

In the end, she did. And then she called me the next day to say she'd spent half the night on her computer and that she was sorry for not understanding and for not trusting my decision. She'd do the same, she realised. And so now, after my surgery, I had Bec's support more than ever because she knew, if it were her, she would have made exactly the same choice.

◆ ◆ ◆

As for my mum, well, she was incredible. Mum bathed me and fed me and, when she wasn't looking after me, then she was bathing and feeding my children, too. Moreover, she was upbeat and optimistic and cheery whenever I needed it most (which was every day at this point in time). It was like having my own personal cheerleader.

So you can imagine my surprise when, years later, Mum told me that watching me go through my mastectomy was the worst thing that had ever happened in her life. For a woman who has endured so much—who'd had a mastectomy herself, and survived breast cancer, plus an ovarian cancer scare, and who'd nursed her mother through cancer before that—Mum doesn't use the term 'worst' very lightly.

Even now Mum finds it hard to talk about my surgery (and the recovery afterwards) without crying. For her, the saddest

The Lucky One

day came a week or so after my operation, when I was recuperating at home and a nurse arrived from the hospital to remove my bandages for the first time. Mum and Nan sat on one couch and the nurse sat facing them on the couch opposite, while I stood in the middle, my arms outstretched, as the nurse slowly unwound me. On and on and on it went, the bandages slithering to the floor like some sort of white crepe serpent shedding its skin. And beneath it all, I looked horrendous.

My chest was speckled with yellowing bruises that stood out angrily from my ashen skin. My four drains were still attached, two on either side, only now I could see the train tracks of neat black stitches puncturing my skin where they were holding the drains in place. But worse than that: my chest was flat. During my mastectomy, when my own breast tissue was removed and the hard silicone expanders were inserted in its place, the expanders were filled with less than 100 millilitres of fluid. In the weeks and months to come, my plastic surgeon would begin a process of regular saline injections into the expanders, like slowly, painstakingly blowing up a balloon. Only it was too soon to start injections yet so, on the day the nurse removed my bandages, my chest looked like that of a 12-year-old boy.

◆ ◆ ◆

However, that horror was nothing compared to having my drains removed. Surgical drains, I had learned at some point during my BRCA journey, were affectionately known by those that needed them as 'hand grenades'. I guess their bulb shape, plus the drainage tube coming out the top, makes them not unlike a hand grenade to look at. What struck me, though, was that a woman could joke about having handheld bombs attached to her bra, when her own breasts were ticking time bombs—cancer victims, I had fast discovered, often had a wonderfully black sense of humour. Time and time again I would meet super-inspiring women in surgical waiting rooms or familial cancer clinics who could somehow find the strength to laugh in the face of cancer.

I, however, wasn't at the laughing stage quite yet when it came to my own 'hand grenades'. At about the time I was due to go back into hospital to have my drains taken out, the drains that were inserted into my left-hand side somehow got caught around one of my nerves. I don't know if it was something I did—if I'd moved the wrong way and caused it to become entangled—but what I *do* know was that the pain was unbearable. Absolute agony. I felt like I was being stabbed in some raw wound in the side of my breast with a hot rusty knife. I could barely breathe for the pain it sent into my chest whenever I took in air. So, after several hours of watching me fight to draw breath, my parents and Chris gingerly packed me up and took me to the hospital, two days earlier than planned.

Dad double-parked right outside the entrance and Mum and Chris were forced to take me inside in a wheelchair because I was well past walking by this stage. I must have looked like a wizened little old lady, all grey-faced and doubled-over in pain, as they wheeled me back into hospital that day. Even though it was only a few metres from the entrance bay to the foyer, I certainly couldn't have walked. It seemed grossly unfair that I'd walked proudly out through this same archway a few weeks earlier, fresh from my operation and so determined to make a

The Lucky One

new start, and yet here I was heading back into hospital, and having to be *wheeled* this time because I was too sick to make it on my own.

As all the pamphlets on breast removal surgery will tell you, surgical drains aren't necessarily painful but 'you will probably be aware of the discomfort they have caused you after you have had them removed'. *Aware of discomfort?* Oh, I was aware of discomfort, alright. My tangled nerve meant that the process of removing my drains was horrific. Chris was by my side at the time and he swears some gloopy part of my insides came out with the plastic tubing. But then the relief I felt the *instant* my drains were gone was quite simply incredible. *I didn't hurt! I could breathe freely again! They didn't call these babies grenade-drains for nothing, I thought—it was as if all the pain in my breast had been annihilated!*

◆ ◆ ◆

It was at this point that I felt like I could go on again; I could do this thing. I would get out of this hospital and I would piece my life back together; I would recover and grow strong and I would be able to lift my boys again and to hug them to my chest. Sure, this whole experience hadn't been much fun. In fact, it was hands-down the hardest thing I've ever had to do in my entire life. But I had undergone a double mastectomy and I'd survived. What's more, I was one of the lucky ones; I didn't have cancer. And so the only way from here was up.

Or so I thought, until I got my new breasts.

◆ ◆ ◆

'They're saggy!' I sobbed, cupping the teardrop-shaped globules of silicone that sat heavily in my palms. 'Oh, my god, they're so ugly.'

I shouldn't have been surprised. Although Megan had done an incredible job, my breasts were much smaller than I'd been expecting (which is why, I guess, it's so common for people to have corrective surgery after they have breast reconstructions). More surgery, however, was the furthest thing from my mind right now. Over the last three months I had undergone a process of expander inflation, achieved through regular percutaneous injections. In short, every three weeks Chris would drive me to the surgery of Dr Megan Hassall, whereby she would come at me with a needle best suited to a racehorse and inject it into my breast. From here, Megan would inject saline solution into my breast expanders in order to pump them up. It was a hair-raising experience—not so much painful as stressful—as Megan was required to inject the saline solution into the hard, plastic expanders. This required force but Megan was always very gentle. On Mum's good advice I popped half an Ativan before each session to calm my nerves. Still, the actual process of pumping up my pectoralis muscles (the main muscle under the breast) didn't hurt too much, nor did the gradual stretching of my skin over the three-month period as my breasts were inflated. It just made me feel somewhat like a pincushion.

On the upside, being able to choose my boobs was like being some sort of mammary Goldilocks at a silicone smorgasbord. C-cup? D-cup? *This one is too small; that one is too hard; but this one? This one is just right!* My options were mindboggling. There was, however, one option I didn't have to ponder—and that was size. Because if I was going to go through the pain of a double mastectomy and then a breast reconstruction, there was no way I wasn't coming out of it with amazing boobs. So I had Megan pump me up to a fulsome C-cup, and didn't my cup of happiness overflow with it! I would walk down the street to meet Chris after each injection session, pumped up with saline and sporting a tight T-shirt, flaunting my babies for the world to admire. In fact, it wasn't until I had my second and final surgery—when my saline-filled expanders were removed and my permanent implants were inserted in their place—that things went wrong.

This final surgery was much less complicated than the original mastectomy as the procedure mostly takes place through the existing scars. Consequently, my expanders were whipped out and my silicone implants put in and I was home and recuperating before I even knew it. I arrived home with permission from Megan to take off my own bandages after a 48-hour period. What I uncovered when I did was devastating. My new breasts were much flatter and more natural-looking than I had hoped for and, despite having elected to go up a size to a 12C, they were now no bigger than the real 12Bs that I'd been through so much heartache to have removed. It wasn't that anything had gone *wrong* with the implant surgery; just that once the round expanders were removed my breasts appeared much smaller than the 12Cs I'd been parading around. It was only the expanders that made me look like I'd gone up a size. Apparently this is a common complaint and revisional procedures (either to fix breast appearance or to re-match breasts where only one breast has been remade) are relatively frequent in the world of reconstruction. My new boobs were teardrop-shaped, as planned, but rather than making them look more natural somehow this only seemed to make them appear saggy after the 'round' look of the expanders that I'd grown used to. They looked like they were someone else's boobs stuffed into my body. I cried for two days when I saw them.

'I hate them ...' I sobbed quietly in the bath, my hair piled up on top of my head and my body sunk low to try to submerge my breasts under the foam so I didn't have to look at them. 'This is so unfair!'

Mum and Chris sat patiently on the cold tiles next to the bath; Chris tried to calm me down, while Mum cried quietly at having to see me so upset.

'They're so ugly,' I cried. 'I hate them!'

'They're not ugly, babe. You look beautiful,' Chris said.

'Megan is amazing. We can always go back and she'll give you the breasts that you want,' Mum encouraged.

But I wasn't having a bar of this. 'No; no way. I've had so much surgery, there's no way I'm going back again.'

And there wasn't. After a double mastectomy and a breast reconstruction, after drains and expanders and injections and implants, there was no way I was going back for more. Eventually, I realised that I could live with boring B-cups if it meant living without cancer and returning to normalcy.

CHAPTER 18

Still, it was weird seeing my breasts without nipples. At first I found it hugely confronting, like I was some sort of life-sized Barbie Doll, all smooth plastic contours, fresh off a factory conveyor belt. I felt it acutely, those two small but very essential parts of me that were now missing; parts I never really appreciated until they were gone. I mourned my lost nipples whenever I stepped out of the shower and caught a glimpse of my android-curved chest in the mirror, or when I slipped into seductive lingerie for my husband and couldn't feel the lacy mesh prickling against my nipples. It was strange. Of course, having no nipples has its perks, too. T-shirt bras are a thing of the past and I never have to worry about seedy old men ogling my chest when I'm cold. And I've reached a point now where

I can be critical of my nipples in a way I never could when I was (literally) more attached to them. They were too big, for a start. But, still, it took me a long time to arrive at this point where I could find any positives to not having them around (despite the fact I had elected not to replace them). For the first few months, my missing nipples bothered me more than I cared to admit.

I distracted myself from this, and from my post-op recovery, by throwing everything I had into Pink Hope. Before long I was working up to 50 hours each week, in between looking after my two young children, and still there always seemed to be so much more I could be doing. Responding to the emails alone was huge. In the twelve months since I first registered the domain name, Pink Hope was fast becoming *the* port of call for the 120 000 women in Australia at high-risk of developing breast or ovarian cancer. We'd grown from being a single-page website to a multi-platform community, where women and their daughters (some as young as fifteen) were accessing information and resources and very practical advice on being high-risk. (Advice as diverse as: 'How to deal with inconclusive gene test results' to 'How to host your own boob farewell', complete with boob-bake-off, boob-themed decorations, pin-the-tail-on-the-boob and, of course, a booby piñata.) Then, we had online state groups which put Pink Hope members in touch with each other within their local area. There was even an ambassador program where young women could nominate to represent their local Pink Hope community. But the thing I was most proud of was our online community, which allowed any high-risk woman, wherever she lived, the chance to chat to other women just like her at any time of the day or night. It was *exactly* what I'd craved when I first learned I was BRCA mutation positive.

On top of all this, I was becoming more and more involved in the lives of our Pink Hope members. It was impossible not to. I started going along to medical appointments with some of the women when their own families or friends couldn't make it; dropping them off at their surgeons or sitting with them during chemo treatments. I was on the phone nearly every night, offering advice or tips or listening while one of our members unleashed her darkest fears to me, relieved at being able to talk freely to someone who wasn't a family member and therefore not directly involved, or effected, themselves. In that first year alone I must have spoken to around 400 women, talking them through their mastectomies or helping them plan how to tell their children about hereditary cancer or just listening to them cry as they told me they were terminal. It was heartbreaking and awe-inspiring—I was crying on a near-daily basis—and it sure as hell made me forget about my nipples.

◆ ◆ ◆

One of the most memorable women I encountered was Rachel Rogan from the South Coast of New South Wales. Rachel was a young mum with advanced breast cancer and, though she was one of the first people to ever contact Pink Hope, I've never forgotten the email she sent me:

Hi Krystal,
My name is Rachel and I've just found out that I have triple negative breast cancer and that it's metastasised to other parts of

my body. Although I didn't know it until recently, I have a BRCA2 gene fault that was passed down to me via my grandad and my dad. I have three children under the age of six—three beautiful baby boys—and now that I have cancer I don't know what I'll do. I've never felt so helpless and alone and I'm writing to you in case Pink Hope can do something ...

I was devastated by Rachel's story. I couldn't believe that life could be so cruel to one woman and to her (incredibly young) family and so I spent the next four days on the phone trying to see if I could help. I chased up local support services and coordinated volunteers in her area into a visiting schedule; I phoned Woolworths and arranged for food drop-offs to feed her family, then coerced other small businesses in her town to donate various goods and services where needed, given that her medical treatment wouldn't come cheap. I even managed to recruit a lovely team of locals to come in and help clean her house on a regular basis. I felt if I could make this woman's life just a little bit easier then somehow my own genetic journey had a purpose.

But Rachel was a battler and, thankfully, she survived. It wasn't till a few years later that I got the chance to meet her face-to-face when she came along to our first Bright Pink Lipstick Day event. Bright Pink Lipstick Day has fast become the biggest day of the year on the Pink Hope calendar. It's a day when celebrities and Pink Hope members, plus friends, supporters and family members alike, all slick on their brightest pink lippie and donate hard to help raise funds for our charity. The idea is to 'wear', then 'share' (posting photos of yourself on social media), in order to show you 'care'. It was a simple concept, and one I dreamed up in my pyjamas in front of my laptop while Bonnie was raiding my lipsticks, but since our launch day at The Star at Pyrmont on 28 September 2012, Bright Pink Lipstick Day seems to have taken on a life of its own.

That first year alone we got 17.5 million imprints from our social media campaign; we trended on Twitter; and a host of generous celebrities jumped onboard to lend their support. Lara Bingle, who has been a long-time friend of Pink Hope, couldn't make it to our launch event so she snapped a pic of herself in her car, boasting hot pink lips, and that helped to spread the word even faster. Nowadays, Bright Pink Lipstick Day has become so popular that in 2013 we received 92 million imprints in media and social media and had celebs like Olivia Wilde and Sally Obermeder supporting our campaign. With any luck, Bright Pink Lipstick Day will become the first globally recognised fundraising day supporting hereditary cancer.

Back in 2012, however, our beginnings were a little more humble. On the day of our launch, around 200 members of the Pink Hope family (media, ambassadors and celebrities) came together for morning tea at The Star, our sea of hot-pink lips clashing brilliantly with the sparkling blue of Pyrmont Bay behind us. Our hosts that day were Karl Stefanovic, Australian television personality, and Whitney Port, American television personality, who happened to be in Australia at just the right time to attend our event. (I've always been obsessed with Whitney, with her TV shows and with her clothing line, Whitney Eve; I still have to pinch myself when I think about her support of Bright Pink Lipstick Day.)

Our launch was a blast of a day—still one of the best I've ever had with Pink Hope—but the highlight for me was always going to be meeting Rachel.

The moment she saw me she threw herself into my arms and hugged me tight.

'OMG! Krystal!' she cried, as I started to tell her how thrilled I was to see her, too.

'No—Karl Stefanovic is here!' she squealed, having spied the breakfast television presenter over my shoulder. 'You didn't tell me Karl Stefanovic was coming! I *love* Karl!'

And with that Rachel disappeared and I barely saw her again for the rest of the morning! Rachel and Karl happily shot the breeze and posed for photos and generally got on like a house on fire for the next couple of hours. It was kind of like the movie *When Harry Met Sally* but without that famous dessert scene. Meeting Karl was better medicine than anything Rachel's doctors could ever have prescribed for her. (And it sure brought me more satisfaction than any number of website hits or marketing dollars ever could. This is what Pink Hope was all about: giving hope.)

I should mention here that Karl has gone on to become one of Pink Hope's secret weapons. He's a tireless supporter of our charity and the lengths he goes to in helping us are astonishing. I first met Karl on the set of the Nine Network's *Today* in 2006, when I appeared on the show with Mum and Nan. Karl maintains that, after meeting the three of us and hearing our story, he felt compelled to help support my family and he started the very next day by wearing a pink ribbon on his lapel—a ribbon he wore every morning for the next six months or so. (I have my suspicions, however, that it was the cookies Nan baked for him, rather than anything I or Mum or Nan said, that made such an impression!) Here's a piece Karl penned for *Pink Ribbon* magazine, published by the *Australian Women's Weekly,* which illustrates just what an exceptional supporter, and all-round nice guy, Karl is:

When I was growing up, pink was associated with girls, women and Miss Piggy. Ignorance, some say, is bliss. These days, its meaning is associated with so much more than just a colour.

For four years, I have been presenting Today *on the Nine Network, and have been introduced to pink's other, more serious meaning—breast cancer. Over that time, I've met some truly inspirational women. Women such as Sarah Murdoch, who campaign tirelessly for the cause. Women like Jane McGrath, who stared the disease down and said, 'You will not beat me'. And women who carry the genes of this disease like some ticking time bomb.*

A couple of years ago, I met Valerie, Julie-Anne and Krystal—three generations of women from the same family, all living with the disease in some way. Krystal, 24, was about to be married when she found out she was carrying the BRCA1 breast cancer gene that had been passed down through her family. Krystal bought a pink dress for her special day and said at the time, 'Some people would wear pink because it's a beautiful colour. I wear it because it's the colour of my family. I wear it to honour my mother, grandmother and great-grandmother, so I'll be taking a part of those three special women down the aisle with me.'

But Krystal's mum almost didn't make the wedding day. Two months before, she and the family were told that she probably only had a few months to live. Scans showed a tumour and it looked like it had spread. She was operated on and finally cut a break. The cancer was non-malignant—even the doctors were cheering in surgery.

It was almost a horrible case of history repeating. Valerie, Krystal's grandmother, had cancer when Julie-Anne was getting married. The 69-year-old now lives in New Zealand and, like Julie-Anne, has lost both her breasts. When Valerie comes on the show, she gives me a big hug and a tin of delicious homemade cookies. They have pink icing.

For the moment, cancer is part of these women's lives; and, for the moment, cancer is here to stay. I am a supporter of the Breast Cancer Foundation because I have met these women and because I have a grandmother, a mother, a wife and a daughter. And I hope that, one day soon, a cure for breast cancer is found. Then pink can again be just another colour we all wear and not a life sentence for generations of families.

◆ ◆ ◆

Since founding Pink Hope, I care so much more and love so much deeper than I ever did before. I've found such a true appreciation for my family and my life, and it's finally allowed me to see my BRCA journey in an empowering way. Working for a charity doesn't make me a better person than anyone else, doesn't even mean my work is more worthy than others. But it has made me the best possible version of myself.

Of course, putting yourself in the public eye and also entering the realm of social media does mean you open yourself up to criticism. Not all the feedback I've had over the years has been kind and positive. It only happens very rarely, (in fact, I can count on one hand the negative feedback we've received) but Pink Hope has copped some negative backlash, most commonly with people complaining that breast cancer takes too much of the cancer charity limelight. Then there are the ones who take the time to get in touch to tell us that 'negative thinking causes cancer' or 'there's no such thing as BRCA gene faults; something your family is doing or eating must be causing your cancer'. Or, my personal favourite: 'genes don't exist'. Sure, tell that to modern medical science.

But, above all, Pink Hope has brought into my life some of the bravest and most beautiful women I could ever hope to meet. Women like Sarah-Jane.

Sarah-Jane and I quickly became close, speaking regularly since she first contacted me several years ago through Pink Hope. Sarah-Jane was a brilliant spokesperson for Pink Hope and was easily one of our top ambassadors. Like me, Sarah-Jane was BRCA mutation positive. She was smart and savvy. She had an incredible job—a highly sought-after global HR manager—and travelled all over the world with her work. Plus, she was in a loving relationship. Sarah-Jane had it all.

But what Sarah-Jane never had was time. No time to get sick and certainly no time to get cancer.

Sarah-Jane was still coming to terms with the recent death of her only sister from a BRCA-related breast cancer. Her sister was her best friend and her idol and, having seen her suffer so much, Sarah-Jane wasn't yet ready to deal with her own BRCA mutation positive status and to take preventative action.

It was on the day she found out she was pregnant with her first child that Sarah-Jane also learned she had breast cancer.

Krystal Barter

One of the happiest moments of her life quickly became the most terrifying.

'Make sure no one else goes through this, Krystal,' she said to me from her hospital bed soon after. 'Help them know their risks and *act*. No one should have to go through this.'

It broke my heart to see Sarah and her family suffer so much. In families like Sarah-Jane's (and like mine) there are often more cancer diagnoses than not.

Sarah-Jane gave birth to a beautiful baby boy. I remember seeing photos of him, snuggled up to his bald-headed mum who, despite being exhausted from chemo, somehow managed to give birth to this healthy little cherub. We all thought this was the start of Sarah-Jane's new life.

But soon it emerged that Sarah-Jane's cancer had spread to her spine and from there it went to her brain. Less than two years after her initial diagnosis, Sarah-Jane was terminal. Now, Sarah-Jane's family are doing all they can to make her remaining time bearable. And, while she's still here to do so, Sarah-Jane wants to spread a message of prevention to all the Pink Hopers and the broader community beyond.

Just like Tracey Ryan does. Tracey is mum to Erin (aged 26) and Leigh (aged fourteen) and, as I write this, Tracey is in the final throes of terminal breast cancer. Tracey first discovered a lump in her breast in early 2010, when she was at the Royal Children's Hospital with her son, Leigh (who is chronically ill himself and requires a bowel transplant). Tracey's lump was stage three, grade four cancer when she found it. After a lumpectomy, eight rounds of chemotherapy and, finally, a double mastectomy, Tracey's breast cancer was thought to be removed but had already spread to her spine. She has since

The Lucky One

found another large lump in her breast and, in March 2012, Tracey was told that her cancer was terminal.

Still, she hasn't let this stop her. Tracey told me she wanted to share her story on the Pink Hope website, to help and encourage others, and this is what she wrote:

Hi, my name is Tracey Ryan and I am forty-eight years young. I am married and have two children. I also have advanced breast cancer and, even though I have been told that I cannot be cured, life is good. I am still undergoing treatment and will do so for as long as I can.

I'm still very much alive and, with the help and strength of my wonderful husband and beautiful children, I intend to remain so for a long time. I look at life differently now; I try not to stress as much and I make the most of each beautiful day. I have my wonderful 'Pink Daughters' support group whom I adore and without whom I'd struggle to cope. People like these, and other special friends, get me through the inevitable tough days.

My message for you is: never surrender. Fight for as long as you can because a cure for this disease may be just around the corner. Love your family, love your friends and love your life with everything you've got.

We're women. We're strong. And life is great.

Tracey's cancer has had a devastating effect on her family (a family that has already suffered six other cases of terminal cancer) and this is one of the saddest things we see at Pink Hope: the families left behind. Tracey's husband, Andrew, and teenage son, Leigh, have both written letters to Tracey which she's kindly let me include here. This is the letter from her husband:

Krystal Barter

To my darling Tracey,

The past three years since your diagnosis have been really difficult—there's no other way to say it. The first icy feeling in the pit of my stomach came the day you rang me in Darwin to tell me you had cancer. I wanted to come home right then and there. You told me to stay until I had finished my work but that was a very long three days.

Things happened so quickly after that—or so it seemed. All of a sudden there was hospital and the chemotherapy. The decision to have the double mastectomy was frighteningly immediate. Your hair fell out quicker than I thought it would and it all got very 'real' very fast. I felt bewildered and completely helpless. Other people have cancer; not my wife; not my family. (Especially after all the other crap you'd already been through: the stroke, the hysterectomy and the brain surgery.) I couldn't accept how unfair it was.

Once I had a chance to collect my thoughts, I began to feel more confident that we would beat this thing and I felt a little better. I thought about everything positive I'd read and heard about cancer: it's not necessarily a death sentence anymore; people recover; the treatment options have advanced in leaps and bounds. Plus, you're as tough and—let's face it—as stubborn as they come, and I thought there's no way this was going to beat you. Especially as you just soldiered on, doing your thing—being a mum, over-catering at parties, being a little OCD about the state of the house, and all the other things we love about you and have a chuckle at you about sometimes.

Then came the diagnosis of the secondaries—the one in your spine and then the rib. And then the news that you were terminal. The world changed for me that day. The positives I'd read and heard

The Lucky One

about didn't feel as convincing anymore. It got even more 'real'. I actually acknowledged the possibility that I would lose my wife and our kids would lose their mum.

My first instinct was to ask you how long you had but I honestly don't know why I wanted to know, because—as you know—I tend to just deal with stuff as it comes along. When you told me that your oncologist, Romaine, had tried to tell you how long you had left and that you didn't want to know, I immediately accepted that for two reasons. Firstly, it was your call to make. And, secondly, not knowing made it more 'normal' somehow. Everyone has to die one day and we don't all know when that will happen, so why should you have to know?

I have to admit to having some very conflicting thoughts about your disease and about what was going to happen. At one point I even wondered whether it would be better for 'it' to happen quickly, so you would be beyond the pain I could see you were in (especially knowing that it was only going to get worse over time). That didn't last very long, as I mentally slapped myself, because it kind of meant that I had accepted the 'terminal' thing as inevitable. I even wondered whether I was being selfish—not wanting to watch as you got worse. But you had already decided to fight like anything so I decided that I would support you all the way.

It's been awful seeing you suffer because I can't do anything about it. That's the worst part for me. It hurts me to see your pain when I can't do anything about it. I'm supposed to look after you and protect you but I am helpless against this thing.

So the only thing I can do is try to help. And I know I often drive you nuts, asking if I can do this for you and that for you and, by the same token, it bugs me when you try to do stuff yourself that you *don't need to do. But I understand; it's part of you fighting it and not taking things lying down and not being a victim. (Still, it hurts like hell that I can do so little.)*

You've probably also noticed I've taken to swearing a lot more recently. The reason for that is simple: I swear when I am unhappy. Unhappy about what cancer has done to you and what it's doing to our family. Unhappy with the inevitable mood swings you have, with your tiredness, with sometimes having to walk on eggshells around you when you're feeling lousy—all the stuff that nobody ever seems to mention can happen. Even with how it's affected our physical relationship. It's my way of venting and of letting off steam so that I can cope. So I apologise in advance for the swearing—it will probably keep on happening.

What is also frustrating is having to think about a future without you when I really don't want to. I sometimes find myself about to ask you about funerals and contact details for people so I can tell them when the time comes but then I can't bring myself to do it because I don't want you to think about all that. (Even though I know you must think about it at times, especially when you're having a bad day.)

I want you to know something, too. Sometimes I suspect that you wonder how much I care because I don't often show my emotions. You know only too well that I bottle things up and tend to soldier on without appearing to be too upset by things. Rest assured that I care. I dread the thought of losing you, it's just that sometimes I can't bear thinking about it, let alone talk about it.

I wanted to finish this letter on a more positive note. So firstly, I want to thank you for your incredible courage and grace under fire—you are truly amazing. Part of what amazes me is your love, care and selflessness in helping others, particularly the kids

The Lucky One

and your 'Pink Sisters'. I remember in your most vulnerable moments, when you feared what was to come, that the one thing you would ask me is to promise you that I will look after the kids. Secondly, I want to thank you for your love for me—you are one of the very few people at all who ever ask me how all this is affecting me. I know I don't give much away—but I really do appreciate that you ask.

When we got our latest piece of bad news—that the cancer had spread to your lung and liver—I didn't know what to think or what to say. I watched you on the phone and saw you slump over the kitchen bench when you got the news and I went numb. When the numbness left me, I felt like I had been run over by a truck. It was the most soul-destroying moment I have ever experienced.

But since then you have amazed me even more with how you are facing up to this. I want you to know that your fight is my fight as well. Whatever it takes for you to survive past the time we have been given, we will do. We will fight tooth and nail. We will be positive. We will not wait to die; we will live. And I will be with you all the way—and whenever the day comes, I will be there with you. And I will be okay.

And, yes, I promise to look after the kids ...
With all my love,
Andrew

And from her son, Leigh:

Dear Mum,
The last couple of years have not been the nicest. But we have always stuck together and fought our way through anything this

cruel disease has thrown at us. You're one of the most beautiful people on the face of this planet; you care about others more than yourself; you go out of your way (even on your bad days) to make everyone happy. I don't know how you do it.

When you were diagnosed, it hit me pretty hard. But we talked about it and made choices, planned how we would deal with it. I was and still am very quiet, I haven't expressed my feelings that often, but that's just the way I am. After your reconstruction, I saw you in so much pain, the chemo didn't help either, it just made you look even worse. That was when I realised you were sick. You normally had this glow of... mum. That's the only way I can describe it, but that was gone during your first lot of chemo. Every night at home, I heard you crying out in pain, vomiting over and over, and I would lie in bed and cry.

Sure, the cancer made school a bit harder but we are working through it still. My mates have always been there for me, and I don't know how I would be if they were not there. Everything looked like it was going good for a while, didn't it? You were on chemo tablets, you didn't have to go in for any more operations and you looked healthier. We actually functioned as a normal family for the first time in a long while. So finding out you were terminal hit me like a ton of bricks. Just knowing that you will never be free of cancer made me feel helpless. You always put on a brave face and you tried to smile through the hard moments in the following months and, once again, I don't know how you did it.

But the other night, when Dad, Rara and I were watching TV, Dad told us that you went and saw Romaine. He told us that you were told you only had twelve to twenty-four months left with us. I just sat there silent. I knew that one day, in the distant future, we would have to say goodbye, but I always thought this would be ten

The Lucky One

or so years from now. I feel robbed; robbed of a lifetime with my beautiful mother. But I will be there for you, for as long as you decide to stick around and tell me to clean my room. Never forget that.

I love you,
Leigh

◆ ◆ ◆

Despite these kinds of personal stories, the odds were stacked against Pink Hope. Nothing else like it even *existed* in Australia so I surrounded myself with people who had good medical expertise and business nous, IT support and legal advice just to get it off the ground. Not to mention a helluva lot of time and energy on my part and the part of my family, plus the generous participation of thousands of brave high-risk women. Somehow, together, we managed to make this audacious idea work and there was only one person more surprised about it than me.

Associate Professor Judy Kirk is the director of the Familial Cancer Service at Sydney's Westmead Hospital, a position she has held for near-on twenty years. Professor Kirk specialises in genetics, caring for families whose incidence of cancer suggests a gene fault might be at play. I never met Professor Kirk as a patient, but rather I was introduced to this intelligent, articulate woman when I first dreamed up the idea of Pink Hope and was doing the rounds of Sydney hospitals trying to drum up support and seeking input from experts in the field. Professor Kirk's input was brief.

'It's a big ask,' she said when I'd finished presenting my business plan to her. 'You're a young mum, with limited time and resources, and you're operating from a knowledge base built up strictly from your own clinic appointments as a BRCA patient, is that right?'

I blushed. When she put it like that, you wouldn't back Pink Hope in a pink fit.

'I guess I'm just a little concerned,' she went on. 'I agree there's a need for this sort of community—a huge need. And I hate to be negative, especially when I can see how much work you've already put into this. But I'm just not convinced this is a task for one single person.'

Yet, despite her misgivings, Professor Kirk became an invaluable member of the Pink Hope team from day one. She gave me advice on speaking about familial cancer in public forums and helped me make sure I was using any medical terminology correctly. It was Professor Kirk who taught me to say 'B-R-C-A one' and never '*brac* one', when talking about my gene fault, and to talk about having a 'risk-reducing' and not a 'prophylactic' mastectomy. She was generous with her time and liberal with her expertise and the next time I saw Professor Kirk, at a familial cancer conference in Kingscliff, on the far north coast of New South Wales, we were both thrilled that Pink Hope had proved her initial fears wrong.

♦ ♦ ♦

'Krystal!' she called out when she spotted me standing nervously next to the stage, preparing to present to the assembled conference. The KConFab Conference (hosted by the Kathleen Cuningham Foundation Consortium for research into familial breast cancer) is an annual event and the crowd includes geneticists, clinicians, surgeons, genetic counsellors, researchers and pathologists from all over Australia and New Zealand. Telling *these* people anything new about hereditary cancer is no mean feat, especially for a girl from the Northern Beaches who never got further than six weeks into a university degree. I was daunted, to say the least. So what Professor Kirk said to me that day was a shot in the arm for my confidence at exactly the right moment.

'You did it!' she exclaimed, pointing to the hot pink folder I was clutching. The words 'Pink Hope' and a raft of purple butterflies were emblazoned on the cover. 'I don't know *how* you did it, but you did it! You actually got Pink Hope off the ground!' she said, then she turned briefly to greet Dr Kathy Tucker, clinical geneticist, who was standing with me and who Professor Kirk obviously recognised as a very familiar face in the Sydney hereditary cancer network, having worked closely together.

'You know, Kathy, when I first heard what Krystal was planning with Pink Hope, I didn't dare believe that one woman could pull it off,' Professor Kirk said. 'I'm not even sure *you* believed it, Krystal!' she added, turning to me and laughing. Then she took my hand and looked me square in the face: 'How very wrong I was, Krystal. Congratulations. What an incredible resource you've created in Pink Hope.'

Coming from such a highly regarded medical expert in her field, and someone I personally looked up to so much, this was the single proudest moment in my career.

◆ ◆ ◆

The next time I saw Professor Kirk it was at the Cancer Australia Breast Cancer Breakfast in October 2011, when the theme was familial cancer (a theme I had been petitioning them for three years to include). The two of us were presenting together—Professor Kirk as the medical expert and me as the patient—and I was far less nervous this time than I had been at the KConFab Conference in 2009. I spoke about the need for vigilance among high-risk women, and about the journey towards choosing my *own* preventative mastectomy, while the assembled guests tucked into their continental breakfasts. A few people, I noticed, looked up from their eggs and their orange juice and nodded along; one or two smiled encouragingly as I talked. Still, I could never have predicted the effect my speech may have been having. Finally, it seemed, people were beginning to understand the importance of Pink Hope.

Then, when Professor Kirk took to the microphone after me, what she said was astonishing.

'I had planned to talk to you all today about new research into the genetic mutations affecting the onset of familial cancer,' she began. Then she paused and half-turned towards me. 'But I think you'll all agree that speaking to you now, after we've just heard from Krystal, is one tough act to follow. I mean, didn't she just bring the house down?' Professor Kirk went on and I could feel my face heating up to a colour that must surely be matching my folder.

'What Krystal just gave us was a fantastically powerful and hopeful message. So many of the patients that we see each day have spent years trying to run away from the fact they have a BRCA1 or BRCA2 gene fault. Krystal's message is that "knowledge is power", and we'd all do well to pass that message on to our patients and their families. Because there's so much you can do these days to reduce your risk ...'

It was at this moment that Pink Hope finally felt real.

The Lucky One

◆ ◆ ◆

Pink Hope now has 50 000 people engaged and, at peak times, our website has received more than one million hits. We have a legion of dedicated celebrity supporters, including Whitney Port, Karl Stefanovic, Esther Anderson, Georgie Gardner, Brooke Satchwell and Laura Csortan. And since I first founded Pink Hope five years ago I've been recognised with several awards. (In 2012, I was a finalist for the Young Australian of the Year 2nd, the NSW Woman of the Year and I was an Australia Day Ambassador. I've been a finalist for the 2012 *Instyle* Audi Women of Style Awards, 2012 *Madison* Inspirational Woman, 2011 *Harpers Bazaar* Woman of Influence and 2010 Warringah Young Citizen of the Year.) I've met countless celebrities and made more media appearances than I can remember, plus the footage *60 Minutes* shot of my surgery is now being used as a resource in family cancer clinics Australia-wide.

And yet I would give this all up in a *heartbeat* if it meant sustainable funding for Pink Hope.

The publicity, the celebrities, the need for building a media profile—these things are all necessary for what we do but they mean nothing without the women of Pink Hope. Our ambassadors, the survivors, the 'previvors', and all their family and friends rallying around them: this is the true core of Pink Hope. Pink Hope may have started from a modest idea—to establish a community so high-risk families aren't alone—but one day I hope that an entire generation of women will feel supported and confident enough to make the life-changing decisions that come along with being high-risk. Every day I'm inspired by another Pink Hoper's remarkable story (truly mine pales in comparison, and I feel stupid whenever someone calls me 'brave' or 'courageous'). These women are the brave, courageous ones. Women like Rachel Rogan and Tracey Ryan. They're the reason I can never give up hope.

The other reason is Bonnie.

CHAPTER 19

Bonnie Rose, my precious, beautiful and long-desired daughter, was born in the winter of 2010. On the day Bonnie was born—an unseasonally balmy June day—it was almost twenty months to the day since I'd undergone my mastectomy and I'm not sure what was more amazing: that Chris and I were finally bringing our gorgeous baby girl into the world, or that I was still here myself. After all, if I'd pushed ahead with PGD and IVF back when I'd wanted to in 2008, then I would have necessarily put off my mastectomy, and the pre-cancerous changes detected in my breast at the time may well have developed into full-blown cancer.

Instead, here I was: new boobs and no boob cancer and blissfully bottle-feeding baby Bonnie. It seemed almost too good to be true. I may have lost my breasts but I gained my life. And my daughter's.

Only, things hadn't gone *quite* according to plan along the way to reaching this point. Not by a long shot.

You *might* say that things started to go awry around the time when, less than five months after undergoing my mastectomy, I was back putting my body through the wringer with our first attempt at IVF. Then again, you *might* say it was earlier than that. Back, perhaps, when—only one month after I completed my breast implant surgery—I woke up and decided it was time to start trying to conceive a BRCA1-negative baby. But in truth? In truth, it began even earlier than that, back when I was sitting in the inoffensively neutral office of psychologist Doctor Bronwyn Butler last year, trying to convince myself and Dr Butler that I was okay with my decision *not* to press on with IVF just then. Because I wasn't. I wasn't even *close* to okay with it. I just couldn't let go of the idea of a genetically screened embryo.

One of the main reasons for this was the fact that I was acutely aware I could have ovarian cancer looming in my not too distant future. This might sound dramatic, but women who carry a BRCA gene mutation face a 40 to 60 per cent risk of developing ovarian cancer (as Mum very nearly demonstrated). And, not only is 40 to 60 per cent far too high for my liking, ovarian cancer is a beast of a thing, considered by most medical experts as far deadlier than breast cancer because it's so damn difficult to detect. (In many cases, by the time ovarian cancer is detected, it's often too far progressed to be curable.) And while removing your breasts does seem to reduce the incidence of ovarian cancer (by up to 80 per cent, some studies suggest), it

The Lucky One

was recommended to me that I undergo a prophylactic oophorectomy (or complete removal of my ovaries) within the next five to ten years. Now, an oophorectomy is not something to be entered into lightly as it would mean I was no longer able to have children. But all the best medical advice in my personal case was: that I'd be mad not to do it, and soon. And so I felt something of a sense of urgency when it came to having more children.

As a consequence, when we started down the PGD path for the second time in less than six months, yet again it was probably too soon.

◆ ◆ ◆

'My god, Krystal, you look *terrible*! You're yellow!' Kirsty bustled into the kitchen with her *60 Minutes* camera crew in tow. She assessed me in a glance, and then quickly tried to retract what she'd just said: 'But what would I know? I'm a television producer, not a doctor. I'm sure you're doing just great, babe. Are you doing great, babe?' She plonked herself down at the kitchen table. Her crew jostled for space next to a fridge that was as chaotic outside as in. Electricity bills and council notices and letters from the P&C shouted over one another to be heard.

'Is there a little mini-Krystal cooking in there yet?' Kirsty asked, leaning over and patting my stomach encouragingly.

'Ugh, I hope so,' I grunted, flicking on the kettle and then settling down at the table with her. 'Because I'd hate to feel this bad for no reason.'

Kirsty and her crew were faithfully back following the story of our journey through PGD and IVF. After a false start last time (admittedly, a false start where we offered Kirsty a tale of genetic screening and instead gave her the ratings-winning story of my mastectomy and my unexpected brush with cancer), we were all hoping *this* story would have a happier ending.

'So you're one month in to IVF ...'

'I'm one month in,' I confirmed, trying to ignore the cameras that were capturing my every word.

'And?'

'And it's hell,' I groaned. 'Seriously, Kirsty, I don't know how women do this. I've been through childbirth, I've had my boobs lopped off, but the pain and the discomfort and the emotional upheaval of IVF is *hell*.'

'Hence you look yellow,' Kirsty said, not unkindly.

'Hence I look yellow.'

But resembling the Bananas in Pyjamas was the least of my worries. After just one cycle of IVF I was bloated and sore and crazy with hormones and I really hoped things downstairs were working because I wasn't sure I could do this again any time soon. Since Chris and I had decided to go ahead with PGD and IVF, our lives had been turned upside down. We approached Sydney IVF (now Genea) about the possibility of screening our embryos for a BRCA1-negative baby girl in February (less than four weeks after my implant surgery). By March we had started our first PGD cycle and now six months later (and more than $15 000 poorer) we were about to learn whether our attempt had been successful. I stood and walked to the bench, where I started making Kirsty's coffee.

'If it's okay with you,' Kirsty said, 'what I'd like to do today is just get some background for our story, while the crew get some footage of you and your family at home. Then one of our journalists, Tara Brown probably, should be in touch next week about setting up an interview time with you and Chris.'

I nodded. The smell of the coffee was making me nauseous. *Pregnancy? Morning sickness?* I hoped like hell it wasn't just the IVF drugs talking.

'So why don't we start with the reasons for your decision,' said Kirsty, pulling out her laptop. 'Why did you and Chris decide to try PGD?'

'Oh, that's easy,' I replied. 'After everything that had happened to our family, after all the cancer and the death and the heartbreak and the loss, I wanted to do whatever I could to cut us a break.' Kirsty nodded encouragingly. 'And if that meant conceiving a BRCA1-negative child, a new generation free from breast cancer, then I was prepared to try,' I added.

'Of course. And have doctors given you any indication of your chances of success?'

'They're good,' I said confidently. 'Using PGD, doctors have already found an embryo that doesn't carry the gene fault and this is the embryo that's implanted in me right now. And because Chris and I obviously have no issues with fertility …' Kirsty laughed. She knew I accidentally fell pregnant with Riley when I was just 21. 'Then it's more than likely that our embryo will take first time. In fact, nearly 40 per cent of all patients going through PGD are successful first time around because there are generally no fertility problems to overcome.'

'So you're sitting round waiting to see if you're up the duff?'

Now it was my turn to laugh. 'Pretty much. I had a blood test at the beginning of the week to check if I'm pregnant and I should hear back from the clinic with the results in the next day or two.'

'And so, with any luck, you and Chris will be one of the first Australian couples to use PGD to screen for a baby girl that's BRCA negative?' Here, the camera zoomed in.

'That's right. Our Bonnie will be one of the first girls ever in Australia to have been genetically chosen to live a life without BRCA/hereditary breast cancer.'

◆ ◆ ◆

Or so we thought. When the phone rang later that afternoon, as Mum and Kirsty and I sat around the kitchen table talking locations for next week's shoot, it was Sydney IVF calling to tell me that the result of my blood test had been received and that 'zero' pregnancy hormone had been detected. I wasn't pregnant. Our attempt at in vitro fertilisation had failed. I was devastated.

'I ... I don't understand,' I said, staggered. 'How could the embryo *not* take?' I never expected not to conceive. Chris and I had discussed the possibility that the screening process may not be successful, or that the embryo may not survive the transfer. (However, we knew that it had—IVF Sydney had already confirmed that.) But we'd never considered for one minute that I may not fall pregnant. It was a cruel and complete shock.

The following few weeks were a blur. I was more disappointed than I could ever have imagined. So, too, was Chris, and for the first time that I could ever remember, Chris struggled to summon his usual steely optimism. We were brittle and fragile and we mourned our little girl who never was. (Plus, we were acutely aware that we'd just spent $15 000 and not gained a thing and that this had burned through our savings

The Lucky One

at a frightening rate.) At the time, I was still wild with IVF hormones and my cycle was completely out of whack so, with this in mind, plus our dwindling finances, Chris and I decided to take a month off from IVF while we tried to piece ourselves back together.

And that's when I fell pregnant.

During our month off IVF, Chris and I had unprotected sex one Sunday afternoon after we'd returned home from taking the boys to my parents. It was the first time we'd had sex since we'd learned the IVF had failed and—who knows if it was something to do with our shared sorrow?—but we fell blissfully, thankfully, pregnant.

Of course, it wasn't lost on me and Chris that—having just spent $15 000, plus a hell of a lot more by way of blood, sweat and tears, all trying to conceive a baby through IVF—we'd gone and gotten pregnant the old-fashioned way. Fun, free and, as was our style, accidental. But nor did it escape us that, despite all our efforts to conceive a baby girl that didn't carry our family's gene fault, this unborn child had the same 50 per cent chance as Riley and Jye did of being BRCA1 mutation positive. And yet it was impossible to be anything but elated. After our IVF disappointment, after all the pain of the previous year, to be pregnant again was the most wonderful thing our family could possibly have hoped for.

◆ ◆ ◆

On the day of our eighteen-week ultrasound, when we elected to find out the gender of our baby, I immediately burst into tears at the result.

Krystal Barter

'A girl?' I exclaimed, as I smiled and I sobbed. *After all that we'd tried to do to spare this baby from breast cancer, I couldn't believe we were having a little girl.*

'Krystal! It's okay,' soothed Chris, squeezing my hand as I lay on the ultrasound bed, my swollen belly smeared with cold jelly. 'It'll be alright, I promise.'

'Alright?' I managed through my tears. 'It's a little girl! This is more than alright! It's the most wonderful thing I could ever have wished for!'

And it was. Despite the risks, despite the pain that might lie in the future, to be pregnant with a little girl was everything I had dreamed of. Together Chris and I stared at the wriggling, squirming, black and white image on the screen in front of us in wonder. Finally, we had our Bonnie Rose.

❖ ❖ ❖

As her parents, Chris and I made the decision *not* to have Bonnie tested for the BRCA gene in utero (using pre-natal genetic diagnosis). Nor will we have her tested during her childhood. If Bonnie wants to find out about her BRCA status, then she can choose to do so when she's a consenting adult; it's not something either Chris or I will force on her. It's her body and her choice and we will support her, whatever she decides. Of course, we will always be there to talk to Bonnie about her family genetics, the topic will never be taboo and we'll offer her all the knowledge and the information that we have. Moreover, we'll encourage her to be proactive about her health and to seriously consider getting a gene test when she thinks she's ready. But it's not something we feel we can decide *for* her. And if Bonnie *does*

The Lucky One

turn out to be BRCA1 positive and she *does* have to undergo the same surgery as me, well, our family will be there every step of the way.

Even now, when Bonnie is not quite four years old, I look at her and think: Will Bonnie walk the same path as me? Will her journey be the same or is it just possible she's escaped the curse? Chris reckons it doesn't matter because she'll have us to support her and my experiences to reflect on. In fact, she may even read this book one day and, who knows, it might just help. (Although, she should feel free to skip the first few chapters describing my teenage years. Say, the first twenty-odd years of my life, perhaps Bonnie?) I created Pink Hope especially for Bonnie, and for all the other little girls out there just like her who will grow up in the shadow of hereditary cancer. Hopefully, Pink Hope will mean Bonnie's journey will be a less lonely, less isolating experience. And when she's ready to start asking questions, the Pink Hope community will be there to answer them.

When I look into Bonnie's face, I don't see any gene fault; I don't see a DNA code. I see my funny, charming, spontaneous daughter and I could never imagine any other. Chris and I still have a frozen embryo in storage that's guaranteed BRCA1 negative, but we're reluctant to ever use it. Going through PGD and IVF, even once, was enough to make us realise how lucky we are to even have a child and we will never, ever take that for granted. And in just the same way that having such a strong bond with my mum means that I would go through breast surgery twenty times over in order to have been born her daughter, I only hope that one day Bonnie feels the same about me. Regardless of the genetic inheritance I gift her.

And, who knows? Maybe Bonnie won't carry our gene fault. Wouldn't that be wonderful? But right now Bonnie is busy being a beautiful little girl without a care in the world and that's exactly the way it should be. Perhaps, in the future, there will be medical advancements enough to change Bonnie's fortunes? Or perhaps she will follow in my (tentatively trailblazing) footsteps? Either way, Bonnie will continue what I've begun in breaking our family's cycle of cancer.

CHAPTER 20

Where I *do* hope Bonnie's story differs from mine, if not with breast *cancer*, is with breasts. With any luck Bonnie will avoid having to undergo a preventative mastectomy like I did. This might be through genetic good fortune; it might be through advancements in medical alternatives. But whatever the path her life takes I can only wish, in the eventuality she does require breast implants, that Bonnie's are better than mine.

This was no reflection on Dr Megan Hassall, mind you. Megan did an amazing job with my initial request and with the technology available at the time. Still, having had dramas with my drains, not to mention being so disappointed with my eventual implants, the final hiccup came, about a year after my last breast surgery, when one of my implants rotated, flipped and moved.

In my sleep. Picture this: You go to bed with a pair of normal, matching, apparently happy boobs and you wake up with ... one?

'Oh my god, Chris! Where's my breast gone?' I rifled through our bedsheets frantically as if the runaway boob might be asleep in there with the covers pulled up over its head, while the rest of my body had woken up for the day.

'Wha—your breast? *Gone?*' Chris was yanked awake in the cruellest of ways. (Well, second cruellest. Waking up to find you are missing a body part probably shades it.)

'Yes!' I screeched. 'My breast, my left breast. It's missing!'

And it was. Where yesterday an implant had sat fair and square on the left side of my chest, now there was nothing. Just loose skin. After a brief panicked search, I located my boob camped out upstate, underneath my armpit. It seems my implant had rotated and flipped during the night, popping out of its socket and leaving me flat on one side.

'Does it hurt? Are you in pain?'

'No,' I admitted, grudgingly, once I'd calmed down a little (and woken up some more). 'But how the hell did *this* happen?' I was unimpressed to say the least.

◆ ◆ ◆

As it turned out, 'this' happened when your implants were inserted in an era before traction technology. Nowadays, anyone with lovely, perky silicone sacs can be assured that their breast implants will remain just that: *breast* implants. (As opposed to the armpit variety I was now sporting.) This is because new, textured breast implants are now available that are rough to touch on the outer surface of the implant, practically like sandpaper, and that therefore grip onto your breast cavity. My implants, however, were inserted before adhesive implants were commonplace which meant that during my (apparently energetic) sleep I'd somehow managed to dislodge one from my chest and I now had a boob tucked under my arm.

And, sure, I can see the comedic value *now*. But let me tell you, I wasn't laughing back then because it was a week before I could have surgery to have it corrected. *A week*. Which is a long time for anyone to be walking around with a C-cup wobbling about in your armpit. The phrase 'tuck-shop-lady-arms' took on a whole new meaning and shaving my armpits was a veritable obstacle course by the time I'd dodged the silicone. After everything that I'd been through with my mastectomy and my drains and my expanders and my reconstruction, surely *this* had to be the least sexy of them all?

And so one long week after my left breast left home, I was admitted to North Shore Private Hospital to have both of my breast implants replaced. At the time Bonnie was only seven months old but, as I was unable to breastfeed her as a result of my mastectomy, there was nothing preventing me from having the surgery straight away. And the results were amazing.

My new breasts were 'unveiled' while I was still in hospital. The only people present were Dr Megan Hassall (my ever-faithful plastic surgeon) and my mum and, consequently, the whole affair had the feel of some secret-women's-business ceremony. As I stood nervously next to my starched hospital bed, Megan gently and tenderly unwrapped the bandages from my chest while Mum looked on, holding her breath.

'Wow!' Mum exclaimed once I was exposed. 'They look fantastic!'

Krystal Barter

In my family we refer to breasts as a life-force of their own. It's never '*You* look fantastic' or '*I* feel fantastic', but rather 'they', the breasts, as if they are independent from the rest of you. I guess there's a natural distancing that comes with such traitors as our breasts tend to be. But *fantastic*? Was she sure? While I could generally rely on Mum to be brutally honest (prior to my corrective surgery, Mum described my mismatched breasts thus: 'They used to look like two bright shining headlights but now one has its blinker on and is turning left up and into your armpit ...'), I wasn't so confident now. More than anyone, Mum could see how fragile I was at that moment and I knew she'd be quick to compliment. Instead, I turned to Megan for an honest appraisal.

'Bloody fantastic,' Megan confirmed.

And while this was not quite the clinical assessment I was expecting, it was more than fine with me.

'Really?' I asked dubiously, as I moved towards the mirror.

'Really!' they chorused, and I had to admit they were right. Staring back at me from my semi-naked, reflected image were two perfectly formed, high-set, infinitely feminine D-cups. *My* D-cups. I was thrilled. I fell in love with them the instant I saw them. It was as if they were the breasts I was meant to be born with. After months of surgeries and injections and pain, after years of fear and anxiety and rage, I had at last reached a place I wasn't sure I ever would again: I felt beautiful.

CHAPTER 21

In the eighteen months following my corrective breast surgery, my breasts stayed (mercifully) put. No leaving home; no life on the road; no popping out for some milk and bread never to return again. They were well-behaved and all-accounted for, their wandering spirit having been well and truly quashed. In fact, the only one adding any stamps to their passport at this time (and for practically the first time ever, I might add) was me.

I never *intended* to go on a wildly ambitious and terribly glamorous tour of the United States, let me make that clear from the outset. I'm a homebody and quite happy to be. I had never travelled much before—never been further than across the ditch to visit my extended family in New Zealand—and what's more I'd never had any real desire to do so. Apart from our (aborted) holiday to Phuket, I'd never wanted to go anywhere much. Consequently, when one of Pink Hope's most generous sponsors, and a major international cosmetics company, suggested I jet off State-side as an international envoy to create a USA–Aussie global alliance for high-risk women, well, I was more astonished than anyone else. It went a little something like this:

Me: Milk? Sugar?

Janet from a major international cosmetics company: White with one, thanks.

Me: And is skimmed milk okay?

Janet: Lovely, thanks. Krystal, how would you feel about flying to the USA as an international envoy to create a US–Aussie support network for high-risk women?

Me: Astonished; that's how I'd feel. [Pause] You said 'yes' to sugar, didn't you?

◆ ◆ ◆

I didn't for one second think Janet was serious. I mean, who pops in for a coffee and to discuss the sponsorship details of Bright Pink Lipstick Day and then casually pulls out a free ticket to the States from behind their ear? It was too much. No one organisation could be that generous and no one woman that supportive. But Janet was, and so before I knew it I was renewing my passport and labelling luggage tags and preparing to fly out to America.

The trip was to be something of a cultural exchange. Dubbed the 'Tour of Hope', I would kick things off with four days in New York where I would meet my American sister and all-round

The Lucky One

hero, Lindsay Avner, founder of Pink Hope's USA counterpart, Bright Pink. Together, Lindsay and I would attend fundraising events, meet with sponsors, do the rounds of publicity and, finally, attend New York Fashion Week with Bright Pink's sponsor, TRESemmé. Then, it was off to Chicago and to Bright Pink's HQ where Lindsay and I would talk strategy, pool resources and just generally combine forces to create a more united front in the fight against breast and ovarian cancer. I could *not* wait. Only, there was one small hitch: my pathological fear of flying.

Telling me to cross the Pacific in a plane was like instructing me to fly to the moon. Flapping my own arms. Sure, I may have volunteered to have my own breasts removed and I may have undergone multiple reconstruction surgeries; I might have given birth three times and, yeah, there was the time I had my knee reconstructed, too. But step foot on a modern aircraft? Are you *kidding*? It was near-impossible for me to consider and even more implausible for me to go ahead and do. Even after my ticket had been purchased, my itinerary finalised and my bags packed, I still wasn't sure I had the guts to see this thing through. Could I really swallow my fear (along with some heavy-duty sleeping tablets) and get onboard? It would be terrible to disappoint Janet, and worse to disappoint Lindsay (who was so super-excited you'd think it was Hanukah and New Year's Eve and her birthday all rolled into one). But I would rather be a disappointment than an episode of *Air Crash Investigation*. And so, despite what I was telling everyone around me, my mind wasn't made-up *at all*.

❖ ❖ ❖

And I might still be dithering over the decision even now, if it wasn't for Pink Hopers, Sophie and Amy. Like me, Sophie is a previvor who had surgery after learning she was BRCA positive. Amy, on the other hand, has terminal cancer. The three of us were chatting over lunch one day, in the nervous lead-up to my flight, when Sophie casually leaned back in her chair and asked me if I'd packed my cancer card.

'My cancer—*wha?*'

'Your cancer card. I never leave home without it,' she said. 'You should definitely try it,' she suggested to Amy.

Amy had no idea what she was talking about and said so.

'You're *joking*!' Now it was Sophie's turn to be dumbstruck. 'You've never flashed your cancer card?'

And with that, Sophie came over all misty-eyed as she animatedly explained the 'cancer card' system to Amy and me, talking with the passion of an evangelical.

The 'cancer card' was a pass to better service. Whether an aisle seat on a plane or a discount on a bill, an upgrade in a restaurant or a leg-up in a queue, Sophie simply mentioned the fact she was receiving pro-active treatment for breast cancer, smiled nicely and waited for the sweeteners to roll in.

'I like to think of it as the universe spoiling me in some way,' she explained prosaically and I couldn't stop laughing.

'You really do this? You really tell people about your cancer gene in order to get a golden ticket?'

She shrugged, as if it were the most obvious thing in the world.

'You know what? That's so awesome!' Amy agreed.

And it was. Because I'd seen the god-awful things Amy and others had been through with cancer and she bloody deserved any good things she could come by. But that wasn't what

The Lucky One

impressed me most. What impressed me was Sophie's amazing attitude. Because it wasn't like she was saying: 'My life sucks and the cosmos *owes* me something because I've got a cancer gene.' Rather, she was on the lookout for fun and harmless ways to make her everyday life more bearable despite the hardships she faced. The things she scammed didn't hurt anyone, they didn't cost anyone (other than those corporations that could afford it), and they showed what an all-round positive outlook she had on life. And it was this outlook that made me realise I could get on a plane. I mean, if Sophie could stare down cancer with such good humour and positivity, then surely I could find it within myself to accept a free ticket to the USA? I just had to pull myself together, pull on my flight socks (no point dying of deep-vein thrombosis, right?) and get onboard that plane.

◆ ◆ ◆

In the end, that's exactly what I did. On 1 September 2012, I boarded a flight bound for LAX. I didn't use the cancer card, mind you. I couldn't have brought myself to do that when there were women out there like Amy who deserved it so much more than me. And, anyway, I didn't need to; not when Janet and her people were taking such good care of me. I did, however, think of Sophie as I gritted my teeth and made my way tentatively along the boarding bridge towards the plane, my hand running along the side wall of the tunnel all the way. I wanted to stay connected *terra firma* until the last possible second. Moments earlier, as I'd hugged Chris and the kids and Mum and Dad goodbye, Mum had bawled at the sight of her baby girl jetting off overseas on her own for the first time.

(Sure, her baby girl may have been 29 years old but *you* trying telling that to Mum and her clutch of tissues.)

And so I boarded a fourteen-hour flight to Los Angeles, followed by a transfer to the domestic terminal, and then a six-hour flight to New York. For a normal human being this would be a chore but for someone with as limited travel experience as I had, I may as well have been scaling Everest. Just negotiating my way to the domestic terminal from LAX was life-changing in itself. But what an exhilarating experience! It feels silly to admit it, but getting myself from Sydney to New York on my own, and in one piece, is one of the greatest achievements of my adult life. Conquering my fear, and going it alone without my family around me for the first time ever, was a very big deal to me at the time.

And do you know what I discovered? I discovered that I wasn't really afraid of flying at all. In fact, I quite liked it. I could stretch out and watch a movie and have someone offer *me* snacks (instead of the other way around), all of which are novel when you're a mum to three young children. No; I realised I wasn't really *afraid* of flying, I had just never entertained the possibility before. That might sound strange in a culture like ours, where anyone over the age of eighteen, and therefore legally able to hold a passport *and* to drink, celebrates this happy coincidence by booking themselves on a Contiki tour of some far-off destination. But I had never thought I could go travelling. I had never thought I could do a great many things in life, apart from one day, inevitably, get cancer. In fact, I had always avoided thinking about the future because I never seriously thought that I had one.

But now that I had braved a double mastectomy and been given my breast-cancer-get-out-of-jail-free-card, I was just beginning to see the possibilities in life. Suddenly, I had a great many opportunities ahead of me and travel, apparently, was one of them.

As we began our descent into the city that never sleeps, at just a little before midnight local time, I was overwhelmed with emotion and with the sight of more brilliant, twinkling lights than I had ever seen in my life. *I did it! I actually did it!* I thought. By the time I had stepped off that plane and negotiated customs and found myself alone and alive in New York City, I felt as if I could do anything. Cancer be damned, I was taking my life back, one bite of the Big Apple at a time.

◆ ◆ ◆

The next two weeks were a blur of supersized American amazingness. That, and a lot of pink. Meeting Lindsay was by far the highlight of my trip and we hit it off in person even more than we did online. 'Oh, say that again! You Au*ss*ie's are so cute!' was her constant refrain and she seemed just as enthralled with my Northern Beaches twang as I was with her Chicago drawl. 'You're my little Au*ss*ie sister!' she'd say, giving 'Aussie' that soft 's' sound that only Americans do. But it wasn't all fun and names; Lindsay and I had some serious schmoozing to do.

We visited the cosmetic company's Park Avenue headquarters, where I proudly showed off the photos of Pink Hope's recent Bright Pink Lipstick Day. We met with the editors of *US Weekly* magazine and *Women's Health* magazine, to discuss the issue of hereditary cancer and to talk all things pink. And we spent time with Bright Pink's sponsor, TRESemmé, planning for the year ahead. It was a whirlwind of a trip, highlighted by the fact that I only spied Times Square, home of my beloved Broadway, from behind the dirty glass window of a yellow New York cab as Lindsay and I careened past on our way to our next appointment. We did, however, find time in our busy schedule to pop into New York Fashion Week to see UK fashion designer Jenny Packham's show.

'Oh my god, that's *Joan Rivers*!' I squealed to Lindsay, clutching her arm as the acerbic octogenarian tottered past the catwalk. 'I *love* Joan Rivers!'

'And look! Argh! There's the *E! News* team!' (*E! News* was—still is—my sole source of daily news and current affairs so to see them filming in the same room as me was like watching *Live from the Red Carpet* being enacted for my benefit.)

Later in the week, the two of us headed west to Chicago where I stayed with Lindsay at her home and visited the Bright Pink offices. My time spent at Bright Pink was invaluable and I learnt loads about how Lindsay and the girls created public awareness around the BRCA1 and BRCA2 gene mutations and how they ran their various programs. I sat in on meetings and took copious notes and spent hours talking to Bright Pink's programs coordinator, Mary-Kate. And, most important of all, during my five days in Chicago, Lindsay and I came up with plenty of ideas for strengthening our pink global alliance.

And so, on the final night of my trip, we went out for a celebratory drink (or two). Now, this was no ordinary drink (or two). No, we celebrated that night at RPM Italian restaurant Illinois, part-owned by *E! News* co-anchor Giuliana Rancic. Not only is Giuliana a journalist of some repute, she's also a breast cancer survivor and an ambassador for Bright Pink and to say I'm something of an obsessive fan is putting it lightly.

The Lucky One

I *adore* her to a point that's probably not healthy for a grown woman to adore another woman she's never met. Total girl crush. And as Lindsay and I sat at the bar of this achingly hip River North hotspot, all chrome and black and silver and fabulousness, I only wished I had my childhood autograph book with me.

'You know the menu includes a bunch of dishes inspired by Giuliana's mum, Mama DePandi?' Lindsay said casually, sipping her mojito.

'No! Which ones? Do you know? We'll have to order one in case Giuliana is in the restaurant tonight and she reads our order in the kitchen. Or, imagine if she came over to talk to you about Bright Pink or something and saw us eating one of her mum's own recipes …'

'Oh. My. God. Could you be any more of a stalker?' Lindsay teased me and laughed.

'That's easy for you to say,' I said haughtily. 'Just because you and *Giuliana Rancic* are BFFs.' We were both talking too loudly now, as we were several mojitos in, and the other patrons at the bar turned and looked at me when I made this last pronouncement.

'Shhh.' Lindsay laughed again. And then: 'Oh, hey!' she said, and waved as she spied someone she knew at the end of the bar. 'Hey Mama DePandi! Hey Papa DePandi!'

It was my turn to laugh now. 'Hey Papa DePandi!' I mimicked, and then I turned to see who she was really waving to.

Oh. My. God. It was *Papa DePandi! And his wife!* My idol's parents wandered out of the kitchen as if it were the most natural thing in the world for them to be here. (Which, on reflection, I guess it was, given it was their daughter's restaurant and all, and they were involved in planning the menu. At the time, however, I would have been less surprised to see Santa Clause saunter into the bar.) Lindsay grabbed my hand and dragged me over to meet them.

'Mama DePandi, Papa DePandi, this is Krystal Barter. From Australia. Krystal's here in the States to do some work for her cancer charity, Pink Hope.'

'Nice to meet you,' Giuliana's parents smiled warmly. I grinned like a maniac and shook their arms off.

'What an amazing coincidence that you're in the restaurant tonight,' I enthused. 'I can't believe my luck!'

Giuliana's parents smiled politely.

'I'm such a huge fan of your daughter; I can't begin to tell you …' I began but Papa DePandi cut me short.

'Oh, of course. You should meet her,' he said, and with that he casually motioned to a nearby table where Giuliana and her husband, Bill, were sat as if placed there like guests on her *E! News* set.

'Wow! Oh, wow!' I gushed. 'Giuliana! Bill! It's such a pleasure to meet you!' I was so star-struck that entire solar systems were hurtling by. *I was meeting Giuliana Rancic! And her family!*

'I don't suppose I could get a photo, could I?' I asked shyly. The girls back in the Pink Hope office *had* to see this. And so Giuliana and her family generously posed as Lindsay took several photos of me with Giuliana and Bill.

When it was all over, and Giuliana and her family had gone back to the business of running a restaurant (and after I had run to the bathroom and phoned my assistant, Rebecca, back in

The Lucky One

Sydney and excitedly reported that I'd just met Giuliana Rancic, which resulted in Rebecca bursting into tears and wishing she was with me), I turned to Lindsay to try and explain what this trip to visit her meant to me, but I didn't know where to start. I had to thank her for tonight; to thank her for the last ten days; and to thank her for everything she'd ever done to inspire me and help me and set me on my journey towards Pink Hope. I had to thank her, in short, for helping me to see that being BRCA positive could also be empowering. I owed her a helluva lot. And then when I thought she could surprise me no more, Lindsay had just brought a little Hollywood glamour to my life.

Only, I never expected some of it to follow me home.

CHAPTER 22

Is there anything less fabulous than the afternoon school run? You know the drill. There's the blasting car horns, the scramble for parking, the minibus-sized piece of 'art' that Child A has created and wants you to hold-slash-admire or, even worse, *wear* as you struggle under the weight of two schoolbags and—*who owns this sports kit?*—all the while frantically trying to shepherd Child A, Child B and Toddler C back to your vehicle. Invariably it will rain. Or you'll run into *that* mother from reading groups, *that* father from the canteen committee, or *that* child from your son's soccer team and somehow you'll find yourself railroaded into helping out with the charity sausage sizzle, the canteen fundraising sausage sizzle or the end-of-season gala day sausage sizzle this

The Lucky One

Saturday morning. (Again, probably in the rain.) The whole school pick-up thing couldn't be further from the Hollywood Hills you were sneakily reading about in *OK Magazine* in the car only five minutes ago. And yet, on this day, a little glimmer of Hollywood glamour reached out from the pages of my glossy mag and tapped me on the shoulder.

A little glamour in the (very shapely) form of Angelina Jolie.

◆ ◆ ◆

'Riley! Can you grab Mummy's phone—quick, it's ringing!' I leaned sideways so that Riley could pull my vibrating mobile from out of my jeans pocket for me. As I did, the two school-bags and one child balanced in my arms wobbled precariously. The words 'blocked number' flashed on the screen of my phone. I love a blocked number. There's always a few precious seconds there where I wonder if it's some wildly wealthy benefactor calling up to donate squillions to Pink Hope.

'Thanks, darling,' I said to Riley, bending down further so that he could hold the phone up to my ear. We staggered along like this as Riley hit 'answer' for me. Then I bellowed, 'Jye, don't run too far ahead!' at the same time as Riley got the phone close enough to my mouth for me to deafen the person on the other end.

'Sorry! Sorry!' I said. 'I wasn't talking to you ... my son ... school run,' I finished lamely.

The voice on the other end of the line laughed. 'Tell me about it,' she said, and then she got straight down to business. 'Krystal, it's Kasey, producer, *Mornings*. We need you in-studio first thing tomorrow morning. Wear pink. Can you do it?'

Could I appear on Network Nine's *Mornings*, one of the highest-rating morning shows in the country? And, no doubt, in relation to Pink Hope and hereditary cancer? Hell, I could! Money couldn't buy that sort of publicity for our cause. Plus, I'd been on *Mornings* with Sonia Kruger and David Campbell before and it was always a hoot. But *first thing*? In morning-television parlance that meant *I-should-still-be-sleeping-o'clock* no matter which way you sliced it.

Still, I was about to tell the producer I would be there whatever-the-hell time she wanted, when what she said next floored me: 'We had an alert come through on the newswire seven minutes ago. Angelina Jolie is BRCA1 mutation positive.'

'What?' I said loudly, stopping dead in my tracks, causing my camel-train of children to come to a jerky halt. *Angelina Jolie was BRCA1 mutation positive?* This was huge.

'Yeah, BRCA1. That's your gene, isn't it?' asked the producer, unintentionally gifting the human race's BRCA1 cancer gene to me. 'Well, Ange's positive, too, and she's written an op-ed piece for the *New York Times* revealing she's had a preventative double mastectomy. Although, god knows how she kept *that* quiet …' She said this a little wistfully, no doubt thinking about the missed scoop, but I was busy feeling for Angelina. Sure, she might live a million, trillion light-years away from the rest of us, in her ivory tower with Brad Pitt (*Brad Pitt!*) and all those gorgeous children. Yeah, she was beautiful and successful and wealthy and perfect, but she would have gone through *hell* with her BRCA1 diagnosis and mastectomy. Just like the rest of us Pink Hopers. Suddenly, life from the pages of *OK Magazine* didn't look so glossy after all.

I agreed to the details of tomorrow morning's interview with Kasey and hung up the phone promising to look out for the 'script' she would email me that evening. (Most morning television shows are scripted to avoid anything too offensive or contentious going to air; anything that might leave viewers choking into their Earl Grey at morning tea. While I would have scope to share my opinions on hereditary cancer, the questions, and even the general direction I should take my answers, would be drafted in advance.)

As the kids and I made our way back to the car that afternoon, media outlets around the globe were already running wild with the news that Angelina Jolie was BRCA1 mutation positive. Hers were arguably the most lauded pair of breasts in the world so the fact they had now been lost to a preventative mastectomy was headline-making. So, too, was the BRCA gene. Or the 'Jolie Gene' as it instantly became known.

Angelina Jolie's opinion piece in the *Times* was published on 14 May 2013 and the world of hereditary cancer has never been the same since. No amount of education or funding or charity work or research dollars could ever have thrust the BRCA gene into the global spotlight the way that one woman did. Of course, since finding out she was BRCA1 positive, Angelina's world would never be the same, either, and I really felt for her and for her young family. Even though her surgery was a success, and even though she may well have avoided breast cancer, I understood what a traumatic decision a preventative mastectomy must have been for her and her family. Going public was an incredibly brave thing for her to do, not to mention an incredibly generous one, and I only hope she realises what a positive impact she's had. Angelina's decision to 'bare all' about her battle with the breast cancer gene had ramifications far greater than anyone could ever have expected and so, following her announcement, the next 48 hours became the busiest of my life.

◆ ◆ ◆

'You know, you've always reminded me a little of Ange,' Chris said, as he sat on the couch, mobile phone in one hand, landline phone in the other and a Pink Hope clipboard balanced in his lap.

Angelina Jolie? Well, sure, I thought, surveying the lounge room which was littered with half-empty cereal bowls and video game consoles and small children draped across various pieces of well-worn furniture. My gaze ended at my own, ugg-booted feet. There was a toothpaste stain on one of the boots. Me and Angelina did have alarmingly similar lives, it was true.

'We're both humans,' I conceded. Then I turned back to the run-sheet in front of me. The A4 page of scrawl detailed the radio interviews I had scheduled—at five-minute intervals—for the coming two days. Then there were the TV appearances, the interviews with the *Australian* and the *Sydney Morning Herald* newspapers, plus the various bits and pieces requested by online media outlets, too. Since Angelina's revelations about her breasts, my own boobs had become big news locally and I was working around the clock in the hope of drumming up some publicity for Pink Hope.

'No, really,' Chris persisted. 'You and Ange were both "wild childs", weren't you? And then you both transformed yourselves from teen delinquents into crusading charity queens. And now you're both BRCA1 mutation positive.'

The Lucky One

'Oh, and here I was thinking you meant we're both incredibly good looking,' I joked (but not pausing to look up from my schedule, all the while flicking through emails on my mobile at the same time). 'But if you're strictly talking charity,' I added, 'I'm not sure my work with Pink Hope is *quite* on par with Ange's role as Special Envoy for the UN High Commissioner ...'

Chris threw a cushion at me in disgust. 'Don't belittle what you've achieved with Pink Hope,' he admonished, as the pillow bounced off the side of my unsuspecting head.

'Fine. But how about a little less of the *teenage delinquent*, thanks!' I threw the cushion back at him. 'I may have, um—' Here, I stopped and glanced at the kids who were, thankfully, glued to the TV and ignoring our conversation. 'I may have had a little *fun* in my time. But I never wore a vial of anyone's blood around my neck!'

Chris laughed and dropped the cushion to the ground. 'A little fun, Krystal? I don't think even Ange and Brad, with their Hollywood lifestyles, have *ever* had as much "fun" as you did! I'm just glad you found other ways to enjoy yourself.'

◆ ◆ ◆

We were interrupted by a striking figure walking into the room brandishing a mobile phone and a tube of pink lipstick: 'Krystal, ABC's *7.30* phoned to say they'll be here in ten minutes. Oh, and I found your lipstick—it was in Bonnie's Dora the Explorer lunchbox. Is cleaning out Bonnie's lunchbox part of my job description?'

I smiled gratefully. It was Kim and cleaning out Bonnie's lunchbox was definitely *not* part of her job description. In fact, nothing was. Kim Lockyer was a Pink Hope ambassador, a breast-cancer survivor and a generous volunteer who dropped by the Pink Hope office from time to time to give us a hand filing or answering emails or whatever else we happened to be snowed under with at the time. Now (in addition to being Bonnie's kitchenhand) Kim had very kindly offered to help coordinate the media mayhem in the wake of Angelina's bombshell. Given our house had been turned into Pink Hope media HQ, and given Pink Hope had neither a publicist nor an agent nor a media adviser of *any* description at that point, Kim was a godsend. As were, as always, Chris and Mum, both of whom had been glued to their phones helping out from the instant this thing kicked off.

'And after *7.30* has left,' Kim continued, 'you've got crews from *Seven News* and *Ten News at Five* swinging by. Plus, that guy from SBS *World News*. Here, wanna see the full list?'

I glanced at Kim's outstretched phone and saw it was true; somehow my quaint Californian bungalow was to become a makeshift media hub for all the major networks that day. I suddenly felt overwhelmed.

'And did you get that message from *The Project*?' Chris asked. 'It came through when you were at the Channel Nine studios this morning …'

'Uh, no … I think I wrote down the number here for—wait …' I began rifling through papers in front of me when my mobile sprang to life in my hand. 'Hello, Krystal Barter speaking …' I shrugged at Chris to indicate I couldn't find the message he was talking about but he was already absorbed in his own notes, no doubt making sure I was prepped for the next media interview. Who knew the 'Jolie Gene' would be so very contagious?

The Lucky One

♦ ♦ ♦

Forty minutes later we'd cleared the lounge room of children (and their associated breakfast cereal bowls) and I was being interviewed for ABC television's flagship current affairs program, *7.30*. The reporter, Adam Harvey, had a deep baritone voice that was not unlike that of his late father, respected journalist Peter Harvey. Adam began his report by saying: 'If anyone can raise awareness about a difficult subject, it's Angelina Jolie.' I couldn't have agreed more.

'You know, the scary thing is,' I said to Adam, 'about a week or so ago I was feeling frustrated by the difficulties faced by my charity, Pink Hope. And I commented to my husband: "It's just so hard to get funding. What we need is a major celebrity, someone like, I don't know, Angelina Jolie, to get onboard and get involved. She could make our gene fault famous and for all the right reasons …"'

It was true I'd had this exact conversation with Chris only a week or so earlier. I'd actually mentioned Angelina Jolie and all that. But what I *didn't* say to Adam, while the cameras were rolling, was that I had this conversation with Chris *every week*.

Because, while business was booming insofar as we had more women than ever visiting the Pink Hope website and becoming active members of the 'Pink' community, the truth was, we were broke. Almost five months earlier to the day, at Christmas 2012, I was ready to close the doors on Pink Hope because of insufficient funding. We could barely cover our (modest) costs. Charity donations in general were down, but Pink Hope had suffered near-fatally that Christmas as we'd parted ways with the National Breast Cancer Foundation (NBCF). The NBCF was a much larger, much more powerful organisation than ours. It had millions (and deservedly so). By comparison, we were turning over just $100 000 at that point. Pink Hope had been under the auspices of the NBCF since our inception in 2008 but a change of management at the NBCF meant that it no longer wished to be affiliated with us and we, in return, could no longer retain our sponsorship with it. It was an amicable parting, but brutal all the same (our family had raised thousands for the NBCF during our four years together). But more than hurt feelings, the separation hurt our hip pocket and ever since then Pink Hope had been battling to survive.

Things came to a head early in 2013 when I was due to apply for DGR (deductible gift-recipient) status with the tax office. Previously, Pink Hope had always sat under the umbrella of the NBCF but now I had to decide whether or not we thought we could make it on our own. After several weeks of agonising I finally bit the bullet and applied (and was granted) DGR status. Up until that week, however, I wasn't sure I had made the right decision. Funds were dangerously low, benefactors were thin on the ground and, for much of the year, I wondered whether our DGR status was worth the paper it was written on.

The instant the 'Jolie Gene' hit the headlines, however, Pink Hope's future began to look up. Amazing publicity and media attention aside, our funding increased markedly. Then, there was the fact that so many others in the sector rallied around us in support. The McGrath Foundation, for instance, showed such generosity of spirit by directing any media enquiries our way. (This is one of Australia's leading breast cancer support organisations, founded by cricketer Glenn McGrath in memory of his amazing wife, Jane McGrath, who died of breast cancer in 2008. While the foundation doesn't strictly look after those in the high-risk community, it could easily have swallowed up some of the media attention that was on offer the week Angelina Jolie announced her mastectomy. Instead, the McGrath Foundation pointed the media in our direction and I'll always be grateful for the support it showed us back then.) Cancer Australia, a government-run body headed up by Professor Helen Zorbas AO, did likewise.

Then there was the (frankly heart-warming) response from Pink Hope's celebrity supporters and ambassadors. The divine Mia Freedman ran our story on her website, *mamamia*, before taking the time to email me personally: *You've been such a beacon of light and—yes, hope this week. Congratulations on all that you've done and the rightful attention you've been receiving, xxxxxx*

But most amazing of all was the response from the high-risk women of Australia; the very women Pink Hope was created to help. Our membership base *doubled* in the five days after Angelina's announcement, and the number of families accessing our charity increased by more than 700 per cent. Women from all over the country got in touch to share their stories or join our community or just show support for others. It was truly something to behold. I couldn't keep up with all the messages of love and encouragement and, each and every time my inbox pinged or my phone vibrated, I silently thanked Angelina for what she'd done.

And of all the messages we received at Pink Hope that week, this one from Gena (who is also BRCA1 mutation positive) will stick with me forever:

Krystal Barter

Dear Pink Hope,

I have just spent the best part of the day reading all the information on this great website. How is it that I have all day to do this? Well, I am in hospital recovering from a bilateral mastectomy that was performed four days ago. Performed, in fact, on the very day that Angelina made her own mastectomy announcement to the world. The timing was opportune and I am thankful for the sudden interest in the subject. Previously, I had only told my close friends and some family members that I was undertaking a mastectomy. I was evasive to my work colleagues and most people in my wider circle just thought I was being hospitalised for 'women's problems'.

After Angelina's story broke I thought to myself: 'Why am I being secretive? Why can't I, like Angelina, tell the world?' So I did.

Twelve hours after my operation, when I was high on medication and wide awake at 3 a.m., I started to write my story and I've since published it on my Facebook page. The loving, supportive comments I have received from friends (and from strangers all over the globe) has been a tower of strength for me. It even gave me the courage to share my story with my work colleagues. Again, the response has been amazing and I know this has helped me immensely in my psychological and physical recovery.

I was watching the Morning *show on Friday when Krystal was being interviewed about how she set up Pink Hope. I immediately wrote the website details down. I only wish I had seen the site months ago, in the lead-up to my mastectomy, as I was accessing lots of information on the web but it was mostly from the United States (and not in the user-friendly format of Pink Hope's site).*

The information you provide had been invaluable and the personal stories of your members have really made me feel part

The Lucky One

of a special group. Some of the people I've already met through Pink Hope are going to the same clinics and hospitals as I am and I would love to be able to meet up with them and have a chat over coffee. Who knows? Maybe I will.

Keep up the great work and please let me know how I can help or contribute to this wonderful resource.

Regards
Gena

CHAPTER 23

It seems fitting to end this book with spring. To end with Sydney sunshine and southerly busters and the sight of pink galahs on the front lawn, growing fat and content on grass seeds. Because, that September in 2013, I felt like my own personal springtime had come.

I went to America for a second time, feeling lighter and happier than I had in months. My health was good and my breasts had been problem-free for a while. Mum was all-set for planned surgery on her abdomen in November and Nan was soldiering on. And the kids were as wonderfully raucous as ever. Then, the (pink) icing on the cake? Pink Hope was looking viable once again. So when I boarded a plane to the US that spring, I was feeling optimistic.

The Lucky One

I was headed to the Land of the Free and the Home of the Brave to see Lindsay. She had invited me back to Chicago to speak at FabFest, an event she dreamed up herself. FabFest is both a fundraiser and a way for women affected by hereditary cancer to celebrate health and wellbeing. It's an annual, full-day event offering exercise classes, health seminars, goal-setting workshops and spa treatments, all centred on the idea of living a fabulous life. And the best bit? This year it was hosted by my hero, Giuliana Rancic (or 'G' as she was to me now, given I'd stalked her so much she had no choice but to be my friend).

As the name promised, FabFest was fabulous (so much so that I hope to bring it to Australia one day for all our Pink Hope ladies and their families). My trip, more broadly, was just as brilliant. Albeit a bit of a whirlwind. I took eight flights in two weeks, which is not bad for someone who, only a few years earlier, was almost too afraid to get on a plane. I spent time in Chicago and in New York (including, of course, a stop-off in my spiritual home: Broadway to watch Orlando in Romeo and Juliet. Little did I know I would get to meet him backstage. Highlight!).

Then, two days before I was due to fly home, I woke up to several messages and emails to say that my friend Sarah-Jane Woodford had died. Beautiful, talented, generous Sarah-Jane. Sarah-Jane who was a HR guru and a brand new mum. Dead so soon. Taken by a cancer that had started in her breast and which then spread to her spine and eventually her brain.

I was shattered.

Of course, so were Sarah-Jane's family and friends. When my friends at Pink Hope phoned me in Chicago to tell me the devastating news, they were in deep shock.

'We thought she still had months to live,' they kept saying. 'How did it happen so fast?'

And in many ways it *was* fast.

Sarah-Jane's life ended not just months before doctors predicted it would, but *years* before it ever should have. When her cancer was first diagnosed, it hadn't yet reached her lymph nodes but it was triple negative so her prognosis was not good. Yet, within just two years, Sarah-Jane went from being optimistic about beating cancer, to being told there was nothing anyone could do. She was just 35 years old when she died.

It seems incomprehensible that her poor, poor mum should have to bury both her daughters, and so close together. But in the end Sarah-Jane deteriorated very quickly. She didn't even make it to the wedding she'd planned. Instead she married her husband—the man she'd intended to grow old with—in a service held at her hospice bedside.

Perhaps most heartbreaking of all, though, is the twelve-month-old son Sarah-Jane leaves behind. A son who is too young to know what's going on but who may carry the BRCA1 mutation positive gene, just like his mother and his aunt did before him.

And that is the true horror of hereditary cancer. We're talking about families who have lost their mums and their nans and their aunts and their sisters and their cousins and who then face the prospect of one day losing their precious new generation, too. It's almost too much to bear. It's also an incredibly complex and difficult scientific issue, and one which requires the dedication of our greatest medical minds, plus all the resources we can throw at it. This is why organisations like Pink Hope are so important and why our work will only be done once every family knows their risks and acts upon that knowledge.

The Lucky One

And, in the meantime, we're burying beautiful Sarah-Jane next Monday.

◆ ◆ ◆

While Sarah-Jane's death was not the catalyst for my decision, it certainly focused my mind: I have decided to undergo ovarian surgery. It was something I'd been thinking about for a while now; had been advised by all the experts to do for some time. An 'oophorectomy', they call it. 'Ovary and out', I'm calling it. Because that's the aim. Removing my ovaries means out with the risk of ovarian cancer.

I'm starting with one ovary, not both, because the cancer-minimising effect is still significant and because I'm not ready to go into full-blown menopause just yet. (Not when I'm only 30 years old. And not when some studies suggest early menopause can reduce your lifespan by up to five years. I'm trying to prolong my life, not shorten it.) But I am having my fallopian tubes removed, too—because just like breast cancer so often starts in nipple ducts, ovarian cancers may start in the fallopian tubes.

Of course, removing even one ovary means I'll no longer be able to fall pregnant naturally and this is something Chris and I have thought long and hard about. Chris is much more ready to take this step than I am. His reasoning: we have three happy, healthy children; let's make sure their mum stays happy and healthy, too. And while I do agree, I can't promise I won't regret my decision in future moments of unbearable cluckiness.

But when booties and bunny rugs beckon, I'll only need to remind myself of the stats to know we made the right decision. Like, while around 1.4 per cent of women in the general population will develop ovarian cancer in their lifetime, this can be up to 60 per cent for those of us who are BRCA mutation positive. And at least 15 per cent of epithelial ovarian cancers, the most common type, are thought to be the result of inheriting a faulty gene.

Then, there's the fact that the mortality reduction associated with this type of surgery is massive. One study showed that women who underwent bilateral prophylactic salpingo-oophorectomy (i.e. they had both ovaries and both fallopian tubes removed) reduced their risk of dying from ovarian cancer by almost 50 per cent.

Ovarian cancer is a silent killer. Often, by the time you know you've got it, there's not much anyone can do. And, as if the survival statistics associated with ovarian cancer are not scary enough, my family seems to specialise in the breast and ovarian cancer double-act. My nan's cousin died of ovarian cancer at just 35 years old and there are numerous others dotted throughout our family tree that suffered the same fate. My own mum has had major issues with endometriosis and with ovarian tumours throughout her life. It's like, once a woman in our family gets breast cancer, then that cancer seems pre-programmed to head south to her ovaries. I'm not about to suffer that same fate if I can help it.

So, I have my meeting with Dr Greg Gard next month. He's the gynaecological oncologist who performed my mum's ovarian surgery and he specialises in familial cancer. I might hit him up for a family discount.

Then, assuming my surgery goes well and there are no signs of any pre-cancerous activity in and around my ovaries, I'm going to wait until I'm in my late thirties and then I'll have my other ovary removed, too. There's no point hanging onto it for posterity, after all.

The Lucky One

This might sound cavalier; might even sound brave. But not when you consider the immense bravery of women like Sarah—women who battled cancer to the bitter end. Back when I was 22 and I first found out I was BRCA mutation positive, I was faced with three options. Path one? I could bury my head in the sand and forget I ever knew what a faulty gene was. (For me, this was never a long-term option.) Path two: I could opt for screening and early detection and commit myself to a lifetime of vigilance. Of course, this came with a lifetime of living on perpetual tenterhooks. Or path three: I could put on a surgical gown, have everything whipped out that could potentially (eventually?) kill me, and then get on with the business of enjoying my life. It's not brave to have prophylactic surgery; in my case, it's just sensible.

But this is my story and my path and it may not be the right one for others in similar situations. Every family that faces hereditary cancer is different in its own special way. They have their own stories; their own paths to choose. All I urge is that, if you do run the risk of familial cancer or if you know someone who does, then be aware, be informed, be proactive and be vigilant. Because nowadays we're the lucky ones who know about it and therefore get to do something about it.

◆ ◆ ◆

In the end, I'm nobody. Just a mum from the Northern Beaches. I'm not a celebrity, I'm not a millionaire; I'm just passionate about something and determined to see that thing through. But breaking my family's cancer curse, and then creating Pink Hope, these things have given me cause to see my life as lucky.

Krystal Barter

I may have had some rough times throughout my life. My teenage years were no picnic, that's for sure. But I eventually worked out how to change my path, change my direction. I've learnt in life that you should only ever make time for the people that lift you up and encourage you to be the best you can be. My family have done just that. They've stuck by me always and waited patiently until I emerged as the daughter, the sister, the wife and the mother they always knew I would become.

And there are good times ahead.

My brother underwent genetic mutation testing and his test came back negative for the BRCA1 gene mutation, making his daughter (my niece) the first female in 100 years in our direct lineage not to be affected by our family's gene fault.

For me? I know the future is not without its challenges. There's still a 1–2 per cent chance I could get breast cancer one day. And, far worse than that, is the 50 per cent likelihood that each of my beautiful kids could be BRCA1 mutation positive. But this is something I try not to dwell on. They are beautiful, healthy kids at the moment and that's the most which any parent can ever ask for.

And, sure, I am undergoing ovarian surgery in the coming months, but this is something I'll try to face with dignity and with optimism. Because if there's one thing I've learned in this life, it's that I've got so much to be optimistic about. I'd walk my same journey twenty times over—I'd live this life, with all its hardships and all my mistakes, over and over and over again— in order to have met Chris and to have had my three gorgeous children and to have had the mum and the dad and the nan that I have. Anything to have been born into the family that I have. We might be cursed, but we're lucky to have each other. And I'm the luckiest of them all.

ACKNOWLEDGEMENTS

Mum/Dad – To my incredible parents, you waited patiently for your lost baby girl to find her way home. It took a while! But eventually I became the daughter you both deserved.

My husband – To my amazing husband, Chris, you changed my life just by being in it. Starting my family with you was the single best decision of my life. I look at my beautiful children and I feel so grateful and *lucky*.

To my babies – You make every day better, every decision more meaningful, every cuddle perfect. Being a parent isn't the easiest job in the world but it's by far the most rewarding.

Krystal Barter

My grandparents – To my nans. You provided me with such love and compassion. You are my best friends. The happiest memories of my childhood have you both firmly planted in them.

Lindsay Avner and Stacey Gadd – my BRCA sisters:

Linds – When you answered my email it was the single most defining moment of my BRCA journey. 'You are not alone', you wrote to me. That day you made me feel a little less alone and scared and those words echo in everything I do with Pink Hope.

Stacey – I will never forget talking on the phone to you on the night before my surgery. We were both nervous – I think there were a few laughs and tears! You are such a great friend. I hope you never underestimate the impact you have had on my journey.

Pink Hope Ambassadors – There are too many of you to thank individually but you know who you are. You are the stars of Pink Hope and the reason I wake up so passionate to see Pink Hope through, even during the most difficult days I will always get up and start work again … And all because of you.

Dr Kathy Tucker – Kathy you have held my hand through a pretty tough time. You always gave me the necessary facts and figures but you let me come to the right decision for *me*. You are changing so many lives and yet you always remain humble.

Prof Judy Kirk – Judy I will never forget the moment, in front of so many leaders of the oncology fraternity, when you said:

The Lucky One

'You did it, Krystal. You created Pink Hope and it's such an incredible resource.' That was one of the proudest moments of my career. You gave me such a boost that day!

Dr Megan Hassall – You rebuilt my breasts and my confidence. You have been there throughout my mum's journey and now mine. Thank you for supporting us every step of the way.

Dr Mark Sywak – Having your skills on my team was one of the best decisions I made.

Helen Zorbas & Jane Salisbury – You have been such a professional support for me and Pink Hope. I can remember walking into your office all those years ago with a dream and you believed in me. It gave me the confidence I needed to turn my dream into reality. Look at us now! ☺

Tracey Bevan – Thank you for your guidance and support. You understand, more than anyone else, where true passion comes from. I know Jane would be so proud of everything you have done.

Angelina Jolie – To the woman who made the BRCA gene fault known around the globe: I thank you from the bottom of my heart. Thank you for sharing your story in such an honest manner. I know you care deeply for the plight of women around the world, you have given hope to so many.

Karl Stefanovic – Thank you for giving my nan your personal phone number after our first interview. You offered so much support and kindness to our family. We will always be incredibly grateful to you and Cass.

Krystal Barter

Kirsty Thomson – You shared our story when preventative surgery was rarely discussed. You gave high risk families a voice and you continue to support the cause. Thank you.

Sarah Murdoch – Thank you for your support throughout my years as an ambassador for the NBCF. Your devotion to the cause is something I continue to admire. I still can't believe you invited me onto Australia's Next Top Model (my fave show!). A definite highlight of mine!

Sue Murray – You were my mentor, my friend and my confidant. I attribute Pink Hope's success to your guidance and honesty.

To my girlfriends, Bec, Katy, Jaime, Erin – my bbf's who have supported me through thick and thin. I love you all.

Karin Adcock and Jeff Burnes – When I walked into your office little did I know you would give Pink Hope wings to fly. Thank you.

George Moskos – You are always just a phone call away offering advice and support. I am very grateful.

Heather Thorne – You have been a guiding light through this journey and a dear friend. Thank you for having the passion and dedication to fight hereditary cancer.

The Lucky One

To Pink Hope's board members, volunteers, donors, celeb friends and supporters. Thank you from the bottom of my heart for your continued dedication. I could not do it without you.

Last but not least to Felicity, Jane, Laura, Cheryl Ackle and the team at Allen and Unwin. You have been wonderful. Thank you!